Murder Inc.

The Rise and Fall of Ireland's Most Dangerous Criminal Gang

PAUL WILLIAMS

PENGUIN BOOKS

PENGUIN BOOKS

UK | USA | Canada | Ireland | Australia
India | New Zealand | South Africa

Penguin Books is part of the Penguin Random House group of companies
whose addresses can be found at global.penguinrandomhouse.com.

Penguin
Random House
UK

First published by Penguin Ireland 2014
Published in Penguin Books 2015

002

Set in 11.88/14.17 pt Garamond MT Std
Typeset by Jouve (UK), Milton Keynes
Printed in Great Britain by Clays Ltd, St Ives plc

A CIP catalogue record for this book is available from the British Library

ISBN: 978-0-241-97046-1

www.greenpenguin.co.uk

MIX
Paper from
responsible sources
FSC
www.fsc.org FSC® C018179

Penguin Random House is committed to a
sustainable future for our business, our readers
and our planet. This book is made from Forest
Stewardship Council® certified paper.

In memory of Roy Collins.
And for his family – Steve, Carmel, Steve
Junior, Leanne, Paul and Ryan – who paid a
terrifying price for standing up against evil and
whose remarkable courage won the heart of a nation.

Also in memory of Murder Inc.'s other
innocent victims, including Brian Fitzgerald,
Sean Poland, Baiba Saulite and Shane Geoghegan.

And for the men and women of An Garda
Síochána in Limerick, whose diligence and
determination brought down Murder Inc. after
the longest, most intensive investigation in the
history of Irish criminal justice.

Contents

CONTENTS

Prologue

The gang boss was in his cell when his mobile vibrated to announce another illicit incoming call. It was one of his lieutenants back in Limerick. He was worried about one of their twenty-year-old lackeys. The foot soldier had driven the getaway car used to gun a man down in the street a few hours earlier.

The problem, the anxious caller explained, was that the driver had cried. The wannabe gangster had never been involved in a murder before. He'd realized when it was too late that he wasn't as hard as he tried to make out.

Remorse and regret were emotions alien to the mob members. It was an ominous sign of weakness, and that scared the gang bosses almost as much as the sight of their rivals with Glock automatics. A man weighted down with guilt could easily make a statement of admission in a Garda station. Such feelings were like a cancer that needed to be eradicated.

The lieutenant had a plan to deal with the unexpected crisis, but he needed approval first. There were protocols to observe in these matters. 'I'll ask someone and ring you back,' the imprisoned godfather replied, and went off to talk to another mob member across the prison landing. Ten minutes later the boss rang back. The message was curt and to the point. 'Don't trust him . . . do what you have to do.' The phone went dead.

The lieutenant took his trusted sidekick aside and gave

him his instructions. A short time later the gangster contacted the troubled getaway driver. He wanted help to bury some guns before the cops came to investigate the latest murder. There was nothing unusual in the request – the foot soldiers buried so many guns they could have qualified as grave-diggers.

The pair went to a secluded corner on an area of waste ground. The remorseful young man dug a shallow hole as his 'friend' stood guard. When he finished digging the doomed man looked up to find his associate pointing a pistol at him.

He tried to make a run for it but his assassin was too quick. He hit his victim with the shovel, knocking him to his knees. The lackey began crying again and begged for his life. 'Please don't; please don't,' he pleaded, as he knelt before the hit man.

The 'friend' explained that the problem was that he had cried and shown weakness. The mob couldn't tolerate that. He was a 'loose end' that needed tidying up. The wannabe gangster begged him not to shoot.

The killer got tired of the pleas and wanted to go home. He calmly took aim and fired a single shot into the back of his victim's bowed head. Then he dumped the body into the shallow grave like a dead animal. He threw a few shovels of dirt over the corpse, only partially covering it. The gangster couldn't be bothered concealing it fully. He hoped that wild animals would do the rest.

When the hit man went back to his boss he proudly announced: 'That's done.' In prison the godfather's phone vibrated again. He heard the same two words. 'Good,' he replied and the phone went dead.

Later the gang members callously laughed as the killer described how he'd got rid of the young man who, only a few hours earlier, had been a trusted friend. He helpfully went down on his knees and mimicked his victim's last moments, as he cried and begged for his life. There was no hint of remorse or regret or pity. This was how the mob protected itself from destruction.

It was nothing personal, it was just business.

1. The Arrival of Evil

In the annals of its 1,200-year history there is no precise date for a seemingly unremarkable event that ultimately led to one of the darkest periods in the chronicles of Limerick City and the story of organized crime in Ireland. Exactly when the Dundon brothers – Wayne, John, Dessie and Ger – relocated there is lost in time. The delinquent English-born brothers were gangland nobodies when they drifted back to their parents' home town where the family's traveller roots run deep.

Although some of the brothers already had form as violent criminals, no particular notice was paid to their arrival: they were just four more dysfunctional, feral teenagers. But what is well chronicled in Ireland's recent history is the unprecedented chaos and carnage that was unleashed as soon as they had unpacked their bags and started prowling the streets in one of the city's already troubled ghettoes. Within months the Dundons had formed an alliance with their cousins, the McCarthys. It would prove to be a toxic mix. The newly formed Dundon/McCarthy gang soon emerged from the shadows to wage a war on the people of Limerick. In the pantheon of psychotic mobsters who have stalked gangland, the Dundon brothers stood out from the rest of the rabble as the worst of the worst.

Limerick's motto – 'An ancient city well versed in the arts of war' – was originally adopted to recognize the many pivotal battles the city at the mouth of the mighty River Shannon had endured in its long history. It was borrowed from an epic poem dedicated to the siege of the ancient city of Troy. As the last redoubt of Catholic rule in Ireland, Limerick was also besieged. When Cromwell's brutal army surrounded its walls and King John's Castle in 1651, an estimated 5,000 people died as a result of savage fighting, starvation and plague. Limerick then fell to the army of William of Orange in 1691, after two further sieges and the massacre of over 800 people. It completed England's conquest of Ireland. The resulting Treaty of Limerick precipitated the departure of the Catholic army in what is known as the Flight of the Wild Geese. Violence again erupted during the War of Independence when the infamous Black and Tans, a band of British Army psychopaths sent to stamp out the revolution, were unleashed on Limerick. During a night of savagery in March 1921, known as the night of the 'Curfew murders', the Black and Tans murdered four prominent citizens in their homes.

This spectre of widespread, indiscriminate violence returned eighty years later, bringing with it many more nights of savagery. But this time an undisciplined rabble laid siege to the city from within, plunging it into a decade of unparalleled criminal chaos and bloodshed. This blighted era will live on in infamy as the reign of the Dundon/McCarthys – a horde of primal monsters well versed in the arts of inflicting terror, pain and death. The city's roll call of its most-hated tormentors – Cromwell, William of Orange, the Black and Tans – now includes the Dundon/McCarthys, aka Murder Incorporated.

In the almost five decades that the phenomenon of organized crime has existed in Ireland the Dundon/McCarthy mob hold the awesome distinction of being the most dangerous and ruthless of all the gangs. Daylight executions of underworld rivals and the merciless high-profile murder of innocent people were central to their crude strategy to gain gangland supremacy. The mob blasted their way to the top of the Garda 'Most Wanted List' and were the prime target of the longest, most sustained – and expensive – police investigation in Irish criminal justice history. They also featured in several international police investigations and were classified by the EU policing agency, Europol, as a major criminal organization. The depraved crimes of the Dundon/McCarthy gang threatened to undermine the administration of justice in Limerick and forced the Government to introduce tough anti-gang legislation not seen since the murder of journalist Veronica Guerin in 1996. The names of the Dundons and the McCarthys were etched in the national psyche as the manifestation of what Limerick's State Solicitor, Michael Murray, once described as 'pure evil'.

The State Solicitor played a pivotal role in the administration of criminal justice in Limerick City, with responsibility for the prosecution of all serious criminal offences. Through the mountain of gang-related charges he processed over the years Murray gained a unique insight into the people involved. In an interview at the height of the mayhem, the law officer had no doubt about who had ratcheted up the crime levels – the Dundon/McCarthy mob: 'I think I would put the blame for that on one particular grouping, who have displayed a savagery that I find to this day hard to fathom; they have set the benchmark and the others have followed and it has ratcheted up to the stage now where many killings involve not only murder but the maiming and torturing of somebody in the most horrific of circumstances.'

When asked what he thought drove Murder Inc. he

explained: 'Evil, there is no other word for it. I can't believe that greed does it; it's just these people are pure evil and they have no respect for life.'

The virulent gang culture that evolved around the drug trade in Ireland at the turn of the new Millennium produced a much more dangerous breed of cold-blooded killer. The Dundon brothers' arrival in Ireland coincided with the dawn of a tumultuous era of opportunity for the underworld as the hedonistic Celtic Tiger generation gorged itself on recreational pharmaceuticals, especially cocaine, the 'Devil's dandruff'. The excesses of young, middle Ireland fuelled an unprecedented billion-Euro boom for organized crime. The prodigious profits made gangsters greedy – and dangerous. The gun became the corporate weapon of choice for sorting out disputes over territory and money. Gangland executions spiralled to unprecedented levels as brutal mob wars flared up, mainly in the working-class suburbs of Dublin and Limerick. Over time, the violence seeped from within its natural borders and killings began to occur in once peaceful towns and rural idylls. By the second half of the noughties Ireland had an unenvied record for one of the highest per capita murder rates in Western Europe.

The four Dundon brothers quickly emerged as the most dangerous element in the crime clan. Their unrivalled capacity for savagery made the worst excesses of the Finglas and Crumlin mobs in Dublin look almost harmless by comparison. Untroubled by behavioural boundaries they had no moral qualms about killing on a mere whim, either by accident or design. Devoid of any semblance of empathy or remorse, they were textbook psychopaths. Emotions such as pity, shame or guilt were deleted from their human hard drives and they regarded people only as targets and exploitable opportunities. Instead of friends, they had victims and accomplices who ended up as victims. Empowerment and satisfaction were obtained by inflicting cruelty. Their natural aptitude for terror instilled blind loyalty and a code of *omertà* in their subordinates. The Dundons' principal motivation in life, like all other criminals, was self-aggrandizement, where the end always justified the means – but their means were more outlandish than most.

The Dundons' cousins, former associates and ex-lovers – the majority of them dangerous criminals in their own right – would later describe how the Dundon brothers in particular were driven by a visceral, inexplicable hatred of the world around them. The horrified testimonies of the victims and the case files of their crimes lend themselves to the conclusion that the Dundons were natural born killers. Violence was a trait that ran deep in the veins of the extended Dundon/McCarthy clan through the generations; brutality was in their DNA. But it seemed that in the construction of their genetic make-up the Dundon brothers had received a disproportionate helping of the family poison.

Murder Inc. earned its fitting sobriquet for their ability to cross the line and murder and maim innocent civilians who either stood up to them or were in the wrong place at the wrong time. Among the death toll of the innocent was a security manager, a car dealer, a rugby player, a housewife and a young businessman. And they could just as easily turn on their own. The Dundons casually beat their associates and girlfriends with the same energy they expended on their perceived enemies.

The Dundon/McCarthy gang were obdurately indifferent to the devastation they caused and to the national outcries their callous crimes provoked. Neither were they equipped with the cognitive capacity to realize that their reign of terror would unleash an unprecedented backlash from the forces of law and order. In the warped world they had created, the status of being the country's undisputed Public Enemy Number One was good branding – they believed notoriety would make Murder Inc. untouchable.

Subtlety and sophistication were as absent from the Dundon/McCarthy mob's joint psyche as compassion and mercy, which was amply demonstrated in the way they went about their business. Most criminal gangs, well versed in the arts of survival, put huge effort into operating below the radar and avoiding attention, but Murder Inc. took the opposite approach. After they had been convicted of the abduction and execution of rival gang boss Kieran Keane in 2003, five gang members sniggered and laughed in the dock as a senior detective described the gang's business strategy.

'The motivation and objective was to murder Kieran Keane and Owen Treacy [his nephew] and to lure two other people into a trap from which I believe two other murders would occur. It [the murders] was to eliminate those who stood in their way and those perceived to be their enemies with the objective of totally dominating Limerick City,' Superintendent Gerry Mahon told the court, before the five killers were led away to begin life sentences behind bars.

The murder of Kieran Keane in 2003 was the spark that ignited the gangland firestorm that engulfed Limerick. At the height of the conflagration the city became Ireland's murder capital and had the highest rate of gun crime per capita in Western Europe.

Murder Inc.'s bosses, while intellectually slow, possessed a feral, predatory cunning as they stalked their prey, waiting for the time to pounce with devastating consequences. On the night that they kidnapped Keane and his nephew, the intention was to also lure the Keanes' lieutenants into the trap. It would have been Ireland's version of the St Valentine's Day Massacre; wiping out the rival gang bosses in one decisive act of mass murder. It was the type of strategic savagery that made Corleonesi Mafia boss Toto Riina infamous in the history of Cosa Nostra. The plot failed, however, when Keane and Treacy withstood torture and refused to call their associates.

'If me or my uncle made that call there was four of us going to be killed. At no time were we going to lure the Collopys out the road – at no time,' Owen Treacy would later reveal. After putting a bullet in Kieran Keane's head, the gang made the mistake of leaving the critically injured Owen Treacy for dead. But despite suffering multiple stab wounds, he survived to break with tradition and testify against the killers in court.

Keane's cold-blooded execution sparked a low-intensity urban war for control of the drug trade between the Dundon/McCarthy gang on one side and the Keane/Collopy mob on the other. Driven by blind tribal hatred, the two groups were responsible for an astonishing catalogue of attacks and counter-attacks – there were drive-by shootings, arson attacks, abductions, stabbings, bombings and executions. The war lords strutted through the streets, openly wearing bullet-proof vests and driving armour-plated jeeps. In full view of the police and judiciary in the precincts of the city's courts complex, the two sides threatened and intimidated each other. The courts became a flashpoint for violent clashes and the mobs even tried to burn them down. And whenever a rival gang member was whacked the killers made no secret of who was involved, phoning their enemies to gloat about it. There were no concerns about being charged on foot of such admissions as the belligerents shared their contempt for the law. Both sides were devout practitioners of the primeval doctrine of 'an eye for an eye' and 'a life for a life'. Scoreboards of the body count were smeared in graffiti on walls in the strongholds of the clans.

The warring godfathers had no scruples about sending teenagers as young as fifteen out with AK47 assault rifles, machine-guns and grenades to settle scores. Younger children were used to move drugs and guns because if they were caught they could not be locked up – and had been trained never to open their mouths. In a bid to drastically escalate the mindless butchery, the Dundon/McCarthys set up an international arms deal to buy enough rocket launchers and heavy weaponry to equip a modern military unit. The Keane/Collopys had their own munitions factory to make lethal pipe bombs.

Gardaí who were trying to keep a lid on the madness were openly threatened, assaulted and shot at. In a bid to suppress the prosecutorial process, the offices of State Solicitor Michael Murray were burned down by one of the warring drug factions. When the offices were rebuilt the mobs tried to burn them a second time. As a result of death threats the courageous lawyer received police protection to do his job. The necessity of this step was highlighted when the Dundon/McCarthy gang firebombed the home of a prosecuting lawyer in a bid to undermine a pending murder trial.

The gang war in Limerick became a national crisis which warranted urgent discussions in the Government at numerous Cabinet meetings. Such blatant attempts by organized crime to undermine the authority of the State had not been seen since the reign of Mafia boss Riina in Sicily during the early 1990s, when two investigating judges were murdered.

The sheer volume of prosecutions for murder and attempted murder coming from Limerick meant that the Central Criminal Court began sitting there – the first time it had ever moved from its traditional base in the Four Courts in Dublin. The historic initiative was mooted so that dozens of detectives who would otherwise be required to travel to Dublin to attend trials would have more time to participate in ongoing criminal investigations in Limerick. If the court hadn't moved the backlog of cases would have caused a chronic personnel shortage, hampering the efforts to stop the violence. As the war continued it became extremely difficult to empanel juries to sit in the local Circuit Court for serious crime cases involving the gangs.

The outbreak of violence blighted a positive period in the city's history, which had done much to shed its grim portrayal in Frank McCourt's *Angela's Ashes*. Limerick had emerged as a vibrant, cosmopolitan hub of culture, arts, education and industry. And, of course, it was the proud home of Munster Rugby. But the outside world mostly viewed the city through the prism of the warring clans, prompting the cringe-inducing comment in an international travel guide that 'Limerick is best seen through the rear view mirror!' The corrosive conflict threatened to undermine the commercial and social cohesion of the entire city. The belligerents struck a terror into the citizenry not seen since the English armies descended on its ancient walls.

The situation deteriorated so much in 2003 that for the first time in Ireland the Gardaí felt the need to deploy high-profile firepower on the streets as a deterrent against the criminal gangs. The Emergency Response Unit (ERU), the Gardaí's elite specialist weapons and tactics unit, effectively placed the city under curfew. Backed up by police helicopters, they patrolled the streets after dark in an attempt to quell the raging violence. Dozens more armed detectives were also mobilized from Dublin and Cork to assist the local Gardaí who were struggling to contain the mayhem. The volume of incidents involving improvised explosive devices became so high that an army bomb disposal squad was stationed in Limerick on a semi-permanent basis. In the working-class estates worst hit by the fighting, unarmed police patrols had to be escorted by armed colleagues. The city had the highest concentration of Gardaí, especially armed units, in the country.

All these intensive measures did not stop the feuding. In spite of the unprecedented security operations and mounting convictions, the bitter dispute would continue for several more years, as the body count exceeded twenty and scores more innocent, and not so innocent, were injured and maimed. The death toll in Limerick was the same as a quarter of the total number of gangland killings occurring in Dublin, a city with a population thirteen times larger. There was one factor in the conflict on which all the various participants – the Gardaí, Murder Inc.'s members and their enemies – could agree: the Dundon brothers provided the murderous momentum behind Ireland's longest-running crime war.

But the reasons for the Dundons' gangland dominance – terror and extreme violence – would ultimately precipitate the implosion of Murder Inc. The beginning of the end came from within, in the unlikely form of one of their girlfriends, April Collins. She knew where the bodies were buried after spending eight years in the heart of the gang as Ger

Dundon's partner and the mother of his children. Her father and brothers were also key members of the mob. The straw that broke the monster's back came when the Dundons threatened to kill her and her family. She did the unthinkable and went to the Gardaí to tell them everything she knew.

For the investigators who had laid siege to the mob for years it was the breach in the defences that they had patiently awaited. The petite, foul-mouthed young woman gave the detectives a first-hand description of life inside Murder Inc.

'The Dundons are unbelievable people . . . they're monsters. They're very violent people. They terrorize everyone into doing things for them; people are frightened to say no in case they'd be killed. It was no life because they were so controlling. They beat me before. They said they will kill me and I know they will. I am terrified,' she said.

April Collins smashed a sledgehammer-sized hole in the gang's wall of silence as she began spilling Murder Inc.'s bloodiest secrets. And like Cromwell and William of Orange, the breaking of this siege would have historic significance.

April Collins's sister Lisa also came forward with her own hammer – to attack Murder Inc.'s once impenetrable code of omertà. 'Ye have no idea what the Dundons are like; they are vicious and evil. We were just always afraid of them like, they were savages. Ye really have no idea what it was like being around them,' she told the Gardaí. Then she sat back and pondered aloud: 'Jesus . . . when I think back.'

Another person with a first-hand knowledge of the evils of Murder Inc. and who would play a courageous role in their eventual downfall was businessman Steve Collins (no relation to the Collins sisters). In all wars unexpected events occur which turn ordinary anonymous citizens into tragic heroes. Steve Collins was the reluctant hero in the fight to defeat Murder Inc.'s war against their city. His innocent family were subjected to the full force of the gang's demonic rage for simply refusing to breach the licensing laws and allow a child into their pub late at night. Murder Inc. harbour long grudges and their thirst for vengeance is hard to quench. Steve Collins found this out the hard way when one son was shot and seriously injured and another was murdered. A business was burned down and the Collins family, who lived under armed protection, were driven to the verge of penury and despair. Eventually they were forced to leave Ireland as part of a witness relocation programme. Murder Inc. wanted the world to know that no one would be spared their wrath.

To this day Steve Collins struggles to describe the people who turned his life into a living hell: 'It is really hard to describe what you're dealing with here because nobody has ever encountered people like these before. There were already plenty of dangerous psychopaths in Limerick when they arrived but they were a totally different breed of animal altogether. They brought the guns in and the filth in and they brought crime to a new level by showing that they were prepared to slaughter anyone who got in their way.

'I've tried to think of some expression to describe them over the years and pond life is probably the best. Their behaviour is just not normal; words cannot explain what they are like. They infested the area where they lived; they ruined the lives of so many kids and brought the city to its knees. And all the time they seemed to grow stronger on the back of it. They don't get much worse than the Dundons.'

This is the story of Murder Incorporated.

2. An Evil Empire is Born

Limerick has always stood out from the rest of the country when it comes to producing hard, violent men. Long before the outbreak of the gang wars in the noughties the city had a reputation for feuding among its under-privileged class. The genesis of the lethal gangland culture can be traced to the sprawling council estates which were built in the 50s, 60s and 70s to clear the squalid, city-centre tenement slums immortalized in *Angela's Ashes*. But the new housing schemes, like those in Dublin, caused more sociological problems than they solved: the poverty travelled into the suburban concrete jungles with its victims. Apart from improved accommodation, there was little else on offer for the new residents. Grinding unemployment and a lack of basic amenities and proper schools created an atmosphere of despair and apathy. There were high levels of alcoholism and domestic violence. Within a few years of being opened the new estates had become hubs for anti-social behaviour and vandalism.

Retired Chief Superintendent Gerry Mahon witnessed the deprivation first hand when he was posted to Limerick in 1971: 'The first thing that struck you when you went into a home in those estates was unemployment, an absent parent and poor conditions; bad clothing, no heating, no food in the fridge. There was no school, no looking for a job. The people lived in another world really without any support from society.'

The tense atmosphere nourished fierce inter-family feuds,

unique to the Treaty City and which can last for generations. The knife became the tool of choice for sorting out petty squabbles, earning Limerick the hated label of 'Stab City' in the early 80s. The sawn-off shotgun was soon added to the arsenal of the men who bore deadly grudges. Then they opted for assault rifles and automatic pistols. Between 1972 and 1991 Limerick had the second highest rate of homicide in the State. It was second only to the Border area, which was a killing field during the Northern Troubles.

Former Limerick TD and Minister Des O'Malley recalled a much more innocent time in the city – a time before the gangs: 'I practised law in Limerick between 1961 and 1969 and I used to spend at least one day every week on criminal law. But there was really very little crime at all in Limerick. It was petty crime all the time and it was nearly all disposed of in the District Court. I used to appear in the Circuit Court and I can recall at the start of sittings, the County Registrar presenting the judge with a pair of white gloves to signify that there were no indictable crimes in the city or county of Limerick, returned for trial in that term.'

The dangerous young criminals who emerged in the early 70s were the founding fathers of the gangland inherited by Murder Inc. It wasn't long before they ensured that the judges no longer collected white gloves on their visits to the city. One of the frontrunners was a delinquent called Kenneth Dundon.

A settled traveller, Kenneth Dundon was born in April 1957. His family moved to live in St Mary's Park in Southill, on the city's south side, shortly after the sprawling council estate was opened in the late 60s. From an early age he was involved in petty crime but Kenneth also stood out as an extremely violent young thug with a penchant for using knives. His first serious conviction came in 1974, at the age of seventeen, when he was sentenced to two years in a young offenders' home for wounding with intent.

Before he was sent away for his first stint of incarceration, Dundon had been dating Anne 'Doll' McCarthy for three years. Anne, who was a year younger than her vicious boyfriend, was from a large family who lived on Hyde Road in Ballinacurra Weston, also on the city's south side.

Anne's father, John 'The Man' McCarthy, was a hardened criminal who ran a bric-a-brac stall as a cover for the sale of stolen goods. Ballinacurra Weston, which opened in 1950, was the first of the new housing schemes built to relieve the cramped inner-city tenements. Despite the fact that the area had quickly degenerated into a desolate ghetto, crammed with 1,500 citizens, the city's planners continued to build huge, soulless estates. Weston, as it was known, became the stronghold of John 'The Man' McCarthy. Some years later he passed it on to his grateful grandchildren in Murder Inc.

Following his release from detention Kenneth Dundon moved with Anne McCarthy to live in Hackney, North London. Their first son, Wayne, was born on 18 March 1978. A year later they had a second son, Kenneth Junior, the only brother who grew up to eschew the family business.

Kenneth Dundon Senior was the worst father-figure imaginable. He was a violent criminal on the streets and a monster at home, who regularly dished out beatings to his wife and children. Both parents were alcoholics. In 1982 he was convicted of assault causing bodily harm to another man.

In the same year he married Anne McCarthy and the couple had their third son, John, who was born on 26 August. In July 1984 Dessie Dundon was born and three years later, Gerard, the youngest brother, arrived. In 1990 the couple had their only daughter, Annabel. Her father was lucky to escape with his life that year when he was shot a number of times on a visit to Limerick. A man was later charged with attempted murder but the case was dropped when Dundon failed to return from London to give evidence. The family regularly went back to their native Limerick on holidays and were close to their cousins, the McCarthys. Despite the fact that the Dundon brothers spent their formative years in London, strangely they all had strong Limerick accents.

Wayne, John, Dessie and Ger would soon display their father's violent traits. School wasn't a priority in the dysfunctional Dundon household and the kids could barely read and write, opting instead to spend their time on the streets. Wayne and John began getting into trouble with the police from their early teens. Even then they exhibited the behavioural traits that would define their careers as violent criminals. The brothers preyed on the vulnerable elderly who they targeted and robbed.

The teenage thugs feared no one and Wayne was a particularly dangerous individual. While he rarely drank, smoked or took drugs, his passion in life was inflicting pain and fear. When he was still a teenager he once gave his alcoholic mother such a severe beating that she was hospitalized for three weeks. At eighteen years old, the eldest Dundon brother was jailed for four years for a series of robberies. During one burglary, Wayne Dundon savagely beat a wheelchair-bound pensioner, and in another he terrorized a ninety-year-old woman in her home.

By the late 90s Kenneth Dundon and his chaotic family were attracting extensive police attention. In 1997 he was convicted for another assault and considered moving his family back to Limerick.

When twenty-two-year-old Wayne Dundon was released from prison in June 2000 the British Home Office considered him to be so dangerous that it issued a deportation order against him. The Dundons made the fateful decision to return to live in Limerick; the havoc began soon afterwards.

The Dundon family moved to a local authority house on Hyde Road in Ballinacurra Weston where their mother had grown up. The immigrants were surrounded by a large extended family. The four young brothers, aged between twenty-two and thirteen, were soon making their presence felt. The volatile grandchildren of John 'The Man' McCarthy formed the nucleus of what would soon be one of the most dangerous gangs in the country.

On his deathbed in 1998, McCarthy had passed over his son Larry to anoint his twenty-year-old grandson, Larry McCarthy Junior, as head of the family business. It had expanded to include robbery, extortion and low-level drug dealing. The new leader of the McCarthy family was already well known to Gardaí as a dangerous thug. A year after his grandfather's death he received a suspended six-year jail sentence when he was convicted on a charge of violent disorder. During a fracas McCarthy Junior used a pitchfork to stab another criminal, Johnny McNamara. The McCarthys and McNamaras were involved in a feud that had begun when McCarthy's aunt was badly assaulted by a McNamara, losing an eye in the attack. Johnny McNamara earned the nickname 'Pitchfork' after the stabbing. Several cousins in the extended McCarthy clan were members of the mob, including brothers Christopher and Anthony 'Noddy' McCarthy.

As soon as the Dundons arrived they teamed up with their relations under the leadership of Larry McCarthy Junior. This was the origin of the Dundon/McCarthy mob. The gang soon emerged as a new threat on the streets of the city. The Dundons and the McCarthys shared a tribal, siege mentality and were implacable enemies. They had long, unforgiving memories; grudges were never allowed to be forgotten.

One Limerick detective commented: 'They are so dangerous that they would be shaking your hand one minute and then shoot you in the back, as soon as you turn away from them. They hold grudges for years. In one case the Dundon/ McCarthy gang shot a man who had assaulted one of their aunts ten years earlier. They don't care about doing time or being shot and injured, although they would prefer to avoid both if they could. They accept the danger as part of everyday life, like it is an occupational hazard. It is fair to say that they brought a level of savagery not seen anywhere else in this country or indeed a lot of other countries.'

Behind their backs, and safely out of earshot, associates nicknamed the Dundon/McCarthy gang the 'Piranhas' because of their propensity for treachery. The following is a graphic description of the young gangsters from an experienced local detective who watched their development: 'They are the most devious and dangerous bastards that we ever encountered in Limerick, which is saying something. They were called the Piranhas because they would eat each other if they were hungry enough. They run with the hares and hunt with the hounds. Killing or maiming comes like second nature to all of them and they have absolutely no fear of the law.'

The Dundon/McCarthy mob had big ambitions and began plotting a path to gangland domination. Larry McCarthy Junior started building a criminal network, establishing links with crime gangs in Ireland and the UK. Operating from a base in west Dublin, settled traveller Stephen 'Dougie' Moran, a second cousin of McCarthy's, became a key member of the organization. Regarded as a violent and clever criminal, he was involved with dissident Republican groups, the INLA and the Continuity IRA. Moran used a security company as a front for his criminal rackets, which included drug dealing and the supply of firearms to criminals and terrorists.

Larry Junior's strategy in Limerick was to conceal the gang's avaricious designs until they were ready to strike. He continued to buy his drugs from the Keane/Collopy gang, steering clear of a confrontation with the mob that controlled the trade in the Midwest region. The Piranhas focused instead on building a powerbase in Ballinacurra Weston. The first people to suffer were those living in the south side ghetto, which was already run-down and overwhelmed by anti-social behaviour. Over a few short years the Dundon/McCarthys turned the area into a smouldering wasteland which they ruled with an iron fist. The gang created a safe enclave for Murder Inc. with all their family and gang members living around them. As they came of age the Young Turks moved into their own houses in the tight geographical area, marking out their territory by painting the houses in garish pinks, reds and yellows.

To gain effective control of the area they employed their own crude version of social engineering by driving the terrified people out of their homes. Businessman Steve Collins recalled how they did it. 'They offered people about €10,000 for a house that was worth about €80,000, and when the people wouldn't take it the gang burned them out. They took over whole blocks of houses, marking their territory, so they'd all be living in a square in what they called their stronghold. The area was already neglected but they finished off the destruction.'

As the Dundon/McCarthys made their malevolent presence felt in Weston the new mob inevitably came to the attention of the Gardaí based at the nearby Roxboro Road station. On 5 September 2000, Gardaí from Roxboro Station, who were investigating the theft of circus horses, called to the home of the Dundons at Hyde Road to arrest Dessie Dundon – who was then aged sixteen. Trying to free his brother, Wayne Dundon launched a savage attack on Detective Garda Pat Cox and his partner, Detective Garda Brian Lynch. During the incident, Dessie shouted to Wayne to get him his knife so he could stab one of the arresting officers.

Wayne Dundon dumped a concrete pillar cap and a bag of rocks on Detective Garda Pat Cox. The officer suffered serious injuries to his arm and shoulder, as he tried to protect himself. His injuries were so acute he never worked in active service again. The brothers, who had only been in Limerick for three months, were arrested when reinforcements were called and later charged with assault. It would be the first of many altercations with the police – and the Gardaí were not the only ones to suffer.

The experience of residents in one small cul-de-sac provides an example of what families throughout the area were going through. When the Dundons returned to live in Hyde Road there were nine houses at Weston Gardens around the corner from their new house. Within eighteen months three were burned out. The new gang offered the remaining occupants €20,000 cash for their homes – which was little more than half their true market value. When the residents refused to sell, a campaign of intimidation and violence ensued.

Groups of youths began drinking outside the home of one man who refused to sell, regularly breaking his windows.

When he was mugged in his front garden, the man put the house on the market for €40,000. The day the 'For Sale' sign went up, the house was burned down. The youths even set fire to the sign to reinforce Murder Inc.'s point – no one else would be buying the property. When the owner fled the area, the shell of his home became a magnet for drug addicts and drunken teenage tearaways. They tore the copper piping out of the house before burning it again.

The gang then shifted their malign attention to the terrified pensioner who lived next door. His house was vandalized, horses were put in his garden and there were nightly drug parties in the derelict house next door. After a fire was set under his stairs the elderly man packed his belongings and abandoned his home. The family living in the next house then found themselves in the full glare of the unruly mob. They returned from holidays to find their house boarded up, following a failed arson attack. The house had also been ransacked. The family left in a taxi with whatever possessions they could carry, never to return. Another neighbour also fled, after enduring two years of relentless abuse, threats at knifepoint and several attacks on her property, including the demolition of the front garden wall by a stolen car. The residents were often too scared to call the police, and if they did the harassment got even worse. When the Gardaí did go into the enclave to investigate crimes and anti-social behaviour they had to do so in force or be attacked.

The social depredation spread like a cancer. Gaping, burned-out skeletons of houses gave the ghetto the image of a war zone. Menacing gangs of riotous youths wandered the streets where drugs were openly sold. The growing number of derelict houses provided accommodation for parties and for hiding drugs and guns. Horses used for sulky racing – popular among criminals and travellers – roamed the overgrown, debris-strewn gardens. Greens became dumping grounds for household waste and burned-out stolen cars used for joyriding or armed robberies.

One former resident recalled: 'We were being targeted one by one, with kids as young as five throwing stones and bottles, battering the houses. It was like living in a war zone. There was one bizarre incident where young children collected bottles into bags in the green, as if they were going to recycle them. Then they came to my house and smashed them off the front. It was surreal.'

The people who were determined to remain, or simply had no alternative but to stay, were prisoners in their homes. The chairman of one local Residents' Association, who tried to stop the drug dealing and anti-social behaviour in his estate, was stabbed and seriously injured. A number of youths were convicted for the incident but it did nothing to stop the rot.

The local authorities seemed powerless to do anything about the situation either. Another local resident commented: 'It was like a domino effect. One by one houses got boarded up and the parties started. Gangs stripped the houses of copper pipes and burned them down. People started dumping rubbish. Then the people in the next house can't take it any more, and the council buys that, boards it up. People were terrorized and beaten in their own homes and there seemed nothing that the police could do about it. They turned the area into a burned-out smouldering wreck.'

From the beginning the members of the extended family gang displayed an implacable hatred for the police and all authority. In their sub-cultural world there was only one law to be observed – mob law. The Dundons regularly set up ambushes for passing patrols and attacked officers. They erected a powerful spotlight on the front of the family home on Hyde Road, built on an embankment overlooking the road, to blind Gardaí when they arrived to investigate crimes. Fusillades of stones and bottles would rain down on the officers from above.

In late 2001 and early 2002, the Dundon/McCarthy crew also began a terrifying campaign of intimidation targeting Gardaí and prison officers based in Limerick Prison. The young gang members developed an intense dislike for the prison officers during their regular stints behind bars. Wayne Dundon was charged with threatening a prison officer, and in August 2001 John Dundon swore he'd burn down the home of another guard. In January 2002 an officer's car was petrol-bombed and two weeks later shots were fired at his home and his car. In the same week, paint was thrown over the car of another prison guard living on the other side of the city. Hoax bombs were planted at the homes of two other officers. John Dundon was later charged with over twenty offences, including assaults on three prison officers and threatening to kill a fourth in September and December 2001. On another occasion Wayne Dundon attacked two detectives who were questioning him, breaking one officer's jaw in the process.

The Piranhas didn't confine their hatred of authority to the Gardaí or the prison service. When they were in the dock it was normal for Murder Inc. members to shout abuse and threats at the presiding judges who were sending the thugs for well-earned sojourns behind bars. During one court appearance Wayne Dundon expressed the family's attitude to the criminal justice system when he sprang from the bench and dropped his tracksuit bottoms.

The Dundon/McCarthys fed like parasites on the innate despair and apathy that pervaded the bleak council estates they held in their grip. There was a rich supply of vulnerable young kids with little prospects in life. For these children a lucky break meant not being caught breaking into someone's house or car. Like paedophiles, the gangsters groomed impressionable boys as young as twelve, transforming them into killers and drug dealers. They flattered the children, playing on their low self-esteem, and gave the kids money and drugs, seducing them with the bling lifestyle of the family's gangster paradise. While the kids' parents drove around in bangers, the Dundon/McCarthy gang had top-of-the-range cars and jeeps. Their houses were decked out with the finest fixtures and fittings, including large, flat-screen TVs and sound systems that the youngsters' parents could not afford.

Defenceless children were lured into a dark world from which there were only two exits: death or a prison sentence. The young protégés of evil were then sent out to murder and shoot on Murder Inc.'s behalf and they were too terrified to refuse orders. These foot soldiers often found themselves in an impossible situation where they had only two stark choices: to obey orders and kill or else be killed themselves. And when they were caught the same kids opted for prison sentences, sometimes for life, rather than turning on their bosses. On the streets where they grew up, in the mob's menacing dark shadow, there was an existential threat that loved ones would pay dearly for any infringement of the code of silence. Four young men who became embroiled in the gang resorted to suicide as their only means of escape from the torment and fear. Others were executed by the Dundon/

McCarthys because they were seen as disloyal or potential State witnesses.

After a few years the Dundon/McCarthys had a stranglehold on Weston. The Dundons were particularly loud, coarse individuals with strong, flat Limerick accents. They spoke fast, like verbal machine-guns, in a vernacular used by travellers that was hard for the untrained ear to understand. They were prone to terrifying outbursts of unpredictable maniacal rage which often left family and friends requiring a visit to the local accident and emergency department. Their associates described how the brothers shared a similar frightening trait where they would froth at the mouth as they screamed obscenities and threats at the objects of their tirades. Their cousin, Anthony 'Noddy' McCarthy, once described how Wayne Dundon became incoherent when he flew into an 'excitable' rage. He said everyone in the gang was afraid of the brothers' casual propensity for bloodshed.

Domestic violence was endemic in the households occupied by the gangland hard men and their partners. April Collins in particular seemed to fare worst out of the mob's girlfriends. She suffered regular vicious beatings at the hands of her boyfriend, Ger Dundon, with whom she'd had a relationship since the age of fifteen. On numerous occasions she was hospitalized as a result of her injuries. She was also beaten by his brothers. At the same time her father, Jimmy, and brother Gareth were key members of the gang's inner-circle. The father and son shared the same appetite for terror and violence as their friends. They never lifted a finger to protect April. Jimmy Collins was a wife beater himself and his wife, Alice, had obtained protection orders against him in the courts. In the world of the Dundon/McCarthy mob spousal abuse was an accepted norm, but Jimmy Collins was not completely devoid of compassion; he would visit his daughter in hospital. When Gardaí asked him why he tolerated Ger Dundon's abuse of his daughter, the loving father would tell them to fuck off and mind their own business. For their part the women seemed to accept their lot and remained loyal to their depraved lovers and husbands.

If relatives stepped out of line they could even find themselves at risk of losing their lives. Twenty-seven-year-old John Creamer was a cousin of the Dundons. From Southill, he had a long history of violent crime and in 1995 had been left on a life support machine after a vicious assault. But he survived to fight another day and a year later was charged with the murder of another criminal. The charges were dropped when the prosecuting Garda was killed in an accident. Creamer was involved in a number of armed robberies with his Dundon cousins after they returned to Limerick. On 11 October 2001, he went to see John Dundon at the family home on Hyde Road to collect his share of the loot from an earlier heist at a city jeweller. On 25 September the gang had got away with over €100,000 in cash and diamonds. Creamer got more than he bargained for when his nineteen-year-old cousin produced a Mac 10 machine-gun and opened fire at close range. John Creamer was shot fourteen times, leaving twenty-eight entry and exit wounds in his body. He was hit in the head, neck, chest, left arm and leg. One of the bullets hit him in the jaw and travelled through his mouth, taking a piece of his tongue and smashing his teeth in the process.

Doctors battled to save his life during twelve hours of surgery and he was in intensive care for several weeks. It took him almost two months to regain consciousness; his eventual recovery defied science and astounded doctors. But despite his near-death experience, and the fact that he could clearly identify his attacker, Creamer refused to co-operate with investigating Gardaí. He had been visited in hospital by his relations and left in no doubt that if he ever opened his mouth he would not survive the next machine-gun attack. Murder Inc. had laid down an important marker. When it came to killing it wasn't personal, it was just business – of the most primal kind.

3. Tribal Feuds

As the new Millennium advanced, the Dundon/McCarthy mob was at war on four fronts. They were waging a campaign of intimidation against Gardaí, prison officers and their neighbours, while also becoming embroiled in a bitter and complex inter-family feud. At the centre of the tangled web of hatred were five families – the Dundons, McCarthys, Caseys, Kellys and McNamaras. They in turn dragged in distant relatives and friends as the contagion spread. It typified the dynamic of family rows that are unique to the Treaty City. The exact origins of the feud are almost impossible to trace but locals claim it stemmed from the assault on the McCarthys' aunt by a McNamara in the early 80s. In Limerick long, bitter, murderous feuds can be sparked by ostensibly innocuous incidents such as damage to a car. Another distinctive trait common to the feuds are the involvement of women, who often goad their menfolk into battle. Enmities fester for years, with each side provoking and taunting the other, leading to eruptions of sporadic bouts of tit-for-tat attacks.

To the outsider the family feuds are labyrinthine. The hatred is driven by a siege mentality and a predisposition for extreme violence among the fighting clans. Local historians have claimed these are traits genetically inherited from the city's warlike ancestry. The bloodlines of some of the participants in the ongoing violence can be traced directly to the British Army and the most violent elements of the traveller community. The poison is passed like a cherished heirloom from generation to generation, with children reared on a diet of unconditional hatred for the other side. When the Dundon/McCarthys got involved in the south side feuds the violence escalated to a new level. It would serve as a foretaste of the nightmare just over the horizon. The outcome of this particular spate of blood-letting would contribute in no small way to a much bloodier conflagration the following year.

All the other criminal families involved in the feuding were also from the south side. The longest-running dispute was between the Caseys and the McNamaras. A bar room assault had led to intense bad feeling that had simmered for years before finally boiling over early in 2000, when members of the two families attacked each other in a night-club. Within twenty-four hours a seventeen-year-old was shot in the leg and, in retaliation, a man from the other side was shot at while sitting in his car, narrowly escaping injury.

The Dundon/McCarthys waded in on the side of the Caseys, a large extended traveller family living on a halting site at Clonlong in Southill. They went after the McNamaras who lived in nearby O'Malley Park in the Southill Estate. In turn the Caseys were feuding with the Kellys who also lived in Southill. The number of arson attacks, shootings, stabbings and assaults spiralled. Several people, including a teenage girl, were injured in drive-by and horseback shootings, but there were no fatalities. On 15 October 2000, a group of seven thugs, including John Dundon and three members of the Casey clan, gave Johnny 'Pitchfork' McNamara a severe beating in a take-away restaurant in the city centre. Then they took his car away and burned it. McNamara, who had convictions for drug dealing and firearms offences, was an equally violent gangster.

After the attack McNamara made a statement to the Gardaí and John Dundon and his associates were arrested and charged. The seven assailants were remanded in custody but were released on bail on 6 November, despite strenuous objections from the Gardaí and State Solicitor Michael Murray.

In the meantime the shootings and assaults continued. Even during the festive season there was no respite from the violence. On Christmas Day one of the Dundon/McCarthy gang walked into the front garden at the home of 'Pitchfork' McNamara's uncle, Eugene McNamara, in O'Malley Park where children were playing with their toys. He produced a shotgun and fired two shots through the front sitting-room window. It was the fourth gun attack on Eugene McNamara's home in as many months. His daughter Natalie had been injured when shots were fired into the house in November, and her father suffered a serious head wound when he was attacked by the McCarthys. A petrol bomb had also been thrown at the house. In another feud-related incident the previous May, two gunmen on horseback shot a youth close to McNamara's house. One of the 'cowboys' was the Dundons' cousin Anthony 'Noddy' McCarthy, who was living with a Casey. Luckily no one was injured in the Christmas Day attack but the children were left deeply traumatized.

The McNamaras also had a terrifying start to the New Year. On 2 January 2001, gunmen burst into the house and opened fire with a sawn-off shotgun. Johnny McNamara who was visiting at the time took the brunt of the blast and was hit in the face with pellets. He later lost an eye. Eugene McNamara's fourteen-year-old daughter Stacey was also hit in the hand and face as she watched TV. An associate of the Dundon/McCarthys was arrested for the shooting shortly after the incident and was charged with possession of firearms. He was later convicted and jailed.

On the same day John, Dessie and Wayne Dundon celebrated the New Year by abducting Terence Casey (no relation to the Caseys already mentioned), a close associate of 'Pitchfork' McNamara. The brothers and their accomplice, Gary Campion, stripped Casey and tied a rope around his neck. They planned to shoot him. Luckily for Terence Casey, Gardaí had been alerted to the incident and rushed to the scene. When they saw the Gardaí approaching the Dundons released their victim. Casey ran into Roxboro Road Garda Station, seeking refuge. In a brazen act of defiance the Dundons went to the Garda station looking for Casey and told Gardaí that it was only a prank. But the victim made a statement to the Gardaí about the abduction, and two days later John Dundon, who was already on bail, was again arrested. He was charged with false imprisonment. Together with Dessie and Wayne he was also later charged with assault. The Dundons were making a name for themselves among Limerick's law enforcement community, especially John.

When John Dundon was formally charged in the District Court, the eighteen-year-old psychopath openly sneered and verbally abused Stacey McNamara, who was in the court to see her attacker being charged with shooting her and her cousin on the same date. Local Garda Inspector Jim Browne objected to bail on the grounds that if John Dundon was released the Gardaí had serious fears for the safety of the McNamaras and their neighbours in O'Malley Park. Dundon was refused bail.

To complicate matters further a subsidiary feud then erupted around this time between the Dundon/McCarthys and their erstwhile allies, the Caseys. This dispute also descended into shooting and assaults. The fact that Wayne Dundon was married to Anne Casey and her brother was married to one of the McCarthys did not deter either side. In June 2001, shortly after he had again been released from custody, John Dundon and Larry McCarthy Junior tried to shoot brothers Martin and James Casey. They hit an innocent passer-by instead. The Casey brothers identified the pair and John Dundon was charged with that offence. He was again placed in custody without bail.

In retaliation for the attempted shooting the Caseys blasted in the windows of Larry McCarthy Senior's house. They were subsequently charged after McCarthy made a statement to police identifying the attackers. Two houses the Dundons owned on Hyde Road were also burned out. Most of the houses being attacked and burned, however, belonged to the city council, which meant that the taxpayer had to fund the huge costs of repairing and reconstructing the damaged properties.

The Gardaí based at Roxboro Road Station were left with the Herculean task of keeping a lid on the escalating madness. The Garda district that covered Southill and Ballinacurra Weston had one of the highest murder rates in the country. But they also enjoyed the highest success rate when it came to solving homicide cases. In 1995 there had been five murders in Southill alone, all of which were the result of petty feuds. The dead had been dispatched by the knife and the gun. In the same year a Garda officer based at Roxboro was transferred when a plot to murder him was exposed. But the current cycle of sustained inter-family violence was the worst in many years. It became obvious that the levels of serious crime had escalated dramatically. The continuing feuds were threatening to engulf the entire area and it was only a matter of time before someone was killed. The involvement of the Dundon/McCarthys, who thrived on mayhem, was the most worrying development yet.

Garda resources were being stretched to the limit as extra patrols were mobilized to keep the peace and officers investigated dozens of serious incidents. In December 2000 a major operation was launched in a bid to put a stop to the feuding. In charge was Garda Inspector Jim Browne, one of the city's most respected police officers. He had been stationed in Limerick since 1978. Inspector Browne and his colleagues in Roxboro were the first to realize the deadly potential of Murder Inc.

By the summer of 2001 Gardaí had charged dozens of the combatants with serious offences, including attempted murder, wounding, assault, criminal damage, false imprisonment, possession of firearms and making threats to kill. The myriad charges created the bizarre situation where the victim in one case was the accused in another. As a result of police objections to bail most of the thugs were also now locked up while awaiting trial. This restored a degree of uneasy calm to the streets of the south side estates. But then a local city councillor called Michael 'Mikey' Kelly stepped in to make peace – and in the process he contributed to the establishment of the country's most dangerous criminal gang.

On 4 July 2001, Michael Kelly called a press conference to announce he had negotiated a 'peace deal' between the Dundon/McCarthys and the Caseys. The heads of the families, Kenneth Dundon Senior and Paddy Casey, were photographed shaking hands with Kelly and a local priest. Kelly told the local newspaper that the sides had agreed to stop the 'stupid fighting'. It was the second time in six months that the violent-killer-turned-public-representative had announced a peace pact to maximum fanfare. In January he had presided over another peace deal, this time between his own family and the Caseys and McNamaras. The momentous event was also recorded for posterity on the front pages of the local newspapers. In order to 'end the terror' Kelly said that the various belligerents had agreed to withdraw their allegations against each other. On the surface it appeared to be a positive move, but the real motive for the outbreak of harmony was much simpler: to get the violent men off the hook.

Michael Kelly, who was a contemporary of Kenneth Dundon, had the reputation of being one of the most violent criminals to emerge in Limerick's new gangland in the 70s. Born in 1955, his family were among the first new residents to move into the Southill council estate. Mikey Kelly was a vicious thug with a string of convictions for serious violent crime, including wounding, robbery, demanding money with menaces, possession of firearms and shooting at a person with intent to maim and endanger life. His younger brother Anthony was equally volatile. It was the Kelly brothers who earned the city the detested soubriquet Stab City, as a result of their involvement in family feuds. In 1982 Mikey Kelly had a pint glass smashed into his face by another local criminal called Ronnie Coleman. Coleman was associated with the McNamara and Duffy families who were feuding with the Kellys at the time. On 12 October that same year Mikey exacted his revenge when he stabbed Coleman several times in the chest, killing him. Kelly was charged with the murder but was subsequently acquitted.

Two months later, on 11 December 1982, twenty-two-year-old Anthony Kelly ran into another family with whom the Kellys were feuding – the McCarthys (relatives of the

McCarthys in Ballinacurra Weston). Kelly, who was on the run from the Gardaí, was drinking in the Treaty Bar in Thomondgate in the heart of the ancient city. The bar was named after the Treaty Stone across the road, on which Patrick Sarsfield had signed the Treaty of Limerick to end the 1691 siege. The site where the pub stood in the shadows of King John's Castle had been a battleground during the war. Almost 300 years later it became the scene of another bloody skirmish.

The feud between the Kellys and the McCarthy family began when Mikey gave some of the McCarthys a severe beating during a street row. The McCarthys were from St Mary's Park, the oldest council estate in the city. It was built in the 30s on the Island Field beside King John's Castle, across the bridge from the Treaty Bar. Anthony Kelly had made the mistake of entering the McCarthys' home ground and was quickly spotted. He was attacked by three of the brothers who were armed with knives. When the row was over, Sammy and Tommy McCarthy had been stabbed to death. Anthony Kelly was subsequently charged with the killings but was acquitted after he testified that he was acting in self-defence. Locals recall that the killings ratcheted up the level of violence at the time and introduced guns into the conflict. Luckily there was no further loss of life or serious injury. The feud was finally resolved some years later when the two families agreed to bury the hatchet. But the enduring effect of that conflict was that sawn-off shotguns had become the weapon of choice among the grudge-bearing families.

By the 90s Mikey Kelly had become an adept media manipulator who portrayed himself as an ordinary decent criminal who had turned his back on a life of crime to give something back to his beloved community. He was the subject of a flattering TV documentary shown in 1995, *The Hard Man*. It told of his journey from violent brute to born-again good guy. In 1991 Mikey and Anthony Kelly had established a security company which served as a cover for protection rackets. If M and A Kelly Security were not hired to protect a building then it was likely to be burgled or burned down. The poachers-turned-gamekeepers inveigled lucrative contracts from businesses and the local Corporation. Mikey Kelly also supervised a community project organized by the Gardaí in Roxboro. By making Kelly seemingly 'respectable' the authorities had sent out a toxic signal – in Limerick crime pays.

Behind the scenes nothing had changed – and the Gardaí were well aware of that. In 1995 Kelly hatched a plot to murder a Garda based in Roxboro Road because he had been paying too much attention to the reformed criminal's dodgy business. The allegations were made by a former Kelly associate called James O'Gorman and were aired in a special RTÉ *Prime Time* programme, which was a less flattering portrayal of the Southill Hard Man. However, despite a major investigation, Kelly was never charged in connection with the conspiracy because O'Gorman withdrew his allegations. O'Gorman's brother Paul, who lived in Manchester, had received an unwelcome visit from Kelly's henchmen. It had left him on a life support machine in hospital. A close associate of Kelly's was charged with the attack but the charges were dropped when the victim withdrew his statement. Mikey Kelly had visited Paul O'Gorman's partner to remind her that she had little children to think about. Kelly then held an emotional press conference, declaring his innocence and claiming that he was the victim of a mendacious plot at the hands of the Gardaí.

The Hard Man began using the media as a tool in his attempts to undermine Gardaí and alienate them from the communities they policed. Kelly got plenty of coverage because he was always good for a headline-grabbing story. At one stage he even announced in the local newspapers and radio that he was setting up a private police force in Southill because the Gardaí were not doing their jobs. The charade paid off when Kelly topped the poll in the 1999 local elections, giving him the new title of Alderman. The fact that a criminal thug had been elected to the city council was seen as validation for the city's growing gangland culture.

As soon as Kelly had his feet under the benches in City Hall he did everything in his power to create as much chaos as possible. His signature approach was to make outrageous allegations in the local media in a bid to smear local politicians, business people and Gardaí who crossed him or his family. There would be no evidence to back up his claims, which he invariably dropped once the seed of doubt had been sown. For the benefit of the emerging Limerick crime gangs he stepped up his campaign to undermine the police at every opportunity and began to see himself as a Mafia Don in the mould of the celluloid Godfather. It was against this backdrop that Kelly became a supposed peacemaker.

The real motivation for Kelly's version of a 'peace process' in 2001 was to get his brother Anthony off charges connected with the violence. Anthony had been charged with shooting nineteen-year-old Paddy Casey in the head on 9 May 2000. The young man was walking home to the halting site at Clonlong when he was attacked; a humane killer was pushed against his jaw and fired. He suffered a circular wound to his cheek and bones in his upper jaw, nose and eye socket were shattered. Four days later Paddy Casey made a complaint to Inspector Jim Browne, naming Anthony Kelly as the man who had attacked him. When his brother was charged, Mikey claimed in the local media that he was living in fear of his life and was being forced into hiding because of a feud with the Casey family.

As the case progressed the 'reformed' criminal resorted to intimidation to save his brother from jail. On 24 October 2000, depositions were taken in the District Court in which Paddy Casey, under oath, identified Anthony Kelly as his attacker. Mikey Kelly attended the hearing in the company of three men who were described by State Solicitor Michael Murray in a letter to the Director of Public Prosecutions (DPP) as 'heavies'. Murray said they were acting 'in what I can only describe as a menacing fashion'. The scare tactic didn't work and Anthony Kelly was returned for trial. It was then that Mikey Kelly tried his last resort – becoming a peacemaker.

Kelly's much-publicized peace process between all the combatants was a clever bid to pervert the course of justice. He negotiated firstly with the combatants in the Casey and McNamara families. Kelly needed to obtain agreement that they would drop all charges against each other. The large volume of serious criminal offences pending before the courts gave everyone an incentive to agree. Following the first peace announcement in January 2001 the Caseys, Kellys and McNamaras withdrew their complaints as the various cases came on for hearing in court. The Dundon/McCarthys, the Caseys and McNamaras also all saw the obvious benefits of the so-called deal and, following their peace 'agreement' in July, began withdrawing the statements they had all made against each other.

When Anthony Kelly's case came before Limerick Circuit

Criminal Court Paddy Casey became a hostile witness and the charges against Kelly were also dropped. The Caseys withdrew their statements against Larry McCarthy Junior and John Dundon and refused to testify. Larry McCarthy Senior then dropped the charges against the Caseys for the gun attack on his house. And so it went on. As each feud-related trial came on for hearing at the Circuit Criminal Court and the District Court, the witnesses turned hostile or said they were too afraid to testify. All the protagonists, including the McCarthys and the Dundon brothers, walked from court free men. The Alderman's efforts to undermine the rule of law in the city had proved spectacularly successful. The 'peace process' had served to embolden the young gangsters while the Gardaí could only look on in utter frustration.

Gardaí launched a major investigation into allegations of intimidation of witnesses and perverting the course of justice but in the absence of witnesses the DPP had no choice but to instruct that there be no prosecutions. By thwarting the criminal justice process Mikey Kelly had assisted in the development of the Dundon/McCarthy gang – whom he once described as 'the most dangerous people in Limerick'. If the Gardaí had succeeded in putting the main players behind bars, it is argued that it would have prevented the subsequent gang wars a few years later. This is the view of the long-serving Fianna Fáil TD and former Minister Willie O'Dea who has represented the people of Limerick for over thirty years.

He commented: 'Kelly interfered in the Gardaí's business and ensured that certain people, especially the Dundon/McCarthys, could operate freely and become proficient in crime. These people formed the basis of the membership of the future gangs. There is no doubt that Mikey Kelly was a very significant figure in the evolution of organized crime in this city.'

Buoyed by his success over the Gardaí Mikey Kelly continued his campaign to undermine them. Every time a member of his family or an associate was arrested Kelly organized protest vigils outside Roxboro Garda Station. The harassment came to a head in the autumn of 2001 when Kelly was charged with beating his wife, Majella. She was subsequently forced to withdraw her complaint. A few months later he bullied her into making outrageous false allegations against the officer-in-charge of the wife-beating investigation, Inspector Jim Browne. Browne, who was one of the most active criminal investigators in the city, had become a serious problem for Mikey Kelly and his friends in organized crime. Majella Kelly brought a malicious private prosecution against the officer in the District Court, claiming sexual assault. But when a tape was produced in which she had admitted being forced to tell lies by her husband, the case was dismissed. Judge Peter Smithwick commented: 'This is an evil conspiracy of the Kelly family to denigrate members of the Gardaí, particularly Inspector Browne who is innocent of the charges against him.' Judge Smithwick said he believed Kelly had coerced his terrified wife into taking the action.

The vexatious case brought more than its fair share of bad karma to the Southill killer. It turned the public against him and finished his political career. In the general election of 2002, when he hoped to be elected as a TD, he got a mere 700 votes and later resigned his seat on the city council. He was subsequently jailed for eight months for tax offences following an investigation by the Criminal Assets Bureau and his business closed down. Kelly had become a pariah.

In May 2004 Mikey Kelly was found unconscious in his bed with a gunshot wound to the head. He never regained consciousness and died in hospital a month later. It is still not known if he shot himself or was assassinated. Gardaí believe his death was by suicide and someone hid the gun. Media speculation, suggesting that the weapon might have been buried with Kelly, led his family to carry out a macabre exhumation of his corpse to prove there was nothing there.

By the time of Kelly's demise the peace deal was long forgotten and Limerick was already in the grip of war. In the wake of the peace pacts the Dundon/McCarthy mob continued to establish themselves as a major criminal organization with tentacles that spread across Ireland and overseas. As relative newcomers to the drug trade they had to plot their course to dominance with care. The Ryan, Keane and Collopy families had set the standard for the Dundon/McCarthys to surpass.

But the north side clans were temporarily distracted with their own problems. While the south side families had been negotiating peace deals to stay out of jail, on the north side another series of feuds had exploded, which would eventually drag the whole city into the fray – and would present a huge opportunity for Murder Inc. In the meantime they were content to be seen as third-rate players, as they watched and schemed from the shadows. Like vultures, they lurked in the background, waiting for the right time to swoop and pick up the spoils.

4. The War Begins

On the evening of 12 November 2000, the Keanes' gangland enforcer, Eddie Ryan, had good reason to be watching over his shoulder. Two days earlier he had attempted to murder his long-time friend and north side crime boss, Christy Keane. Ryan had fled Limerick after the gun he aimed at Keane's head failed to fire as he knew that he was a dead man walking. But the would-be killer had returned to attend the removal of his brother-in-law's remains to St John's Cathedral. In recognition of the solemnity of the event he ignored his brother's advice and decided not to wear his customary bullet-proof vest.

At 9 p.m. he went with his son and some friends to the Moose Bar at Cathedral Place. He sat inside the front door with his back to it. Fifty-three minutes later two masked men armed with handguns suddenly appeared in the pub doorway. One of them shouted at Ryan: 'You bastard, come out ya bastard.' Then they started shooting.

The gunmen fired fourteen rounds in the direction of their former friend and associate. Ryan instinctively rose from his seat to get away and took the full brunt of the murderous fusillade. The deafening explosions sent the terrified patrons diving for cover, toppling tables and breaking glasses in the confusion. Ten seconds later the hit men fled after firing another volley of indiscriminate shots into the front of the premises. Inside there was a stunned silence as the dazed punters tried to comprehend the carnage around them; the smell of cordite and gun smoke wafting in the air. Screams and cries of pain then filled the room.

Eddie Ryan lay slouched sideways on a seat as blood oozed from his wounds. The forty-year-old enforcer had been hit eleven times at close range: two rounds hit him in the right shoulder, seven in the back and one each in the hip and left arm. The bullets travelled through Ryan's chest penetrating both lungs. Another shot severed his spinal cord. Forensics would later show that some of the bullets had been specially designed for use by the German Police to shoot out car tyres.

Ryan's friend ran to his side and tried to straighten him up. 'Eddie, Eddie where are you hit?' he frantically asked.

'Everywhere,' Ryan gasped. Then he slid off the seat onto the floor and died.

The murder of Eddie Ryan was one of the seminal events in the history of gangland in Limerick. The dramatic execution of one of the most feared gangsters in the city was the spark that lit the powder-keg which would open up new opportunities for Murder Inc. The family feuds had provided a convenient excuse for the hit men – Christy Keane's psychotic thirty-four-year-old brother Kieran and nineteen-year-old Philip Collopy – both key members of the notorious Keane/Collopy mob. The indiscriminate nature of the attack in the Moose Bar was a brutal announcement of how the gangs would deal with anyone who dared to take them on. The shocking incident could easily have turned into a massacre of the innocent, but the killers clearly didn't care about collateral damage.

Sixty-three-year-old Mary Reddan and her daughter Deirdre, who had been sitting close to Ryan, were also shot and seriously injured in the hail of bullets. Mary Reddan was hit in the abdomen and lower chest and her daughter was also hit in the chest. Both women underwent emergency surgery for the life-threatening wounds. Mary Reddan was airlifted by helicopter to be treated at Cork University Hospital. Doctors later said the women were lucky to survive. The fact that Mary Reddan was Philip Collopy's aunt-in-law underlined the shooters' ruthless disregard for anyone caught in the crossfire.

Ryan's sixteen-year-old son Kieran, who was in the toilet when the executioners burst through the doors, had also been lucky. The gunmen would have had no compunction about killing the teenager as well; that would have been a bonus. Failing to kill young Ryan would ultimately prove fatal for Kieran Keane.

Eddie Ryan had been the Keane gang's enforcer from when they moved into the drug trade in the early 90s. He was a childhood friend and the most trusted lieutenant of gang leader Christy Keane, who was a year younger. Born in December 1959, Eddie grew up close to the Keanes in Hogan Avenue, Kileely, just across the River Shannon from King John's Castle, on the city's north side. Ryan had a long record for armed robbery, theft and violence, dating back to when he was twelve years old. He was described by Gardaí as a vicious, extremely dangerous hoodlum who enjoyed inflicting pain. Ryan was seventeen when he was convicted of the manslaughter of another teenager, Christy Jackson, in 1977. He stabbed Jackson to death in a row outside the Savoy cinema. On 27 February 1978, he received a five-year jail sentence for the killing. Four months later he was also convicted of five counts of breaking and entering and got another three years.

In prison Ryan became a close friend of Mikey Kelly and

the pair often 'worked' together after they were released, pulling off armed robberies and burglaries. (Kelly, the peace-maker, later claimed that he had offered to broker peace between his friend and the Keanes on the day of the murder, but Ryan refused.) In November 1984, Eddie Ryan was jailed again for six years for three counts of receiving the proceeds of an armed robbery he'd carried out with Kelly. By the time he was released from prison Christy Keane was building a major criminal empire and Eddie Ryan became his loyal acolyte.

Ryan's fearsome reputation as a hard man proved extremely useful to Keane who was also a very violent man. Ryan collected drug debts and carried out 'enquiries' of the very painful type, to uncover Garda informants and gener-ally keep everyone in line. 'When Eddie Ryan called to your door looking for something you gave it to him or else he'd give you something you didn't want. He was a ferociously violent bastard and everyone was scared of him,' one former associate recalled.

The enforcer also had close links to the Republican groups, the IRA and the INLA, and was a regular prison visitor to convicted Provo cop killers Noel and Marie Murray and kid-napper Eddie Gallagher. Gardaí suspected that he was a hit man for hire for other gangs around the country. His rela-tionship with the Keanes began and ended in bloodshed.

Christy Keane was the man credited with bringing organ-ized crime to Limerick, and by the time of his henchman's murder he had been the city's undisputed *capo dei capi* or boss of bosses for a decade. Born in 1960 he was the third young-est of a family of ten – six boys and four girls – born to Theresa and Richard Keane. The family grew up at St Munchin's Street in St Mary's Park, a run-down corporation estate in the shadow of King John's Castle, just north of the city centre. It was the first local authority estate built by the Government in 1936 as part of a programme of slum clearance. The area, also known as the Island Field, is in the heart of the old city.

Through the centuries the Island Field was used by the various conquering armies to billet soldiers and keep their animals. In the twentieth century, as the Keane family's personal fiefdom, it had again become the stronghold of another violent army. Geographically the Island was perfect as a territorial HQ. Encircled by the Shannon and connected to the rest of the city by a single road, it was an extremely difficult location for the police to keep under surveillance. Strangers and Gardaí entering the domain were quickly spotted, and the Keanes controlled everything and everyone in the concrete enclave. And just like the Dundon/McCarthy approach, if certain local residents were not to their liking, the Keane gang ran them out of the place. Christy Keane was described by Gardaí as 'ruthless, extremely violent and highly strung'. With the help of Eddie Ryan, he ruled his patch with an iron fist.

Keane's father Richard, a casual worker at Limerick docks, married his mother Theresa in 1948 when she was sixteen years old. A short time later she gave birth to her eldest son, Seanie. Richard Keane was an alcoholic and it was left to Theresa to provide for her young family. She was known as a hard worker and a dedicated mother. According to local people, Theresa passed on her work ethic to her sons who started a successful coal business in the Island. People in the area believe that the Keanes could have been hugely successful legitimate businessmen. Instead, Christy Keane decided to play both sides of the fence, selling coal and robbing at the same time. By the time he was seventeen, Keane had been in and out of prison for a string of convictions, mostly for larceny and burglary.

Keane used his business acumen to set up a well-organized criminal enterprise centred on his family. They were involved in practically every type of illegal activity that could turn a dishonest profit, including prostitution and protection rackets, smuggling, handling stolen goods, car theft, counterfeit money, fake motoring documents and hiring out firearms to their associates.

Limerick's State Solicitor Michael Murray recalled that the Keanes were not driven into a life of crime through deprivation – it was a business decision: 'I have no doubt that there are people involved in crime who would not have been involved in crime if they had got a better start in life. Poverty can be very grinding and it can be very demoralizing and I can understand why that would cause somebody to drift into crime, but none of these people can use that excuse. They were short of nothing when they were growing up.'

By the early 90s most of Ireland's criminal gangs were beginning to realize the extraordinary financial potential of the drug trade. As the numbers of Irish people using recreational drugs soared, the underworld experienced their own Celtic Tiger-style boom. Dublin gangsters, such as John Gilligan and George 'the Penguin' Mitchell, graduated from armed robbery into the more profitable and less hazardous business of narcotics, dealing particularly in cannabis. Christy Keane was a natural businessman, with an eye for a good deal. Together with his brother Kieran, who was six years his junior, they added drug dealing to their extensive criminal operation. Within a few short years the Keanes controlled a large chunk of the drug trade in the Midwest region. They had operated largely under the radar as they built their power-base, but that all changed in the dying days of 1993 when they demonstrated their capacity for shocking brutality. In the process they introduced gangland violence to the streets of Limerick and set the standard for the type of barbarity for which the city would become known a decade later.

In a seventy-two-hour period leading up to New Year's Eve 1993, Eddie Ryan and the Keanes were responsible for the murder of two men and the attempted massacre of an entire family. The cause of the blood-letting was a tragic road accident in February 1993. Kathleen O'Shea, the partner of traveller Patrick 'Pa' McCarthy, was killed when she stumbled out in front of a van being driven by Daniel Treacy, Christy Keane's nephew. Pa McCarthy's father, 'Miko' McCarthy, was a brother of John 'The Man' McCarthy, which made him a second cousin of Wayne Dundon and Larry McCarthy Junior. A Garda investigation found that Kathleen's death had been an accident and Daniel Treacy was exonerated. Afterwards the Keanes paid for the dead woman's funeral and gave money to McCarthy as a form of compensation. But Pa McCarthy, who was a chronic alcoholic and habitual thief, made the fatal mistake of continuing to harass the Keanes and the Treacys, looking for more money.

On the night of 28 December, in a drunken haze, thirty-two-year-old McCarthy drove his van into St Mary's Park accompanied by his two brothers, William and Joseph, and David Ryan (no relation to Eddie Ryan). McCarthy encountered Christy Keane and his twenty-one-year-old nephew Owen Treacy, Daniel's brother, on St Ita's Street. Pa McCarthy wanted Keane to change foreign currency he had stolen earlier. But the meeting quickly degenerated into demands for money and a fight ensued. McCarthy's brothers later told

Gardaí that they saw Keane stabbing Pa twice through the heart. He died a short time later in the back of the van as his brothers rushed him to hospital. Keane and Treacy were arrested for questioning about the incident a few hours later and released pending further investigations. William and Joseph McCarthy and David Ryan gave detectives statements describing the incident. In the meantime Pa McCarthy, whose four young children were now orphans, was buried on New Year's Eve.

After the funeral Pa's family gathered in Martin McCarthy's caravan, which was parked in a halting site at the Cooperage Canal Bank on Clare Street, a short walk from the Island Field. Ten adults and two sleeping children crowded into the cramped space. The group drank cider and beer as they huddled around a small fire under the light of a single candle. Around 10.30 p.m., two of the mourners left the caravan to collect more drink at a local off-licence. As they walked off, two masked men armed with a sawn-off shotgun and a handgun stepped out from the shadows and challenged them. A third man appeared and looked closely at the couple. 'They had nothing to do with it,' the man told his accomplices. The man and woman were warned to go away and keep their mouths shut while they had the chance. Eddie Ryan and Kieran Keane then stood in the caravan door and began blasting the terrified group in front of them. A fusillade of seven shots was fired in what was a clear attempt to kill the remainder of the McCarthy family. The shooting only stopped because the ammunition the killers were using was faulty and misfired.

When police and ambulance crews arrived they found a scene of carnage and bloody chaos. Michael McCarthy was bleeding to death with a gaping gunshot wound to the neck and died before he got to hospital. His brother Joseph was hit in the back and leg and his sister Nora in the hip. Their cousin Noreen was also shot in the leg. Miraculously the two young children were uninjured. If the gunmen had lifted their aim a few inches the death toll would have been higher.

The outrage was the first major news item of 1994 and was greeted with shock and revulsion across a country where gangland violence was still rare and such acts of terror were confined to the streets of Northern Ireland. Gerry Mahon, who retired as Limerick's Garda chief in 2009, was one of the detectives who investigated the attempted massacre. He recalled: 'It was a shock to the whole system and a wake-up call. This was the first time that a criminal gang had stooped to such a level of sheer violence and brutality. That incident in 1993 announced the arrival of gangland in its most brutal form in Limerick. It was a taste of what we would be facing on a regular basis a few years down the road. The clear intent was to wipe out the McCarthy family so there would be no witnesses to testify against the suspect for the death of Pa McCarthy [Christy Keane]. The only reason that they weren't all killed that night was that the ammunition used by the gunmen was defective and they had to stop firing after seven shots.'

Local Gardaí didn't have to look far for suspects. Eddie Ryan and his wife Mary, Christy and Kieran Keane and another gang member, Declan 'Darby' Sheehy, were all arrested in connection with the cold-blooded ambush. There wasn't enough evidence with which to prosecute a case against Ryan or his accomplices, although detectives were satisfied that Ryan and Kieran Keane were the gunmen.

On 4 January 1994, Christy Keane was charged with the murder of Pa McCarthy, based on the statements of the three eyewitnesses to the stabbing. The following morning Michael McCarthy was laid to rest alongside his brother in Mount Saint Lawrence Cemetery. At the funeral Mass, Canon William Fitzmaurice said the dead man had been the victim of 'senseless and mindless' violence. 'Violence begets violence, leading inevitably to more suffering and more grief and more loss of lives,' he told the congregation. Although he didn't know it at the time, the clergyman was predicting the future for several local criminals, including the two men who had tried to wipe out the McCarthys. Less than ten years later Canon Fitzmaurice's comment was a paradigm for life in Limerick's seedy underworld.

At a subsequent High Court bail hearing on 10 January, Superintendent Liam Quinn asked the court to keep Christy Keane in custody because he believed that the murder suspect would 'interfere with witnesses' if he was released. Nevertheless, Keane was granted bail. Following the murders the Keanes and their henchmen subjected the McCarthy family to intense intimidation, forcing them to leave Limerick for good. In March 1995, the gang boss was tried for the murder of Patrick 'Pa' McCarthy, but was acquitted after the witnesses proved to be unreliable.

One result of the investigation into the McCarthy murders was that Gardaí began to realize the full extent of the empire controlled by the Keanes and they were soon classified as one of the biggest criminal gangs in the country. In a search of one of the brothers' homes, detectives found a floor safe containing over €30,000 in cash. In the years before the Criminal Assets Bureau (established in 1996), the police had no choice but to return the money to the owner, even though it was clearly the proceeds of crime. But it did alert them to the fact that the gang were already making huge profits. However, they realized that instigating an operation to destroy them would be fraught with difficulty. Surveillance was almost impossible and the murder of the McCarthys had also illustrated how potential witnesses and informers would be dealt with. Eddie Ryan let it be known that there would be no protection for anyone suspected of 'touting' to the cops. The McCarthy incident had provided an impenetrable wall of silence around the gang. In the tense atmosphere the Keanes' drug business flourished.

By the late 90s the Gardaí launched a major investigation into the gang, codenamed Operation Coalface. It revealed that Christy Keane had become one of the biggest drug traffickers in Ireland, supplying millions of Euros' worth of drugs to gangs throughout Munster and the Midwest region each year. The Dundon/McCarthys were among the Keanes' growing number of customers.

Christy Keane presided over a highly efficient criminal organization made up of staunchly loyal family members and associates. Within the network individuals specialized in various aspects of the business. Some organized the movement and storage of drugs and guns; others were involved in distribution and the collection of money; while more handled the laundering of the cash through front companies. The mob operated a number of cash counting centres in the secure environs of St Mary's Park. The money was rolling in so fast that at one stage Keane resorted to storing cash in wheelie bins. He used a horse-trading business to move cash out of the country hidden in horse boxes.

As the business prospered, Christy Keane began dealing directly with major drug suppliers on the Continent, buying product in bulk at more competitive prices. He also formed alliances with other gangs around the country, including

Dublin drug traffickers Troy and Arthur Jordan. The Jordans, from Tallaght, west Dublin, cut their teeth with John Gilligan's gang. When that gang was busted in the wake of the murder of journalist Veronica Guerin, the Jordans built their own empire. Keane's long list of associates included Anthony 'Fanta' Gorman and Declan 'Whacker' Duffy, the leaders of the Republican terror gang the INLA, which was heavily involved in the drug trade. George 'the Penguin' Mitchell was a major business associate, as was the second biggest drug syndicate in the country, headed by veteran Cork villain Paddy McSweeney. Another partner-in-crime was Anthony Kelly (no relation to Mikey Kelly), a shadowy godfather who operated a nationwide criminal network from Kilrush, County Clare.

The demand for drugs grew dramatically on the back of the hedonistic days of the Celtic Tiger and the gang branched out into the sale of cocaine. State Solicitor Michael Murray revealed how the Keanes also developed a market for heroin in the region: 'One of the things that they did was to starve this city of what I call recreational drugs, ecstasy and cannabis, and they made sure that the only available drug was heroin and now heroin is a huge problem in this city. They have a lot of people recruited who are dependent upon heroin and that is probably the nastiest thing that has happened in Limerick in the last ten years or so.'

The increased trade was reflected in a commensurate increase in the size of drug seizures being made by local Gardaí. In 1990 the street value of drugs seized in Limerick was €2,500; by 1999 it had risen to over €4 million.

Operation Coalface resulted in a number of significant drug seizures and the conviction of a handful of gang members, but the godfathers controlling the enterprise remained untouched. At a meeting of Limerick City Council in 2002 independent Councillor John Gilligan, an anti-drugs campaigner who represented Keane's home turf of St Mary's Park, made a shocking revelation. He stated that over the previous six years European police forces had intercepted drugs valued at €300 million which had been destined for Limerick as the main distribution centre for the Midwest region. In 2000 the total value of all drugs seized in Limerick was over €3 million. Using the internationally accepted hypothesis that police intercept an average of 10 per cent of total supply, it followed that the overall value of the trade was conservatively worth in excess of €30 million per year. The gangland bonanza had arrived in Limerick and with it came trouble.

It wasn't long before Eddie Ryan got fed up with being a leg breaker and branched out to set up his own lucrative distribution racket. The psychopath joined forces with long-time friend and drug dealer Sean 'Cowboy' Hanley, who was originally from Kileely. Hanley ran a farm at Meelick, outside the city in County Clare, which he subsequently sold for €3 million. Cowboy earned his nickname in the early 80s when he imported ponies from Welsh coal mines and sold them to children in Limerick. He had developed his own network of criminal contacts through his horse dealing business. Initially, Ryan's drug business with Hanley didn't bother the Keanes because they were supplying Ryan with the product. But the relationship gradually became more strained as the enforcer pushed for a larger slice of the cake. By 2000 a row was simmering between the hit man and his former partners over a €40,000 drug debt he owed them. A festering series of petty family feuds provided the catalyst for the outbreak of hostilities.

Eddie Ryan's thirty-five-year-old brother John was married to Christina McCarthy. In 1990, John Ryan's in-laws blamed Jack Collopy's children for slashing the tyres on a car. The two families lived around the corner from each other in the Island Field. The Collopys denied the charge but the row escalated when one of the McCarthys assaulted Jack Collopy's wife in the Moose Bar at Cathedral Place. She ended up requiring five stitches for a facial wound. An hour later Jack Collopy, an ex-soldier, was attacked at his home by John Ryan and the McCarthys. Ryan stabbed Collopy in the gut and shoulder with a knife and beat him over the head with an iron bar. The victim was critically injured and spent two weeks on a life support machine. He had to learn how to walk again. He identified his attackers to Gardaí but the DPP decided there was insufficient evidence to proceed with charges against the men. Collopy would claim years later that it was this incident which turned his then young sons – Vincent, Brian, Philip and Kieran – into dangerous criminals.

In October 1997 the Collopy boys demonstrated their criminal credentials when they sought revenge on the McCarthys. John Ryan's brother-in-law, 'Pa' McCarthy, was hit in the back when the brothers opened fire on his car with a shotgun as he drove past their home. Three young children sitting in the back seat narrowly escaped injury. McCarthy and his brother identified the attackers as Kieran, Philip and Vincent Collopy. The brothers, then aged between fifteen and twenty-one, were each charged with assault and possession of a firearm with intent to endanger life. Two years later they were found not guilty, following a trial at Limerick Circuit Criminal Court. By then the Collopy brothers had become loyal members of the Keane gang.

In the meantime the feuding between the McCarthys and

Collopys and the Ryans and Keanes continued. The women in both families were blamed locally for fanning the flames. The situation was exacerbated through gossip and rumours, which were spread by both sides. The younger children were poisoned by their parents' senseless hate and were actively encouraged to get involved in the fighting. When John Ryan's daughter had a schoolyard row with one of the Collopys, her father retaliated by firing shots at their home.

Eddie Ryan and the Keanes had an unwritten agreement to remain neutral in the ongoing disputes, which were becoming a major problem. But it didn't bode well that Eddie Ryan was with his brother when the Collopy home was shot at. The volatility of both sides made a fatal confrontation inevitable.

By the summer of 2000 the bitterness had reached boiling point. There was another schoolyard row at St Mary's Secondary School in Corbally between John Ryan's daughter Samantha and Christy Keane's daughter Natalie. The fathers agreed that the only way to resolve the dispute was for an arranged fight between the two girls. After a half hour of fighting Natalie Keane gave up. The teenager had had a piece of her ear bitten off and the victory went to Samantha Ryan.

Eddie Ryan found himself being inexorably dragged into the vortex of evil. On 25 October 2000, there was another schoolyard confrontation, this time between Samantha Ryan and Christy Keane's niece. The following day the girl's mother, Anne Keane, the wife of Christy's brother Anthony, called to the primary school in Bishop Street to collect her younger daughter. She ran into John Ryan's daughters Samantha and Debbie and a fight ensued. Anne Keane was knocked to the ground, punched, kicked and slashed in the face with a Stanley blade. The two young women were subsequently charged with assault but the case never went to court.

Later that same evening a number of shots were fired through the front window of John Ryan's home at the Lee Estate, situated in the heart of the Keane territory. He called Eddie who immediately went to the house to find out what had happened. Eddie Ryan went to confront Christy Keane and the former friends had a fist-fight. Not content with that, Eddie and John Ryan later drove to the home of Owen Treacy on Colmcille Street, armed with a sawn-off shotgun. A gun battle resulted as Eddie Ryan fired several shots at the house and Treacy returned fire with a handgun. As the Ryans sped away, Treacy's bullets shattered the rear window of the car. What had begun as an apparently innocuous schoolyard row had suddenly escalated into a full-blown shooting war. But it was also a convenient excuse to deal with the bitter issue of control of the drug trade and the unpaid €40,000 debt. The former partners-in-crime were on a one-way collision course, hell-bent on spilling each other's blood. There was no longer any chance of reconciliation. The war was about to begin – and the Dundon/McCarthys were ready and waiting to seize control in the aftermath.

On the afternoon of Friday, 10 November 2000, Christy Keane was collecting his sixteen-year-old son Liam from school. Eddie Ryan and his sixteen-year-old son Kieran were waiting for him. When Christy Keane spotted Ryan walking towards him, he rolled down his window to talk to his former enforcer. But Ryan was not in a talkative mood. He produced a powerful Magnum revolver which he pointed directly at Keane's head. The weapon jammed as he squeezed the trigger. Ryan tried to shoot again but Keane drove off at speed down a pavement, sending children and parents scrambling out of the way.

As a disciple of the doctrine of an eye for an eye, Eddie Ryan didn't need a soothsayer to predict his fate. He immediately left Limerick and travelled to stay with his girlfriend in Newcastle, County Down in Northern Ireland. His wife Mary had just discovered she was seven weeks pregnant with their fourth child. Ryan stayed in County Down for the rest of the weekend. He returned to Limerick on Sunday evening for the funeral of his wife's brother, 'Pa' Collins, who had died from kidney failure the previous Friday. It was a big mistake.

Ryan was late for the ceremony, arriving at 8.45 p.m., where he spoke briefly with his wife. Then he set off for a drink to the Moose Bar with his two sons, Edward and Kieran, and a number of friends. Seventeen-year-old Edward borrowed his father's car to drive someone home. It would prove to be a life-saving decision. Eddie Ryan was only back in Limerick fifteen minutes and he had already been spotted by gangland spies. As soon as Ryan entered the pub, Christy Keane's brother Kieran got a call on his mobile phone informing him that the target was in the bar. The Keanes knew that the sudden death of Ryan's brother-in-law was fortuitous as it would bring their former friend out into the open. An assassination plan was readied for when Ryan turned up for the funeral. Keane's minions had stolen the getaway car from a pub at Murroe, County Limerick the night before. Kieran Keane was determined that Ryan would not escape. To ensure a successful outcome he recruited nineteen-year-old Philip Collopy for the job. Described as the most dangerous of the Collopy brothers, Philip had a fascination for firearms and no problem using them to kill. The getaway driver was twenty-three-year-old gang member

Paul Coffey, a close associate of the Collopys, who was unlawfully at large from prison. When the call came in they were ready.

Keane armed himself with the .357 Magnum revolver that had been used to shoot up John Ryan's home on 27 October. He sat in the back of the car while Collopy, who carried a 9mm automatic pistol, sat in the front. Kieran Keane instructed Coffey to drive to the Moose Bar. They parked in a yard across from the pub as Keane made one more phone call to his spy to find out where Ryan was sitting. He told Coffey to pull across in front of the pub for 'a few minutes'. As the car stopped, Keane and Collopy pulled balaclavas over their faces, jumped out and ran into the pub. Their enemy was sitting with his back to them when they opened fire. Within minutes they were back into the car after firing another seven shots at the front of the bar. Keane shouted, 'Drive, drive!' and Coffey sped away. Keane was elated by his night's work. He was shouting and cheering in the back of the car: 'Eddie is dead; Eddie Ryan is dead; he's gone.' Coffey dropped the killers at a nearby house. He then dumped the car on a deserted lane and set it on fire.

The murder of Eddie Ryan was greeted with shock and outrage. The fact that two innocent women had been seriously injured illustrated how close the attack had come to mass slaughter. Unfortunately for Kieran Keane and his mob they had missed Ryan's two sons. Despite their tender ages the Ryan brothers were violent thugs, like their father. The Keanes had given the brothers good reason to continue the family feud tradition and they immediately set about seeking vengeance. Gardaí at Mayorstone Station launched a major investigation assisted by officers from the specialist National Bureau of Criminal Investigation in Dublin. The Gardaí were now dealing with family feuds on both sides of Limerick City and knew Ryan's execution would result in more violence and death.

Within a few days local detectives had established through their informants who was responsible for the murder of Eddie Ryan. On 7 December, a large force of seventy armed officers invaded the Keanes' Island Field stronghold and raided several houses. Seven suspects, including Kieran Keane, Philip Collopy and Paul Coffey, were arrested for questioning. Keane and Collopy were hard men who denied any involvement in the outrage, but Coffey was not so resilient. He broke down under interrogation and gave detectives a detailed statement admitting his role in the murder and naming the killers. Coffey was charged with murder and Gardaí were hopeful that he would become a State witness against the hit men. However, his family were subjected to intimidation and threats by the Keane/Collopy mob and Coffey repudiated his statement during his trial. He opted instead to plead guilty to manslaughter and was later sentenced to fifteen years in prison.

The murder of Eddie Ryan sparked a major upsurge in violence in the north side of the city. The Ryans, backed up by Sean 'Cowboy' Hanley, went to war with the Keanes and Collopys in an orgy of tit-for-tat shootings and arson attacks. The conflict involved over seventy people, drawn in from the extended families and friends of the various combatants. Over the following year there were at least thirty petrol bomb and gun attacks on John Ryan's house alone. His wife and children were living in sheer terror. The house was nicknamed 'the Alamo' due to the number of assaults it had sustained. And for each attack there was retaliation. In one incident, in May 2001, Owen Treacy's father Philip, a baker with no involvement in crime, suffered serious burns when two petrol bombs were thrown through the front window of his home in County Clare. Two associates of the Ryan family, twenty-five-year-old Noel Price from Kileely and nineteen-year-old Michael Stanners of Delmege Park, were later charged with the attack. In May 2003, they were convicted of arson and were each jailed for twelve years. Price had more than ten previous convictions, including for an arson attack on the car of an off-duty Garda, assault, possession of a fire-arm and drug offences.

A deeply sinister twist in the gang war occurred in January 2001 with the discovery of an elaborate booby-trap bomb. It had been attached to a car driven by an associate of the Ryans. The device failed to explode and was discovered when it fell off the car. An army bomb expert said the viable device had been designed to kill anyone who was in the vehicle when it exploded. Gardaí suspected that the device had been made by the Keanes' INLA bomb-making associates in Dublin. The incident heralded the introduction of the bomb to gang wars in Ireland. Over subsequent years the number of such incidents spiralled into the hundreds as hoodlums all over the country tried to wipe each other out.

As the violence intensified between the Keane/Collopys and the Ryans, Chief Superintendent Gerry Kelly ordered a virtual lock-down of the Island Field. A full-time static police checkpoint was placed on the road at the entrance to the Keanes' kingdom. The neighbourhoods at the centre of the violence were also saturated with extra armed patrols. Christy Keane grew so accustomed to the intense Garda presence that he grew careless. On 21 August 2001, one of the Garda patrols spotted the godfather walking along St Senan Street carrying a coal sack. The bag appeared heavy and Keane was bent over holding the top of the bag with one hand and supporting it with the other. Detective Garda Ronan McDonagh, one of the most experienced serious crime investigators in the city, was immediately suspicious. When he and his colleagues pulled over to talk to Keane, the gang boss made a run for it, struggling to hold on to the sack.

When Detective Garda McDonagh caught up with him and searched the bag he found €240,000 worth of hashish. Keane, the clever hoodlum who had evaded justice for so long, was stunned that he had been caught so easily. It was a major victory for the Gardaí and a devastating blow to the city's biggest crime gang. Keane was subsequently charged with drug-trafficking offences and remanded in custody. A few weeks earlier the Dundon/McCarthys had agreed to Mikey Kelly's putative peace pact to end their feud on the other side of the city. The arrest of their main drug supplier couldn't have come at a better time; they began to monitor developments on the north side very closely.

August 2001 was a bleak month for the city. Five men were either beaten or stabbed to death, although none of the murders was a direct consequence of the feud. One of the victims was Brian Hanley, the son of Cowboy Hanley. He was out on bail at the time, having been caught with over €1 million worth of ecstasy the previous June. Four days after Christy Keane's arrest, Hanley was fatally stabbed when he and his father attacked a couple at their home following a drunken row. A woman subsequently received a suspended sentence for the attack.

Three days after Hanley's death, Christy Keane's seventeen-year-old son Liam also found himself in trouble with the police – as the prime suspect for stabbing nineteen-year-old Eric Leamy to death. Liam was following in the footsteps of his father, uncle and the other psychopaths who had been his role models since birth. Like most of his peers, he was born into a life of crime and displayed an unhealthy propensity for violence from an early age. He was being groomed to assume his father's mantle when he retired. Liam Keane's foray into serious crime had nothing to do with the feuds, however. It all began as an innocuous row over a dog.

On 27 August 2001, Keane's friend Jonathan Edwards visited the Lee Estate where he collected an Alsatian pup. On his way home he bumped into a group of youths including Eric Leamy who accused him of kicking the animal. Edwards left the area but returned later that night with Liam Keane. They ran into Leamy and a row ensued. Keane produced a knife and the nineteen-year-old was stabbed a number of times. He died a few days later in hospital. The day after the murder, Willie Moran Junior, a friend of Leamy's, hit Jonathan Edwards over the head with an iron bar during a revenge fight. Edwards was seriously injured and fell into a coma. He later developed pneumonia and died in hospital. In a subsequent trial Moran was acquitted, on the grounds that he was defending himself. Liam Keane was charged with Eric Leamy's murder after a number of people gave Gardaí statements saying they had witnessed the attack.

Liam Keane's case would cause a national outcry two years later, when it collapsed in the Central Criminal Court in Dublin. One of the petrified witnesses later revealed that he had been threatened at gunpoint by Kieran Keane and offered cash not to testify. In the meantime the bitter feuds continued to thrive on visceral hatred.

The Keanes and their allies took pleasure in taunting the Ryans about Eddie's murder. Mary Ryan was even jeered and abused by the Keanes when she brought her newborn baby to visit her husband's grave for the first time. 'The maggots are atin' Eddie,' they shouted across the street.

In January 2002 Mary Ryan was walking from the courts one afternoon when she bumped into Kieran Keane. In full view of the Gardaí he began verbally abusing the widow about her family, but she gave as good as she got. The gangland thug then head-butted the widow twice and shouted at her: 'I got your husband. Now I'm going to get you.' Gardaí arrested Keane for assault and he was subsequently jailed for three months. On 5 March Eddie's son Kieran Ryan stabbed Liam Keane as he walked through the city centre. Keane gave Gardaí a statement and Ryan was subsequently charged with assault and two counts of being in possession of a knife.

In May 2002, Christy Keane pleaded not guilty when he stood trial on drug-trafficking charges. He tried everything he could to get off the hook. On the first day of the hearing, the presiding judge ordered one of Keane's henchmen out of court for acting in an intimidatory manner towards the jury. Gardaí also discovered that another member of the gang had threatened the bus driver transporting the jurors to their lunch. Several of Keane's associates, including members of the INLA from Dublin, were present for the trial. Christy Keane offered a preposterous defence, claiming that the Gardaí had got the wrong man. Daniel Braddish, a drug addict and inmate in Limerick Prison, stated that he had been carrying the sack of hash when Keane's arrest took place. Braddish maintained that he had paid for the drugs with stolen money. When prosecution counsel put it to him that he was being paid to take the rap for Keane, Braddish replied: 'The State should reward me with money for owning up to this. I expect him [Keane] to go free because he is innocent.' The witness was laughed out of court.

On Monday, 3 June 2002, the court sentenced Christy Keane to ten years. Garda Superintendent Gerry Mahon told the court that the criminal was not a courier but a major league crime boss. He was taken to serve his sentence in Portlaoise maximum security prison, in the company of the country's most serious gangsters. Back in Limerick the feuding on the north side continued.

Two months later there was another sinister incident which illustrated how the situation was escalating all the time. Eddie Ryan's nephew and criminal associate, 'Fat' John McCarthy, had a lucky escape when his house was wracked by gunfire from an AK47 assault rifle. One of the bullets narrowly missed his nine-year-old son. McCarthy's attackers, cousins Ross Cantillon (aged nineteen) and Roy Woodland (aged twenty), typified the calibre of thugs created by the culture of mindless hate that existed between the feuding sides. The two Keane gang members already had the battle scars to prove their loyalty to the cause. On 1 December 2001, Woodland, who had previously been stabbed in the head, was ambushed by Kieran Ryan and his pal Christopher 'Smokey' Costelloe. Costelloe shot Woodland twice in the legs. His injuries were so severe that his right leg was amputated. Cantillon had also been shot in the leg and on another occasion sustained two perforated lungs when he was stabbed. The pair were consumed with a thirst for vengeance and happy to oblige when Kieran Keane sent them out to kill. As the hit team drove by in a stolen car Woodland fired a burst of eleven rounds at McCarthy's house. The use of a deadly weapon normally associated with terrorism was yet another new precedent set by the continuing warfare. The following day the shooters were rounded up by Gardaí who also located the weapon. The cousins were charged and remanded in custody. In February 2003 they were jailed for seven years each for their troubles.

Following the arrest of his brother, Kieran Keane had taken over the reins of the drug-trafficking operation. He was a lot more volatile than Christy and he soon let everyone in town know that he was, quite literally, calling the shots. The Dundon/McCarthys were careful to stay on good terms with both the Ryans and the Keane/Collopys. They were still buying drugs from the Keanes and were even supplying both sides with guns to shoot each other. With Christy Keane out of the picture, the Piranhas saw that one less obstacle stood in their way to gangland domination. The feuding maelstrom had created sufficient confusion to blur the lines between a turf war and internecine hatred. If the Dundon/McCarthys picked the right side they could further their dark ambitions. The treacherous Piranhas began forming deadly alliances behind the scenes – and drawing up battle plans for an underworld coup.

5. The Man Who Said 'No'

While the feuds were simmering, Murder Inc. made the breakthrough into the big league. Their way in was Larry McCarthy Junior's business relationship with Sean 'Cowboy' Hanley and Eddie Ryan. Hanley was a major drug trafficker in his own right. The seizure in June 2001 of €1 million worth of ecstasy at Hanley's property was an indication of how successful the former horse dealer had become. Hanley's son Brian and another man were arrested when the Garda National Drug Unit found the drugs in a shed behind Cowboy's house. After the murder of Eddie Ryan the veteran villain took Ryan's two sons under his wing. Cowboy Hanley had sworn bloody vengeance on his friend's killers and co-ordinated the spate of retaliatory shootings and arson attacks. He also had a lot of influence over the younger members of Murder Inc. who treated him as a mentor. Ostensibly the dealings between Cowboy and the Dundon/McCarthys were confined to the drug trade, as Larry Junior was careful to keep the gang's true allegiances under wraps. Secretly the Dundon/McCarthys had agreed to help Hanley get his eye for an eye – but only when the time was right. Through Cowboy Hanley, the narco-terrorists from Ballinacurra Weston also joined forces with two other major Irish criminals – James (Jim) 'Chaser' O'Brien and veteran County Clare gangster Anthony Kelly.

On the surface Chaser O'Brien was an unlikely gangland player and seemed to be the polar opposite to the uncultured savages in Murder Inc. Born in June 1963, he was the son of a farmer from Rawlinstown, Grange in County Limerick. O'Brien was from a respectable family and had a privileged upbringing when compared to the atavistic thugs he was dealing with. He was educated by the Christian Brothers in Hospital, County Limerick and entered the bar trade when he left school. He worked in a number of well-known pubs around the city and then bought his own premises in Pallas-green, on the Limerick–Tipperary Road, naming it Chaser O'Brien's. He was a greedy man with a taste for the high life – Chaser liked designer clothes, fast cars and glamorous women. And he had no scruples about where the cash came from to pay for it all. For him, becoming a drug trafficker was a calculated career choice.

O'Brien ingratiated himself with the top gangsters in Lim-erick and Dublin and by the mid-90s he was dabbling in the drug trade. As he prospered, he bought the Henry Cecil night-club and bar in the city centre. It soon became a popu-lar haunt for drug dealers. In 2000 Garda intelligence reports identified Chaser as being involved in the large-scale impor-tation and distribution of cannabis, cocaine, ecstasy and heroin. He and his partner-in-crime, gang boss Anthony Kelly, had links to major gangs in Ireland, the UK, Holland, Belgium and Spain.

Born in 1957, Kelly (no relation to the Kellys in Southill) was rated as one of the country's most serious criminals. From Kilrush he ran a large second-hand furniture business which was a front for a huge criminal operation, specializing in everything from stolen goods to drugs. A multi-millionaire, with an extensive international property portfolio, Kelly was a clever criminal who managed to remain one step ahead of the law. This was reflected in the fact that he had just six previous convictions to his name, for larceny, assault and receiving stolen goods.

In 1984, he was jailed for nine months for running a rather novel prostitution racket for the benefit of lonely bachelor farmers in the wilds of rural County Clare and Limerick. Kelly and his ladies toured the country back roads in a former mobile bank which he had converted into a brothel on wheels. Clients were entertained in the back of the 'passion wagon' as Kelly trundled around the bumpy roads. The businessman had been targeted in several major Garda investigations over the years but this was one of the few occasions when he was caught out.

On another occasion Kelly and O'Brien were arrested in Manchester after police uncovered a multi-million Euro haul of stolen computer components. However, they were never charged. In recognition of his status in the underworld, Kelly was one of the first crime figures targeted by the newly formed Criminal Assets Bureau in 1996. He was forced to pay over €1 million in taxes based on his criminal earnings.

Kelly was in a relationship with a Limerick woman, Marie Cronin from Ballinacurra Weston. Marie's criminal brother Mark was an associate of Larry McCarthy Junior and was also a foot soldier for Kelly and O'Brien. He was a violent thug who had done time for assault, possession of an offensive weapon and criminal damage. The father-of-three was also a monster at home and subjected his wife, Angela Collins, to nine years of appalling abuse. He once stabbed her when she was heavily pregnant and left her bleeding on the side of a street. Following another row he threw her out of a first-storey window. In 1998 he took the violence to a new level when the couple had an argument on a night out in O'Brien's club. Cronin head-butted his wife and stormed out. He returned to the packed Henry Cecil's around 1 a.m., armed with a handgun which he aimed at her. Cronin fired a shot which hit a totally innocent bystander, Georgina O'Donnell, in the eye. She died the following day and Cronin was subsequently jailed for life. As a result of the horrific incident business dropped off dramatically in O'Brien's night-club and he closed it down. By then he was already earning a lot more money in the drug trade.

The Dundon/McCarthys provided the army for the formidable new alliance: a gang of young, depraved hooligans who were utterly loyal to their bosses. Apart from the core membership from the Dundon and McCarthy families, their organized crime group was made up of cousins and individuals related through marriage. The gang had up to fifty members including drug couriers, street dealers and general foot soldiers. Also in the ranks were a few natural born killers who were happy to spill blood, anyone's blood, as long as the price was right.

One of the Dundons' closest friends was Gary Campion. They had a lot in common with him as the description most often used by his peers was that Gary was 'pure evil'. According to Gardaí, Campion was probably the only man the psychotic Dundon brothers and their McCarthy cousins were actually ever afraid of. In a warped world where respect really meant fear, Campion was revered. The local cops also acknowledged his lethality by classifying him as someone to be 'approached with extreme caution' and preferably with a loaded pistol on the hip.

Born in May 1983, Campion was the youngest of three brothers who grew up in Moyross. It was an urban sprawl built in the 70s on the north side of the city, close to the border with County Clare. Even by the standards of the

Dundons, Campion and his brothers, William and Noel, were a breed apart when it came to extreme violence. William and Noel had been in and out of prison for assaults and robbery with violence since they were children. When Gary was ten years old his poisonous siblings were in their mid-twenties and, in the absence of a father, were the worst role models imaginable. Under the tutorship of his psychopathic brothers, the youngster realized his true potential as a malevolent, cold-blooded killer, a role he took to with relish. Campion was the quintessential assassin. Before the age of twenty-three he had been implicated in at least five murders and countless shootings.

Gary Campion was fourteen when he was 'blooded' by his thirty-year-old brother William. He brought the teenager on a rampage of robberies, targeting the isolated rural homes of vulnerable old people who were living alone. Late on the night of Holy Thursday, 9 April 1998, the Campions burst into the home of sixty-eight-year-old Patrick 'Paud' Skehan at Bridgetown in County Clare. The helpless bachelor farmer, described by friends as a shy and intensely private man, was savagely beaten as he lay in his bed upstairs. Medical evidence would later show that the gang had smashed Paud Skehan's head several times, with a hard object, causing extensive brain injuries. He suffered several fractures to his skull and his nose was broken. In an act of mind-boggling savagery the Campions then dragged the pensioner from his bed and brought him downstairs. Skehan was blindfolded and his hands and legs were bound with TV cable. They then doused their seriously injured victim in petrol and hung him upside down from the banisters of the stairs in his kitchen.

When he was found by a neighbour, some twenty-four hours later, the farmer was barely alive and the only word he could utter was his dog's name, 'Puppy'. He was dressed only in a shirt and underpants and his face was caked in blood. The farmer survived on a life support machine for seven weeks but died on 3 June. The merciless act of barbarism caused outrage and fear throughout rural Ireland. Gardaí later arrested William Campion after matching his shoes to bloody footprints found at the scene. In March 2000, he was jailed for life for the murder but there was insufficient evidence to link anyone else to the crime.

Two months after Paud Skehan's murder, Noel Campion, who was in prison for armed robbery, threatened to kill a prison officer in Limerick jail. Noel told the officer he knew where he lived and would burn his house down. Two days later, fifteen-year-old Gary Campion duly petrol-bombed the officer's home in the middle of the night. When the Dundons returned from London in 2000, Gary Campion, then seventeen, began running with them and enthusiastically participated in their campaign of intimidation against Gardaí and prison officers. As a key player in Murder Inc. he was also responsible for several shootings and stabbings in the inter-family feuds and was with the Dundon brothers when they kidnapped Terence Casey in January 2001. One young criminal that the hit man tried to kill on a number of occasions was so fearful that he ended up killing himself.

Camion's blood-curdling description of what it is like to kill someone appears in retired prison officer Philip Bray's memoir, *Inside Man*: 'When you shoot a man, he drops down. He doesn't go flying backwards. It doesn't matter if it's a shotgun or a nine mil., that stuff you see in the pictures is pure crap. I never saw anyone move more than a few inches in my life. I'll tell you another thing. If you shoot a man in the back of the head, a funny thing happens. His two eyeballs will pop out of the front of his head and just hang there on stalks – ha ha!'

A seasoned Limerick City detective described the dangerous young man: 'Gary Campion was a pure evil monster and he would kill for anyone who would pay him; even the Dundons were afraid of him. There were no boundaries or limits for that creature. He had been shooting and killing when kids his age were still at school. He was responsible for at least five murders before the age of twenty-three; he was a natural born killer.'

With Christy Keane locked up on drug charges and his gang distracted by the ongoing feuds, the Dundon/McCarthys grew more cocky and confident. The Piranhas had been on the lookout for a new opportunity and began expanding their market and flexing their muscles. In a vibrant city with a large youth population, including over 20,000 third-level students, there was a huge demand for recreational drugs. Night-clubs and pubs frequented by young people with plenty of cash became much-sought-after pitches for cocaine, hash and ecstasy dealers to ply their trade. One of the city's most popular night spots was Doc's, a trendy club in the city centre which catered for over 800 patrons on an average night.

Larry McCarthy Junior and his depraved cousins decided that Doc's was going to be their exclusive patch. If they could establish themselves in the club their ill-gotten gains would be worth at least €30,000 a week. The gang reckoned that taking over Doc's night-club would be a pushover, but they were wrong. When Murder Inc. made their move they ran into an unexpected – and intolerable – obstacle: Doc's Head of Security, Brian Fitzgerald. When Fitzgerald stood in the way of the Dundon/McCarthys' plans he found himself in the path of a murderous juggernaut. His fate would be a dark omen of what was to come and it would encapsulate the savagery that made Murder Inc. a household name.

Brian Fitzgerald was literally a giant of a man. Born in 1967, he stood over six feet tall and was a former Munster power-lifting champion. He didn't drink or smoke and had three passions in life – his family, work and rugby. He regularly lined out for St Mary's Rugby Club and had played one season with Thomond Rugby Club. Brian had grown up in St Mary's Park, the Keanes' domain, and knew a lot of the local criminal fraternity, but he had opted for life on the honest side of the tracks. In 1995 he married his childhood sweetheart, Alice McNamara, and a year later they bought their first home, a semi-detached house at Brookhaven Walk, in the middle-class suburb of Corbally on the northern outskirts of the city. Fitzgerald was totally devoted to his wife and two little boys, Aaron and Evan. After leaving school he worked in Krupp's, the German household electrical appliance manufacturer. He also worked as a doorman at clubs and pubs around Limerick, a job he seemed naturally suited to.

Fitzgerald got a job as a bouncer at Doc's in 1997 and soon moved up to the position of the club's security manager, heading a team of thirteen staff. He became the public face of the club, the first person patrons met at the front door. Brian Fitzgerald didn't like the tradition of the menacing bouncer and insisted that his staff maintained an informal and welcoming demeanour. Fitzgerald also adopted a diplomatic, cool-headed approach when faced with trouble. His main concern was for the safety of the young patrons who came through the doors every night. He enforced a strict no-drugs policy and barred anyone suspected of selling drugs on the premises. Among the people refused entry were pushers working for the Dundon/McCarthys.

It was already well known in Brian Fitzgerald's security circle that the Dundon/McCarthys were extremely dangerous. The streetwise security manager knew who and what he was dealing with – and he instantly recognized what they were up to. In 2001 Brian Fitzgerald took the life-altering decision to bar Larry McCarthy Junior and the Dundons from the premises.

Around 2 a.m. one September morning McCarthy Junior drove up to the front door of Doc's in his red BMW. When he tried to go into the club Brian Fitzgerald told him it was closing. He knew McCarthy Junior and what he was involved in. The red-haired diminutive gangster wasn't happy and he asked the security man if he realized who he was talking to. Brian later told Gardaí in a statement: 'I said I know the name but we're still closed. He said he would be taking it further.' The Murder Inc. boss later sent a message to Fitzgerald, demanding that he meet McCarthy and his cousins, but the security manager refused to go.

Two weeks later Larry McCarthy Junior and John Dundon were sitting in a white van when Brian Fitzgerald arrived for work. Dundon made the shape of a gun with his hand and asked the security manager who he thought he was, refusing to meet them. Fitzgerald later recalled: 'I said to them, "Who the hell are you?" and Dundon said, "We're the Dundon/McCarthys and you're getting it tonight," with his fingers pointed at me like a gun.'

McCarthy Junior then told him all they wanted was to be allowed into the club for an hour because that was all they needed. Fitzgerald's wife Alice told Gardaí in a statement: 'Brian told me they said, "Leave us in there for an hour, turn a blind eye and you'll be a rich man."' The security manager bluntly told them that they would not be selling drugs to kids in his night-club. The matter was closed – and so was the front door.

The arrogant thugs were infuriated by the temerity of Brian Fitzgerald. They had been confident that their menacing presence would be enough to convince him of the wisdom of reversing Doc's drug policy.

Fitzgerald's impertinence astonished the dangerous thugs and from that moment he found himself in a living nightmare as he became the focus of the gang's obsessive hatred. Larry McCarthy and the Dundons began to intimidate and threaten him on a daily basis. They would drive by the front door of the club at night, where the security manager was on duty, just to let him know they were watching him. The gang could not, and would not, forget the man who had stood up to them; instead they decided to show him what they were capable of. A month after being barred from Doc's, John Dundon shot his cousin, John Creamer, fourteen times with a machine-gun. It served as a chilling message to anyone who dared to even consider crossing them.

Around 12.30 a.m. on 7 December 2001, seventeen-year-old Dessie Dundon arrived at Doc's with three other people, but Brian Fitzgerald told him he was barred. Later that day Dessie brushed shoulders with Brian on the street. The security manager told Gardaí: 'He then turned to me and said, "You're getting it soon, Fitz." My understanding of that was I was going to be shot. I didn't say anything to him.'

Around 12.50 a.m. on the morning of 18 December, the mob increased the pressure on their target. A shotgun blast was fired through the front sitting-room window of Fitzgerald's home, which was decked out in Christmas lights. The pellets from the blast landed on the couch where his sick child had been resting a short time earlier.

Two days later, at 11.30 p.m., Larry McCarthy Junior and John Dundon approached Brian Fitzgerald at Doc's to make sure he'd got the message. He told them to go away and that they weren't welcome in his club.

'John Dundon made a gesture with his hand, as if he was firing a gun, and said: "Fitz, you're going to get it soon,"' the security manager told Gardaí afterwards. At the same time, Larry McCarthy was running his fingers across his throat indicating that Fitzgerald was about to be killed. The deadly cousins then drove away and returned about fifteen minutes later and parked across the road. One of them shouted over: 'Rudolph got it.' It was a reference to the ornament in Brian's front window which had been blasted in. The security manager decided that he would not be intimidated. Brian Fitzgerald made an official complaint to the Gardaí who moved quickly to intercede.

On 26 January 2002, Larry McCarthy Junior and John Dundon were arrested and charged with making death threats against the security manager. John Dundon was also charged with over twenty offences, relating to his ongoing intimidation of prison officers and Gardaí. In that January alone Dundon had been involved in a spate of arson and gun attacks on the homes of prison officers in the city. The cousins were remanded in custody. McCarthy Junior was incensed that Brian Fitzgerald had 'the cheek' to get up in court and testify against him. The up-and-coming crime lord, who celebrated his twenty-third birthday behind bars, was facing at least four and a half years in prison if Fitzgerald didn't drop his complaint. If he was convicted on the intimidation charges it would also reactivate a suspended six-year sentence McCarthy had received on 2 February 1999, for violent disorder. The gang boss decided that he wasn't prepared to let that happen.

On 11 February, McCarthy Junior applied for bail in the High Court in Dublin. Gardaí objected and Brian Fitzgerald testified that he had feared for his life when McCarthy had threatened him in December. The court refused the application. In the meantime, McCarthy and his associates made several approaches to a number of Brian Fitzgerald's friends, urging them to tell him to drop the charges. His wife later revealed that he was in a state of turmoil and found himself in an impossible bind. He was afraid to go to court and she told Gardaí he said: 'What's the point? When they come out they will get me anyway.' But the night-club security manager also told one of his friends that he was determined to make a stand against the Dundon/McCarthys. Alice said that the attack on their home had had a profound effect on her husband and he was clearly fearful for his own and his family's safety.

Larry McCarthy Senior offered Brian money if he dropped the charges against his son and nephew. He told his wife about the offer. 'Brian said McCarthy Senior told him: "I'll offer you my word that my son won't touch you and some day if you are ever in a spot, I'll owe you one." He refused point blank to take money off them,' Alice later said. 'I'll always remember his words to me: "Take money off them and you always owe them a favour."'

While Larry McCarthy Junior and John Dundon were languishing in prison, Gardaí got an insight into the extent of the gang's burgeoning drug trade when they busted the distribution network operated by Jim 'Chaser' O'Brien and Anthony Kelly. On 13 March 2002, undercover cops watched as fifty-four-year-old grandmother Ann Keane delivered €30,000 worth of cocaine and ecstasy to Ger Dundon. It was the eve of his fifteenth birthday and he was already heavily involved in organized crime. At the meeting Dundon handed over a Luger 9mm pistol as part payment for the drugs haul. The arrests of Keane, her twenty-six-year-old boyfriend Brian Aherne and fourteen-year-old Ger Dundon were the culmination of an investigation – appropriately codenamed 'Hillbilly' – involving officers from the Limerick Division.

In a follow-up search of Ann Keane's rented house near Newport, County Tipperary, detectives found a major distribution centre. They seized over €500,000 worth of cocaine, ecstasy and cannabis, and two firearms. A ledger found on the kitchen table showed that over the previous nine months alone Murder Inc. had moved drugs worth millions of Euros. Ann Keane was subsequently jailed for six years and Aherne got three years. Ger Dundon also got a three-year sentence, which was suspended in recognition of his tender age – and to give him a chance to mend his ways. One of the conditions of the suspension was that he remained living in Waterford and did not return to Limerick. However, in 2004, the sentence was activated after Ger Dundon was convicted of assaulting a Garda. Dundon had attacked the officer after he spotted the young hood acting suspiciously in Limerick.

Meanwhile the intimidation case involving Brian Fitzgerald took an unexpected twist on 23 April 2002, when McCarthy Junior appeared for a remand hearing before Limerick District Court. The court was told that the Book of Evidence relating to the charges had not yet been completed. The charge was struck out although the State could re-enter the charges when the book was finalized. McCarthy was free to go and he promptly left the country and began moving between bases in the UK and Spain. The following day, John Dundon was also released from custody – but not with the consent of a judge.

On 24 April Dundon appeared in Limerick Circuit Criminal Court charged with making threats to kill four prison officers. He was then due to be driven back to Cork Prison in the back of a taxi, under Garda escort. John Dundon was wearing handcuffs and the child locks were activated on the taxi doors to prevent him getting out. But he had other plans. When the taxi stopped at traffic lights near King's Island, Gary Campion ran over and opened the back door. Dundon raced off and vanished, later fleeing back to London. He was not seen for over a year although he and his cousin remained active in the gang and regularly returned to Ireland on secret visits. A few days before their brother's lucky break, Wayne and Dessie Dundon had been convicted of assaulting the Gardaí in September 2000. Wayne was sent down for two years and Dessie got nine months. For a short time Limerick got a reprieve from the scourge of the Dundon brothers and Larry McCarthy Junior, but for the rest of the gang it was business as usual.

Through Larry McCarthy Junior and Stephen 'Dougie' Moran, Murder Inc. had strong links with a number of gangs in Manchester and Birmingham in the UK. They had set up a well-organized supply line of drugs and firearms back to Dublin and Limerick. A Limerick ex-pat called James Patrick Moloney, who was living in Bradford, West Yorkshire, supplied machine-guns, assault rifles and automatic pistols to McCarthy Junior and Dougie Moran, which were then sent on to Murder Inc. in Limerick. The cousins also supplied weapons to a number of Dublin gangs and the Continuity IRA. Moloney sourced the firearms from two members of the Morecambe Rifle and Pistol Club on the Lancashire coast. Robert Naylor (aged forty-nine) and James Greenwood (aged fifty-six) were both gun enthusiasts who collected deactivated weapons, including decommissioned British Army guns, as a hobby. But they discovered a source of easy money by reactivating the weapons and selling them on to criminal gangs.

The drugs and guns were smuggled into the country, predominantly in cars driven by the gang's multiple couriers. One of them was twenty-eight-year-old Philip Michael Dean from Birmingham. Dean had been involved in petty crime, mostly theft, all his life. His only seemingly legitimate activity was when he had a small computer business for a brief period. It sold stolen computer parts supplied by Anthony Kelly and Chaser O'Brien. Dean first met Larry McCarthy Junior in 2000 through Amy Harrison, his partner and the mother of his two children. It was an encounter that the petty criminal would live to regret. He became one of the gang's logistics managers – transporting drugs, guns and gangsters between the two countries. Dean would later claim to Gardaí that Larry McCarthy Junior threatened him with a 'bullet in the back of the head' when he tried to get out of the operation. He said the Dundon/McCarthy gang kept his partner and children 'hostage' to ensure that he continued making the deliveries. McCarthy, who was notoriously miserly, preferred using fear rather than cash to get weaker people to work for him: Dean was paid a pittance for each run.

Between June and December 2002 Dean made five trips from England to Ireland. He delivered a total of twenty-four weapons, including Mac 10 and Uzi submachine-guns, automatic and semi-automatic pistols, silencers, converted torch guns and a large amount of ammunition. He also personally delivered 320 nine-ounce bars of hashish, 250,000 ecstasy tablets and two slabs of crystallized cocaine, with a total street value of over €2 million. Dean later said that he had made the deliveries in person to O'Brien, Kelly, Dougie Moran, the Dundons and other members of the network in Dublin, Newry, Tralee, Kilrush and Limerick. By the end of 2002 the Dundon/McCarthys were running a multi-million Euro enterprise – and they weren't going to let anyone stand in their way.

Larry McCarthy Junior had kept up the pressure on Brian Fitzgerald to withdraw his complaint. The night-club security manager was tipped off that John Dundon had been looking for someone to kill him. Even after his lucky release, McCarthy was extremely aggrieved about his enforced three-month sojourn in prison. Gardaí would later discover evidence of the gang boss's hate-filled obsession with the security manager. In seven handwritten letters sent to a young lover, three of them written while he was on remand, Larry McCarthy Junior portrayed himself as an innocent man but even then he could scarcely hide his contempt for Brian Fitzgerald. One of the letters sent before his release from custody contained the following passage:

> Oh I better tell you why I'm here [prison]. Shooting? Murder? Robbery? No none of the above, for driving my own car and for threatening Brian Fitz in December 01 at Doc's, and 20th I think. I didn't say anything to the dope. I have been sent forward for trial on them both and refused bail. I can't apply for bail again until July. But I might have a chance in 4 to 5 weeks times to get out if not then I don't know what. They are silly charges, but you know what they [police] are trying to do, 6 years!

Another letter contained the remark: 'Doormen. I think I will kill all of them.'

McCarthy also referred to Brian Fitzgerald as a 'lying cunt'. In reference to the possibility that his suspended sentence from 1999 would be activated, he wrote:

> Even if I get six bells [years] does he [Fitzgerald] think I will be happy when I get out? Because I don't fucking think I will. I don't mind being in jail but it drives you mad when you are here for something you didn't do. This is a joke that isn't funny woman. Well not to me anyway!

In another letter he revealed that he had been advised by his partner Chaser O'Brien to get offside and continue making money from their drug business: 'But u know yourself, if I take Jim's advice and stay away from smelly Limk and just work away I will get loads of dosh with him. But that bastard [Fitzgerald] is driving me crazy. He is on my mind worse than you.'

On 16 September 2002 McCarthy phoned Fitzgerald from England and reiterated his demand that his victim withdraw the charges. Brian was at home with his wife Alice at the time and she later related the conversation to Gardaí. 'He [Brian] said: "Larry, I had told your father I wouldn't turn up in court and that was until someone hired two men to bring me down a lane and kill me."' McCarthy Junior denied this and suggested that he forget about his complaint and they could go their separate directions. Alice recalled what her husband said then: 'Ye are the ones that come to me; ye're the ones who threatened my family. I can't walk away from my job Larry. I'm not an educated man; I can't walk in and get an office job. This is my work, this is what I do. Ye go around shooting people, bullying people, being the big hard men and then you want me to stand by and let ye go walk into a club with young boys and girls and give them drugs. I'm telling you this will never, never happen.'

Larry McCarthy Junior phoned Fitzgerald on a number of other occasions to get his answer about what he intended to do. At the time, the security manager had confided to family members and some friends that the pressure was getting to him. McCarthy instructed Brian Fitzgerald to go to a certain solicitor and make a statement withdrawing his complaint.

On 4 October, the security manager visited the solicitor and made the statement. Brian Fitzgerald seemed to believe that his problems with Murder Inc. had ended and his wife said that he was more relaxed after that. He told her that he didn't believe the Dundons would do anything to him without their cousin's imprimatur. But he was wrong. He had crossed swords with a gang who would not forgive or forget. Larry McCarthy Junior was not fully satisfied that the case would be dropped. He feared that Fitzgerald might change his mind and he would be arrested again. If the Gardaí provided the security manager with protection, there was no way he could be got at. The young godfather wasn't prepared to take a chance. The gang's trade in drugs and firearms was also working well and it would be bad for business if he had to go inside for over four years. Brian Fitzgerald had to be eliminated.

On Thursday, 28 November 2002, Brian Fitzgerald bathed his two sons, who were aged one and five, and stayed with them until they fell asleep. He left for work shortly afterwards at 8 p.m. At the same time Murder Inc. were finalizing their plans to kill him that night but at the last moment they had hit an unexpected snag. A stolen motorbike parked at a shopping centre on the outskirts of Limerick, which

Stephen 'Dougie' Moran had organized to transport the hit man, was found by security staff. They called the Gardaí, which threw Murder Inc.'s plans into disarray. The original driver of the getaway bike, a Dublin criminal, got cold feet and decided to pull out of the plot. He was nervous and wanted to get back to Dublin. John Dundon considered shooting him in case he 'grassed' them up but decided to let him leave. At the same time Dessie Dundon contacted Gary Campion, who agreed to get a replacement motorbike and drive it for €10,000. Campion told his pal he had no problem doing the shooting if he wanted. But the hit man had already been hired for the job.

English-born criminal James Martin Cahill had been associated with the Dundon/McCarthy gang for several years. Overweight and completely bald, he certainly didn't look like a gangland executioner. Cahill was born in Birmingham but had been living in Kilrush, County Clare with an uncle from the age of fifteen. He was a depraved individual, with no qualms about killing anyone as long as the price was right. James Cahill had displayed violent tendencies since childhood and had been expelled from school for seriously injuring a teacher. In 1999, he was jailed for ten years for armed robbery and possession of firearms with intent to endanger life in Galway. The Court of Criminal Appeal, however, overturned the conviction on a technicality. He would later claim that Larry McCarthy Junior offered him €10,000 to murder Brian Fitzgerald.

The plot to execute the innocent security manager had been hatched weeks earlier and up to eight members of the gang were involved in the planning and logistics. John Dundon secretly returned from the UK to carry out surveillance on Brian Fitzgerald, along with his brother Dessie and Gary

Campion, while Jim 'Chaser' O'Brien organized a getaway car and other logistics for the 'hit'. In the days leading up to the murder, John and Dessie Dundon drove Cahill out to Brian Fitzgerald's house at Brookhaven Walk on a reconnaissance mission. They also checked out the CCTV security cameras the security manager had erected around his home.

Cahill would later claim in court that after a number of meetings with Chaser O'Brien, he was brought to Anthony Kelly's home in Kilrush the night before the murder. He alleged that Kelly had supplied him with the automatic pistol and a magazine full of bullets. Cahill maintained Kelly showed him how to use the weapon and told him not to 'mess it up'. However, Anthony Kelly was later acquitted by a jury because there was no corroboration to back up Cahill's story. Cahill also alleged that another member of the gang had told him to 'make sure you put one in the cunt's head' because he wanted to make sure it was going to be a closed coffin. In a statement Cahill later told Gardaí, 'I knew that he meant that I was to make sure to put a bullet into Brian Fitzgerald's head.'

The gang met in Chaser O'Brien's house as they made final preparations to do the foul deed. Cahill told Gardaí: 'John and Dessie Dundon were like two generals that day, organizing everything. They were on and off the phone to Larry McCarthy Junior a lot.'

Meanwhile Brian Fitzgerald arrived at Doc's at the usual time. Thursday night was student night and it passed off without incident. The gang's initial plan was to shoot him as he stood at the night-club door. Around midnight Cahill, Dessie Dundon and Gary Campion were outside Doc's. Cahill would later tell the Gardaí: 'As we walked past Doc's Dessie Dundon pointed out Brian Fitzgerald to me. I had the gun with me and I was looking to see if I could do him there, outside the door, to see if I could shoot him there but it was too busy – too many people around.' The three killers walked past the club again with hoodies pulled over their heads. Cahill said he wanted to get a good look at his target. 'I made sure I would know him again,' he said. Campion and Cahill collected their motorbike and went to Brian Fitzgerald's home to wait.

Around 3.30 a.m. on 29 November, Cahill's twenty-eighth birthday, Brian Fitzgerald dropped staff members home in his Opel Frontera jeep and then went home himself. Dessie Dundon had been lurking in the shadows, stalking the victim. He phoned Cahill to alert him that Fitzgerald was on his way. Cahill and Campion were hiding in bushes near the house in Corbally. As they saw the lights of the jeep approaching Campion asked Cahill for the gun and said he would do the shooting, but the hit man refused. It was shortly before 3.50 a.m. when Brian Fitzgerald stopped outside his front door. Cahill and Campion suddenly ran towards him as he got out of the jeep. Cahill was armed with a 9mm semi-automatic pistol, one of the reactivated pistols smuggled into the country by Philip Dean. The corpulent killer tripped and twisted his ankle but he kept going. Brian Fitzgerald saw the two men coming towards him and got ready to defend himself. He shouted at them: 'Come on ye cunts, ye.' Cahill opened fire, hitting Fitzgerald twice in the chest, but the security manager still tried to make a run for it.

Brian Fitzgerald managed to get roughly 65 metres down the road before he fell to the ground beside a car parked outside a neighbour's house. Cahill caught up with his helpless victim and shot him twice in the back of the head. The hit man would later tell a court: 'I shot him in the heart, then after a while I walked round and shot him in the back of the head.' Cahill said he didn't know how many times he fired: 'I just clicked it.'

Brian Fitzgerald was left lying face down in a pool of blood. Campion searched the dead man's body looking for his mobile phone while Cahill searched his jeep. They wanted to get rid of evidence of calls from Larry McCarthy Junior. The hit man had been told to plant bags of heroin in the jeep as a final insult to the memory of their innocent victim. But Cahill said he refused to do this. At that moment Brian's wife, Alice Fitzgerald, knocked at the window to attract Campion's attention. She showed him her phone so he'd know she was calling the police. The killers ran to the motorbike and sped off. Less than eight minutes later, the first Garda unit arrived at the scene. Officers found the body of Murder Inc.'s victim a half hour later.

Within minutes of the shooting, Gary Campion dropped Cahill by a getaway car which was parked some distance away. It was a Ford Mondeo supplied by Chaser O'Brien. Campion dumped the bike, setting it on fire in a laneway, and went to the home of a criminal associate a short distance away. From there he called a taxi to bring him home to Moyross. Meanwhile Cahill drove to Annacotty village on the outskirts of the city where Chaser O'Brien lived. He hid the murder weapon under bushes behind the Jackie Power memorial statue in the village. In O'Brien's home at Willow Crescent he then showered and changed his clothes to get rid of forensic evidence. Chaser had organized transport to get the hit man to Dublin, where he had arranged to meet Dougie Moran. Moran dropped Cahill to catch a train to Belfast, where he met John Dundon and Larry McCarthy Junior. They later travelled on together to Birmingham, by ferry and road.

The brutal execution of Brian Fitzgerald shocked and outraged the people of Limerick. It was an act of narco-terrorism. The sense of horror and revulsion was also expressed by hardened members of the criminal underworld. Even by the standards of the gangland violence already established in the noughties, the murder was seen as a step too far. Politicians and community leaders called for tougher legislation and more Gardaí to take on the gangs. The masters of Murder Inc. didn't care that they were the obvious and only suspects with a clear motive to kill Fitzgerald. They had carefully planned the crime and reckoned there would be no chance of them being caught. It also suited their purpose: the assassination sent a shiver of fear through the underworld and the ordinary citizens of Limerick. Murder Inc. had made it clear that there were no limits to their brutality. The gang had the same warped logic as any other terrorist organization – they wanted the public to be afraid and to know that the same fate awaited anyone who contemplated being a hero and standing up to them. It was also an unequivocal message to the city's security industry to reconsider their anti-drug policies. Gardaí didn't know it at the time but Brian Fitzgerald's execution was to be the first horrific crime in a virtual tsunami of bloodshed coming their way.

Before dawn on that damp November morning the Gardaí had a good idea of who had been responsible for the cold-blooded murder of a totally innocent man. By the following evening, well-placed, reliable informants had confirmed the involvement of the gang in the heinous crime. The first intelligence reports had revealed that Chaser O'Brien had organized transport for two people out of Limerick in the hours immediately before and after the murder. As a result of that information, James Martin Cahill was identified. The investigation team also knew the identity of the man who had robbed the first motorbike for the hit man to use. In turn that led officers to the identities of the rest of the gang. It was clearly a well-planned operation, involving hardened criminals who never talked. Gardaí knew that making a case against the mob would be a struggle.

Gardaí launched the largest murder investigation seen in the region since local Special Branch Detective Jerry McCabe had been gunned down by an IRA gang six years earlier. The Divisional officer-in-charge, Chief Superintendent Gerry Kelly, immediately set up an investigation incident room in Mayorstone Garda Station. His senior officers – Superintendents Willie Keane and Gerry Mahon; Detective Inspector Jim Browne and Inspector John Scanlan; and Detective Sergeants Tom O'Connor, Eamon O'Neill and Paddy O'Callaghan – were appointed as the lead investigators. These men were among the most experienced and respected criminal investigators in the country and it would be their job to take down Murder Inc. over the next decade.

The city's hardened investigators had considerable experience dealing with the most violent criminals in Ireland. They were the team who brought the killers of their colleague Jerry to justice, despite the best efforts of the Provisional IRA to intimidate witnesses. For the Gardaí in the city, many of whom were friendly with Brian Fitzgerald, this was more personal than business. Many of them felt a sense of guilt that they should have done more to protect the victim. By the time Brian Fitzgerald was laid to rest on 2 December, the Gardaí had a clear picture of the gang behind the horror.

Thousands turned out to pay their final respects to the night-club security manager. The Munster rugby family also came out in force to mourn their fallen brother. In his homily Fr Tom Mangan summed up the feelings of the public: 'For his beliefs Brian has paid a heavy price. Nobody deserves to die like that. How can an act like this achieve any benefit, anytime, anywhere? There is no sense to it. But there are people in our society today who seem to make sense of this.'

The heartbreak suffered by Brian's wife and family was incalculable.

Such was the depth of public anger and despair that for the first time ever, hundreds of people took to the streets in an act of solidarity to express their revulsion at the culture of incipient violence which was gaining a stranglehold on the city. Brian Fitzgerald had been the seventeenth person to die violently in Limerick in just two years – sixteen of the deaths had occurred over a twenty-month period. The people staged a silent, candlelit peace march through the city the week before Christmas, to show their abhorrence of mob law. The gangs sat back and laughed at the gesture.

On 3 December, Larry McCarthy Junior, James Cahill and John Dundon arrived at Philip Dean's home in Birmingham. They had travelled on the Lagan Viking ferry from Belfast to Liverpool. The three men discussed the murder of 'Fitz' and Dean later told Gardaí that McCarthy instructed him to immediately return to Limerick and dispose of the weapon. Cahill drew a map, to direct him to the spot where he had hidden the gun. The next day Dean located the hidden weapon and dumped it into the Mulcair River near the salmon weir in the village. But as he was doing so a member of the public spotted him and contacted the Gardaí.

The following day a Garda diver found the 9mm pistol. It would prove to be a significant breakthrough in the case and subsequent investigations would uncover the gang's source of weapons in the UK. But in the meantime the increased heat from the police and the public's revulsion at the Fitzgerald murder did not force the psychopaths in Murder Inc. to go to ground. Less than two weeks after the people took to the streets to pray for peace, Murder Inc. claimed the life of another totally innocent man.

Around 11.30 p.m. on New Year's Eve, thirty-nine-year-old Sean Poland returned to his home at Blackwater near Ardnacrusha in County Clare, with his partner Joanne Lyons. The couple had spent the evening socializing in the Round House Bar in Limerick city centre and went home to ring in the New Year together. The father-of-two had no involvement in crime and didn't have any enemies. So there was no reason why the block-layer and part-time used-car salesman would suspect that he was being stalked by six members of the Dundon/ McCarthy mob, including Dessie Dundon, Anthony 'Noddy' McCarthy and Gary Campion. Sean Poland's only mistake was to sell a car to Gary Campion for €1,000. The treacherous gangland vultures wanted the money back.

The couple were home a short time when Murder Inc. moved in. As Sean Poland answered a knock on the front door, one of the masked gangsters shot him without hesitation in the lower abdomen. The violent criminals stepped across their critically wounded victim and stormed into the house like a horde of wild animals. Inside they beat up Joanne Lyons and tied her up, demanding to know where her partner kept his cash. As the New Year's celebrations blared from the TV, Sean Poland lay bleeding to death in his doorway and the mobsters were ransacking the house. They stayed there for around forty minutes and left when they found the €1,000 cash. The killers stepped over their victim on the way out, completely ignoring him. Joanne Lyons eventually freed herself and raised the alarm. By then it was too late for her partner. In the first minutes of 2003, Sean Poland died as an ambulance crew rushed to get to him.

The investigation of the Sean Poland murder also fell to the Gardaí at Mayorstone Station in Limerick. And from the beginning the intelligence clearly pointed to the Dundon/McCarthys and their associates as the main suspects for the crime. It was now clear to Chief Superintendent Kelly and his staff that they were dealing with a criminal gang who had no boundaries. Gradually the local Garda force in the city, although already backed up by the National Bureau of Criminal Investigation, was being stretched to the limit.

Across the city's three Garda stations detectives were swamped, dealing with at least twenty serious shooting and stabbing incidents associated with the mob feuding alone. At the same time officers were maintaining extra armed patrols to keep a lid on the violence in the north side of the city. Then there was the continuing heavy workload required to complete investigations and prepare court files on the eighteen murders that had taken place in the city in just two years. And in between there were the usual day-to-day crimes, including drug dealing, robberies and burglaries, to be dealt with. The pressure on the Gardaí was immense. But as grim as the situation appeared to be on New Year's Day 2003, it was going to get a whole lot worse. The murder of two innocent men was just a prelude to the main event being planned by the Dundon/McCarthys.

6. A Gangland Coup

The cold-blooded murder of two innocent men shocked not only the law-abiding population but also members of the underworld confraternity. Many of them observed the basic principle that innocent civilian casualties were to be avoided as far as possible. The sentiment was more pragmatic than moral. The investigation of the murder of ordinary decent people by criminals inevitably attracted a much more intensive Garda response – and that was bad for business. The murder of journalist Veronica Guerin in 1996 and the subsequent pummelling meted out to the underworld had been a salutary lesson for the godfathers. The criminals' survival instincts also told them that if the Dundon/McCarthys could carry out such senseless killings they had a limitless capacity for depravity. This combination of fear and revulsion focused the gangsters' minds and loosened their tongues.

In the days and weeks following the murder of Brian Fitzgerald Gardaí received an unusually large amount of good quality information from people on the fringes of Murder Inc. This information gave detectives a clear enough picture of who had been involved and their route out of Limerick afterwards. One informant also made the disturbing revelation that Larry McCarthy Junior had organized a 'gun holiday' in Florida for the gang's trusted lieutenants during the summer of 2002. Posing as a sports team, the group spent a week at a specialist gun school, practising their marksmanship with a wide variety of automatic weapons.

Such 'gun holidays' to the USA and Eastern Europe were a popular activity among most of the country's drug gangs, including the Keane/Collopys. But none of the informants could shed light on the purpose of the training sojourn in the sunshine state: that the Dundon/McCarthys were secretly mobilizing for war.

Murder Inc. and their partners had already agreed a pact with Cowboy Hanley and the Ryans to help them seek vengeance for the death of Eddie Ryan. The devious Piranhas were careful not to be publicly seen to be allied to the Ryans and their ancillary associates. Nor did they show the slightest hint of animosity towards the Keanes and the Collopys, with whom they were still doing business. The Dundon/McCarthys knew that Kieran Keane was determined to have the Ryan brothers murdered, and for Eddie Ryan's sons the feeling was entirely mutual. There were now only two choices left for either side – kill or be killed. With the two main players distracted, the feud provided a rare opportunity for the Dundon/McCarthys to make their move for supremacy in the drug trade.

As the powerful gangland conglomerate weighed up their choices they realized that hitting Keane or his associates on the street was not an option. The mobsters wore bullet-proof vests and were always vigilant. The Piranhas also reasoned that taking out one major player in the mob would not shift the balance of power. Murder Inc. would have to hatch a devious and elaborate ruse to lure their foes into a trap – and it would have to be spectacular. That way they could wipe out all the opposition in one merciless swoop in a conspiracy reminiscent of the infamous 1929 St Valentine's Day Massacre in Chicago. All they needed was an opening to launch their Machiavellian scheme.

The Dundon/McCarthys didn't have to wait for long. Kieran Keane, who was fully aware of their capacity for murder, had sent out tentative feelers to the mob, telling them that he was prepared to pay €60,000 to have the Ryans and Cowboy Hanley assassinated. In early January 2003 Dessie Dundon let him know that his band of brothers might be interested in the proposition, and Keane took the bait. The eighteen-year-old killer was now the de facto head of the gang's operations in Limerick in the absence of Wayne, who was still inside for the attacks on Gardaí and prison officers, and John and Larry McCarthy Junior, who were based in the UK. When Dessie Dundon offered to take up the contract, Keane knew he had the credibility – and the capacity – to do the job. The Dundon/McCarthys agreed to kidnap the Ryan brothers and kill them. But Keane wanted to witness the execution in person and possibly have the pleasure of dispatching Eddie Ryan's sons himself. Dundon didn't mind; after all, Keane was the guy paying the bill and it was his choice. Both sides agreed that the cash would be paid over when the Ryans were captured.

In the meantime the duplicitous psychopaths went back to Hanley and the Ryans and told them the value that had been placed on their heads. The revenge-obsessed gangsters readily agreed to match the bounty if Murder Inc. stayed on their side. The double-crossing Piranhas were delighted with the lucrative arrangement they'd negotiated: both sides were paying them, netting the Dundon/McCarthys a total haul of €120,000. And when it was over they would be the most powerful gang in the Midwest. Despite the increased heat from the Gardaí, who were still investigating various murders and questioning several gang members, the mob set about finalizing their plans for a criminal coup.

As a result of the intelligence gathered in the Brian Fitzgerald murder case, Gardaí had identified Philip Dean's role as one of the gang's transport managers. He returned to Ireland from the UK in the company of James Cahill on 6 January 2003. Dean and the hit man were bringing in another consignment of guns and drugs. The pair spent the following days travelling between Cork, Limerick, Kilrush and Dublin. On 12 January they were summoned to Dublin by Stephen 'Dougie' Moran. He wanted an urgent meeting. Even though Dougie Moran was in the thick of organizing the takeover plot, he had other pressing matters closer to home to deal with. He was immersed in a bitter feud with a former associate, Declan 'Decie' Griffin, a heroin dealer and Garda informant from Coolock.

The two men fell out when Griffin's girlfriend of ten years, Natasha Carberry, started a relationship with Dougie Moran. Griffin was enraged when she and his two children moved in with her Limerick lover. On 3 November 2002, Griffin fired shots into Moran's home in Clondalkin, slightly injuring the gangster and his girlfriend – but they made no complaint to Gardaí. Instead Larry McCarthy's cousin took out a contract to kill Griffin. At the same time the heroin dealer was also offering a bounty for Moran. It was a race against time to see who got killed first. The day after the murder of Brian Fitzgerald, when Moran was helping to get the gunman Cahill out of the jurisdiction, Gardaí arrested two IRA hit men from Northern Ireland. They were on their way to shoot Griffin and had strong links to Moran and the Continuity IRA. The men were carrying €16,000 in cash, a photograph of Griffin, a list of his addresses and a Beretta pistol.

Despite this setback, Moran still wanted the drug dealer killed. When Cahill arrived in Dublin with Philip Dean he offered the hit man €20,000 to take on the contract. Dean would be the getaway driver. One of Moran's associates gave Cahill a picture of Griffin and showed the pair the various addresses and pubs he frequented. Cahill was glad of the work.

The following morning, 13 January, an associate of Dean's arrived into Belfast port on a ferry from Liverpool. The car was transporting another large cache of firearms and ammunition, including machine-guns and automatic pistols. Later that morning Dean's associate delivered the bulk of the arsenal to Chaser O'Brien, when they met near Newry, County Antrim. After that the courier drove to Dublin, where he delivered two Uzi machine-guns and spare magazines to Dougie Moran in Clondalkin. The following day Larry McCarthy Junior sent Philip Dean to Tralee to collect a handgun, ammunition and a mini Maglite torch, adapted to fire .22 bullets, and bring them to Dublin. But by then Gardaí in Limerick were on to Dean. They were waiting for him as he passed through the city on his way to Dublin. Detective Sergeant Eamon O'Neill arrested Dean under the Offences Against the State Act for illegal possession of firearms and brought him in for questioning. It was to prove a lucky break.

Over the next few days in custody Dean decided to come clean and gave officers a detailed account of his activities for the crime gang. He revealed his dealings with McCarthy Junior, Cahill, Chaser O'Brien, the Dundons, Dougie Moran and Anthony Kelly from Kilrush. Most importantly, he shared what he knew about the plot to murder Brian Fitzgerald and admitted that he had been sent by McCarthy Junior to dispose of the murder weapon in the Mulcair River. He confirmed that it was the same weapon retrieved by the Gardaí.

Dean seemed anxious to unburden himself and gave detectives in Mayorstone Station a twenty-five-page detailed statement. He agreed to testify against the gang on the condition that he and his family were placed in the Witness Protection Programme (WPP). It was a stunning development for the police. If their witness testified in court there was a strong possibility they could convict Fitzgerald's killers. His evidence would send the hierarchy of the country's most dangerous criminal gang away for a very long time. It was decided to maintain absolute secrecy about Dean's admissions and on 16 January, he was charged with three counts of possession of firearms and ammunition. He was remanded in custody to Cloverhill Prison in Dublin. For the time being at least, the gang had no idea that their transport manager had turned – the mob had other matters on their minds.

On 23 January 2003, Eddie Ryan's son Kieran stood trial at Limerick Circuit Criminal Court on a charge of stabbing Christy Keane's son Liam. On the way to court Ryan was ambushed on the street and he arrived battered and bruised. When the hearing commenced Liam Keane, the injured party and principal witness, took the stand and was asked by the prosecution who had stabbed him. 'Kieran Ryan. Kieran Ryan stabbed me in the back,' he replied. Then the State's counsel asked if he could identify his attacker. Keane looked around the courtroom, right past his adversary who was sitting in front of him, turned back and blankly replied, 'No.'

In the absence of a formal identification of the defendant, Judge Carroll Moran had no alternative but to direct the jury to find Ryan not guilty. 'It is a very sorry state of affairs that this should happen and if this is going to persist we are

99

going to live in a state of social chaos and anarchy,' the judge angrily declared. The judge's words would very soon prove to be prophetic. As the two sides left the courts complex there was another fist-fight and one of the Keanes stomped on Kieran Ryan's head.

Between 10.30 p.m. and 11.00 p.m. that night, Kieran Ryan, his older brother, twenty-year-old Eddie Junior, and their friend Christopher 'Smokey' Costelloe were walking on Moylish Road in Ballynanty. It was a cold winter night and the streets were empty. An associate of Cowboy Hanley pulled up in a car and the Ryans jumped in. At the same time a few shots were fired in the air for effect. At 11.23 p.m. Gardaí received a frantic call from their mother, Mary Ryan. She told the police Smokey Costelloe had turned up claiming that masked men had abducted her two boys at gunpoint. She was in a genuine panic because she believed Costelloe's story. That was crucial to the plan – the abduction had to be taken seriously by the Gardaí or Keane wouldn't take the bait. As a major Garda operation swung into action the Ryans were being driven by Cowboy Hanley's friend to a safe house near Thurles, County Tipperary. The brothers would remain there for over a week. No one, apart from those directly involved in the scam, knew what was going on.

Costelloe, who was a violent, despicable thug, convinced the Gardaí that his pals had been abducted. He said they had been dragged into a car by masked men who fired shots at him as he escaped. Local residents had reported hearing gunshots around the same time, which seemed to corroborate his story. In any event the kidnapping and murder of the Ryans was not an unexpected incident from the Garda perspective, particularly considering the bitterness and violence of the continuing feud. The city's experienced detectives expected the worst and believed they were searching for bodies.

The investigation again fell to the Gardaí at Mayorstone Station as the bogus abduction had taken place in their area. The detectives were already investigating the murders of Brian Fitzgerald and Sean Poland and Garda resources in the city were under intense pressure. Over the next seven days, the Gardaí, backed up by over 100 soldiers and a Garda helicopter, combed the Cratloe Woods and Woodcock Hill area, just across the County Clare border, outside the city. It was the most likely location where assassins could comfortably dispatch their victims without the fear of being caught in the act. Farms, rivers and fields were also scoured.

Inevitably the focus of Garda attention fell on the most likely culprits – the Keane/Collopy gang. Several of their homes were searched and gang members were constantly stopped, searched and questioned about the missing brothers. Kieran Keane and his mob were totally taken in by the ruse.

As the days went by without any developments, fear and apprehension gripped the city. The public and the police were braced for the worst. The disappearance also became the subject of intense national media coverage. If the Ryans turned up dead it would be an unprecedented escalation of hostilities. Gardaí knew that further bloodshed and mayhem would be inevitable. Limerick was on a knife edge.

As the searches continued, associates of the missing brothers became sure that they were dead. Several houses belonging to the Keane/Collopys were shot at or petrol-bombed. There were serious street-fights between men, women and children, from both sides, as the poisonous hate again seeped into the schoolyard. On 27 January a major fracas erupted outside the city's gleaming new courts complex, during which seven people were arrested. The row began when Keane loyalists taunted John Ryan, saying that his nephews had joined his brother in hell. Mary Ryan was in no doubt who was responsible for the abduction. 'They killed my husband . . . I want my boys back, please give me my boys back, I never wanted this bloodshed,' she told journalists.

Potential combatants began to openly wear bullet-proof vests and the gangs made no effort to conceal the fact that they were preparing for war. The tension in the city was palpable. Limerick had become a powder keg and it was only a matter of time before the fuse was lit. The Dundon/McCarthys sat back and admired the chaos they had created.

Around 4 p.m. on Wednesday, 29 January, Kieran Keane returned to his home in Garryowen with his wife and children. Dessie Dundon was sitting on the garden wall munching a burger, waiting for the gang boss. The two killers spoke for a few minutes. Dundon said they still had the Ryan brothers alive and that things had cooled down enough for them to be moved. Keane agreed to meet the 'abduction gang' later that evening in the home of twenty-one-year-old Anthony 'Noddy' McCarthy, at Fairgreen also in the Garryowen area. After Keane witnessed the execution of his hated young rivals he would hand over the cash.

Around 7 p.m., Keane and his nephew Owen Treacy arrived at Noddy McCarthy's house. They had spent an hour driving around to shake off any potential police tails. Keith Galvin, an eighteen-year-old cousin of Larry McCarthy Junior, was standing guard outside. Galvin told Treacy and Keane: 'The lads are inside.' In the sitting-room they met

Dessie Dundon and Noddy McCarthy. McCarthy suddenly produced a .38 revolver and ordered the two men to get down on the floor. Keane and Treacy realized they had been double-crossed – and that they had walked into a death trap.

The gangsters grabbed the bag containing the agreed fee of €60,000. Keane and Treacy were told that if they played along they would be released unharmed and everything would be 'OK'. Dessie Dundon tied their hands behind their backs and ordered them to sit down. At the same time two other gang members emerged from the kitchen, wearing balaclavas. Treacy recognized one of them as thirty-one-year-old David 'Frog Eyes' Stanners. Frog Eyes' brother Michael had been involved in an arson attack on the home of Treacy's father, Philip. The Stanners had been sucked into the feuds because their sister was living with Eddie Ryan's nephew, 'Fat' John McCarthy. Dundon demanded that Keane phone the two leading members of the Collopy gang, brothers Kieran and Philip Collopy, and arrange to meet them 'out the road'.

Despite being beaten and tortured, Keane and Treacy would not give in to the demand. As ruthless criminals both men were experienced enough to know that their captors had only one plan in mind. Treacy would later tell the Central Criminal Court: 'The four of us were going to be killed. If me or my uncle Kieran made that call there was four of us going to be killed. At no time were we going to lure the Collopys out the road – at no time.' Hoods were placed over their heads and secured with duct tape.

After about an hour, Keane and Treacy were led to a waiting Nissan Micra car and pushed into the boot. Noddy McCarthy and Galvin brought their captives to a house in Roundwood Estate, a middle-class area of Rosbrien. The house was on the outskirts of the city and owned by a relation of Galvin. They drove the car into the garage and ordered the uncle and nephew to get out. Keane and Treacy were brought upstairs and their hoods were taken off. The captors again demanded that they phone the Collopys and arrange to meet them on a country road outside the city. The two men still refused to make the call. The abduction crew were then joined by twenty-four-year-old James McCarthy and Smokey Costelloe. Treacy overheard Dessie Dundon talking to someone on the phone. 'We've got them,' he said.

Ten minutes later the hostages were led down the stairs, at gunpoint, by Noddy McCarthy. Outside they were pushed into the back of a van and ordered to lie on the floor. Blankets were thrown over them. Frog Eyes Stanners drove the van, with James McCarthy in the passenger seat and Smokey Costelloe in the back. The van eventually stopped on a lonely country back road, at an area called Drombanna five miles outside Limerick City. Stanners ordered Kieran Keane out of the van and pushed him to the ground. He stabbed Keane in the side of the head and body. Owen Treacy would later describe what happened. 'I witnessed David "Frog Eyes" Stanners shoot my uncle in the back of the head. He pushed Kieran Keane to the ground and shot him like a dog with his hands tied behind his back,' he said. The gangland hard man collapsed onto the cold, wet road.

Costelloe and Stanners then turned their attention to Keane's terrified nephew and Costelloe stabbed him in the throat. Treacy sliced the palm of his hand when he grabbed the blade in an attempt to wrench the knife from his attacker. Stanners then grabbed the knife from Costelloe and continued stabbing Treacy. Frog Eyes stared into his victim's face and hissed: 'This is the last face you are going to see.' He stabbed Treacy several more times in the ear, neck and chest. In total the gangster suffered seventeen serious stab wounds in the attack. Critically injured, he fell to the ground and pretended to be dead. 'I played dead, because I knew it was the only way to get rid of these men,' Owen Treacy later said.

Treacy heard James McCarthy shouting to the others: 'Come on, come on, he's dead, he's dead.' Despite his horrific injuries Treacy managed to loosen the ties on his hands. When the van left, he staggered to his uncle's side. He could hear Keane faintly breathing. Treacy struggled to his feet and stumbled to a house up the road, to summon help. By the time aid arrived at 9.30 p.m. Keane was dead. An autopsy would later find that he died from a single gunshot wound to the head. He had also suffered six stab wounds near his left ear.

Owen Treacy was rushed to hospital, under armed guard, where he underwent emergency surgery. His survival meant that Murder Inc.'s plan to annihilate the opposition had backfired badly.

Later that night, Gardaí in Roscrea stopped Noddy McCarthy, Dessie Dundon and Keith Galvin. They were driving in a Volvo car registered to Jim 'Chaser' O'Brien. The criminals gave false names, including O'Brien's, and drove on to Dublin, from where they got a ferry to the UK.

Chaser O'Brien was among a group of gang associates rounded up for questioning the day after Keane's murder. As soon as he was released without charge, he fled the country for the Continent and never returned. When word leaked out over the following days that Treacy was expected to survive, other members of the gang also left the country. They escaped to the UK and Spain to keep their heads down and regroup. But the failure of their diabolical plot did not quell their ambitions.

The Dundon/McCarthys clung to the hope that Treacy would succumb to his injuries and die. If he didn't, then they would have to go and finish him off, especially if he was prepared to go to court. There were bitter recriminations among the killers who blamed James McCarthy for the screw-up. The Keanes and Collopys would inevitably strike back and the gang would have to be ready.

Just over five hours after the alarm was raised by Treacy, there was another dramatic development which would soon shed light on the mystery. At 2.53 a.m. on 30 January, the Gardaí at Portlaoise Station received a 999 emergency call from Kieran Ryan. He said he and his brother had been released and they were at a garage in the town. When Gardaí collected the brothers the Ryans were coy about what had happened to them. They said they had been held captive in a van and had only been allowed out to use the toilet. The Ryans wouldn't elaborate because they said their lives were in danger. But their demeanour and appearance stated otherwise. The brothers were calm and collected; they were clean-shaven and washed and there were no injuries on them. Their clothes were also clean and there was no smell of body odour off them, which was inconsistent with them supposedly being held captive in the back of a van for a week. Very quickly Gardaí began to realize that the abduction had been a ruse to lure Keane into a trap.

Later that day when the Ryans were reunited with their mother in Kileely, a very public street party was held to celebrate their return – and the murder of their hated foe. Across the river the Keanes and the Collopys were in deep shock and mourning. It had taken Eddie Ryan's sons two years to reverse the roles of joy and despair. The revellers drank cans of beer and posed for the phalanx of press photographers and TV crews, who had come to cover what was now a major gangland murder-mystery story that had the whole country captivated. The story was even covered by the international media. Among the people celebrating were two members of the murder gang – James McCarthy and Smokey Costelloe. Kieran Ryan stood smirking and laughing with his killer mates as reporters asked him about what had happened to him and his brother. 'I got threatened not to talk to anyone. I don't know where I was held; I couldn't tell you. Our family had no hand, act or part in Kieran Keane's murder. We didn't do it,' he said unconvincingly.

Despite his critical injuries, Owen Treacy was able to identify his attackers. Detective Garda John Nagle visited Treacy in the intensive care ward of Limerick Regional Hospital three hours after the shooting. Although the gangster was very seriously ill, he was coherent. 'Who stabbed you and who shot Kieran Keane?' the detective asked. Treacy replied slowly: 'Green Hiace.' Then he whispered: 'David "Frog Eyes" Stanners, James McCarthy, Moyross and Smokey Costelloe.'

Over the following weeks, Owen Treacy gradually recovered from his dreadful injuries. He agreed to give the Gardaí a full statement of the events on the night of his uncle's murder. He identified the six members of the abduction gang – Frog Eyes Stanners, Smokey Costelloe, James McCarthy, Dessie Dundon, Noddy McCarthy and Keith Galvin. Treacy was determined to testify in court and would later claim that he had no idea what the meeting was about or who it was had contacted his uncle. The criminal was given round the clock, armed police protection.

Word was quickly relayed to the rest of the Keane/Collopy gang about what had happened in the days following the double-cross. From his prison cell, Christy Keane had pieced together the whole ruse and was already plotting revenge. The fact that such an elaborate web of deceit had been constructed by the Dundon/McCarthys to wipe them out chilled the mobster to the bone. It illustrated that they were up against much more formidable enemies than the Ryans. The Keane/Collopy gang were already aware that the Dundons in particular were unhinged psychopaths and now they had just received a first-hand lesson on the Piranhas' capacity for treachery. In such exceptional circumstances Christy Keane's survival instincts told him to compromise on the gang's cherished doctrine of an eye for an eye. He knew that this time they had to straddle both sides of gangland's razor-wire fence. On one side Treacy would co-operate with the police investigation to ensure the killers were convicted; and on the other the mob would plot their bloody revenge. Houses belonging to the Ryans and the Dundon/McCarthys were petrol-bombed and shots were fired, but an unprecedented clampdown by Gardaí forced an eerie peace on the streets. Local wags dubbed it 'the phoney war'.

The Garda top brass found themselves in the midst of a crisis as they tried to prevent the gang violence engulfing the city. Chief Superintendent Kelly and his officers were now on the frontline in a war. The story dominated the national media agenda and was discussed at Cabinet level. Gangland violence had dramatically escalated across the country from the beginning of the new Millennium, but Limerick stood out. Emergency summits were held in Garda HQ in Dublin and the Garda Commissioner of the day, Pat Byrne, briefed the then Justice Minister, Michael McDowell, on the unfolding events. Byrne also sent scores of extra Gardaí from

Dublin and Cork into Limerick, to prevent an all-out blood-bath and to assist in the complex investigations.

In an effort to handle the mammoth workload, all leave for detectives in the city was cancelled. In the months that followed, fatigue and exhaustion were common complaints, as officers worked eighteen-hour days. The ERU was deployed to patrol the streets and a Garda helicopter was based in the city on a semi-permanent basis. On the day after Keane's murder, Commissioner Byrne visited Limerick with his most senior officers. At a press conference that after-noon, Chief Superintendent Kelly described the worsening situation as one of 'utter madness'.

At Kieran Keane's funeral the song 'The Wind Beneath My Wings' blared out in St Mary's Church, as heavily armed Gardaí patrolled the grounds outside to avoid an attack. They knew the Dundon/McCarthys would have no com-punction about shooting mourners at a funeral. Fr Donough O'Malley talked about hatred, violence and death: 'To have peace it is necessary to let go of prejudice and hatred. It requires a change of heart, attitude and behaviour.'

The priest's words of wisdom fell on deaf ears. Christy Keane had declined an offer to make a private visit under escort to the funeral home. Instead the crime boss decided to stay in his cell 'more in temper, than in shock' according to his associates. He was comforted on his loss by fellow drug dealers, including John Gilligan. His henchmen visited to brief him on the situation and to take orders on what to do next.

The funeral was delayed for eight days to allow Owen Treacy time to recover sufficiently so that he could attend. On 6 February he left his hospital bed, under armed police protection, to pay his last respects to his uncle. After the funeral Treacy took his place among the hard men and boys of the Keane clan and their allies, including gang bosses from around Ireland, for the three-mile walk to Kilmurry graveyard. They were all dressed in black and white as a show of force and defiance, prompting one disgusted local to comment aloud: 'What are they trying to prove? That they still own the place.'

The huge Garda investigation that followed soon began to show results. The file on the Keane murder case eventually ran to over 5,000 pages, containing 720 individual statements. By March 2003, the investigation had led to thirty-four people being arrested for questioning. The Ryan brothers, Cowboy Hanley and their Tipperary hosts were also quizzed about the alleged abduction. The investigation had also succeeded in preventing more loss of life. Three members of the Keane gang were arrested on 6 March as they left Dublin with pipe bombs fitted with booby-trap devices, all for use in Limerick. But despite this increased police attention, Stephen 'Dougie' Moran still wanted Declan Griffin murdered. He was so obsessed that he contacted James Cahill and this time agreed to pay €50,000 for the hit. Moran arranged to supply the contract killer with one of the Uzi machine-guns that had arrived from the UK in January.

On the evening of 21 March an associate of Moran's, Graham Dunne, delivered the machine-gun and fifteen rounds of ammunition to Cahill in the car park of the Quality Hotel in Saggart, south Dublin. But the corpulent killer was being secretly watched by the Garda National Surveillance Unit. As the hit man and his accomplice were about to drive off, the ERU moved in and arrested them. While Cahill was detained for questioning at Kevin Street Station in Dublin about the gun find, detectives from Limerick interviewed him about Brian Fitzgerald's murder. They hit him with the damning allegations contained in Philip Dean's statement, but Cahill denied everything. He was then brought before the Special Criminal Court where he was charged with possession of a firearm and ammunition. Cahill and Dunne were both subsequently jailed for five years on the same charge.

Based on the statements of Owen Treacy the investigation team had enough evidence with which to charge the men he had identified. But the six gang members had been in hiding since the incident. Almost two months after the murder, Keane's killers were arrested in dawn swoops in Limerick, Kilkenny and Tipperary. On 23 March, three of the gang – James McCarthy, Frog Eyes Stanners and Smokey Costelloe – were formally charged with the false imprisonment of Kieran Keane and Owen Treacy. A week later, Noddy McCarthy and Dessie Dundon were also caught and charged with the same offences. Keith Galvin left the country and disappeared. He has never returned to Limerick. There was tight security as the accused mobsters were brought before the local courts. A police helicopter hovered overhead as a convoy of heavily armed cops escorted the prison vans carrying them. Detectives in bullet-proof vests, cradling machine-guns, stood guard around the building. The need for such unprecedented security underlined the dangers posed by the warring sides. Scenes like these would become very familiar in the years ahead.

The large police presence was just enough to keep the two feuding sides apart when they congregated outside the courts complex beside King John's Castle. They shouted threats at each other and made the shape of guns with their hands.

There were chants of 'now the game starts', 'you're finished' and 'you're next' as the gangsters were shuffled into the court. The charges against the men were later upgraded to include murder and attempted murder. The arrest of five members of the Dundon/McCarthy organization in such a short time was a devastating blow – and a major victory for the Gardaí. But the war had only just begun.

Meanwhile, despite the fact that the police had clearly infiltrated his organization and already foiled two hits on Declan Griffin, Stephen 'Dougie' Moran hatched a devious plot worthy of his cousins in Limerick. It would prove to be third time lucky. When he learned about the arrest of James Cahill, Declan Griffin approached thirty-three-year-old Shay Wildes and offered him money to murder Moran. Wildes, who had close links with the IRA and other terror gangs, was a hit man for hire with a proven track record. He was on bail for the gangland-style murder of a man in Tallaght, Dublin on 26 December 2001. Wildes was also the prime suspect for the murder of another dissident Republican a year later. The killer accepted Griffin's contract. But unknown to the drug dealer, Dougie Moran had paid the hit man to double-cross him. A plot was hatched that was chillingly similar to the trap set for Kieran Keane.

On 4 April 2003, Moran's brother was reportedly abducted from a site where his company was doing static security. The incident was given extensive media coverage. The following day Wildes contacted Griffin confirming that he had Moran held captive. He said he wanted part-payment of the blood money, €5,000. At 5.45 p.m. on Saturday, 5 April, Griffin arrived to meet the hit man in the Horse and Jockey pub in Inchicore, Dublin. The drug dealer, who knew he was a marked man, was wearing a bullet-proof vest and had a hand-gun tucked inside it for his own protection. Wildes was waiting in the pub with two associates and the four men sat down at a table. Griffin was looking relaxed as he handed Wildes an envelope with the cash. The killer casually put the money in his pocket. Then he pulled out a handgun, leaned across the table and shot Griffin once under the ear, killing him instantly. Then he walked out of the pub. Murder Inc. had claimed another life.

By the time of Griffin's assassination, Moran and his cousins in Limerick, Dublin and the UK had heard from James Cahill that Philip Dean was obviously spilling the beans. The mob had the news confirmed when they discovered that the Englishman had been moved out of the general prison population and put in solitary confinement for his own safety. His testimony could be devastating for the gang, especially for Moran, James Cahill, McCarthy Junior, Anthony Kelly and Chaser O'Brien. The transport manager would have to be stopped at all costs.

On the night of 9 April, a petrol-bomb attack caused extensive damage to Dean's home in Handsworth, Birmingham where his partner and two young children lived. After consultation with the Gardaí in Limerick the family were taken into the British Witness Protection Programme. The following morning Dean was jailed for three years when he pleaded guilty to the three firearms charges. In June, he was formally accepted into the WPP in Ireland, to be enacted at the end of his sentence and in return for his testimony.

Murder Inc. now had another name to add to their death list.

7. Murder and Justice

An eerie calm had descended on Limerick in the three months since the murder of Kieran Keane. The 'phoney war' gave a welcome, albeit uneasy, respite. Between the murders of Eddie Ryan and his former friend there had been over 100 reported incidents of shootings and arson attacks alone. Many more went unreported. The lull in hostilities was partly due to the intensive Garda operations aimed at keeping a lid on the mayhem. Six key members of the Dundon/McCarthy mob were in custody for serious crimes and there had been many significant drugs and guns seizures as a result of the intelligence gleaned from the various investigations now taking place. But containing the violence had come at immense cost to the taxpayer.

In 2002 Gardaí were paid €2.136 million in overtime. In the first half of 2003 the entire overtime budget for that year was gobbled up. Before the end of the year, which was to be one of the most violent on record, half of the 2004 budget had also been spent. The situation was so critical that the Department of Justice allocated an additional €2 million in emergency funding to cover the cost of the city's beleaguered police force. With manpower stretched to breaking point, officers were being forced to work three times the average overtime hours for Gardaí in the rest of the country. Detectives were putting in eighteen-hour days for weeks on end and leave was regularly cancelled. It was clear to the Gardaí that if the exhausting momentum was not maintained then

Limerick would descend into anarchy, with the warring factions taking over the streets. But despite the Gardaí's relentless vigilance the gangs were determined that the uneasy peace would not last.

The end of the 'phoney war' was declared when the Dundon/McCarthys' favourite hit man, Gary Campion, went on a murderous rampage on the streets of his neighbourhood, the sprawling estate of Moyross. On 1 May 2003, he attempted to murder thirty-year-old drug dealer Joseph 'Dodo' McCarthy (no relation to the members of Murder Inc.) in Moyross. Dodo, a violent criminal, made the fatal mistake of using the feud as an excuse to renege on payment for drugs supplied by the Dundons. The Piranhas were quick to take action. If Dodo didn't pay for his heroin then he would have to pay with his life. Around 10 p.m. that evening, Campion burst into the house where Dodo was staying. The hit man blasted him at close range with a sawn-off shotgun, in front of a woman and her young children. McCarthy took the brunt of the blast in the chest and was critically injured. He managed to survive after doctors in Limerick's Regional Hospital carried out life-saving surgery. (Like all medics working in a war zone, they had developed a high level of expertise in treating gunshot and stab wounds.) Three months later Dodo McCarthy had recovered enough to beat another man to death during a drunken brawl, earning himself eight years in prison.

Campion struck again two days after the shooting of Dodo. This time the victim was twenty-four-year-old Wayne Waters, also from Moyross. He suffered serious injuries to his legs and back when Campion shot him a number of times with the same weapon he'd used in the earlier shooting. The second shooting wasn't feud-related. Campion simply didn't like Waters, whom he bullied and threatened. Waters survived the first attack but Campion made a number of other attempts on his life and the young man couldn't take the pressure any more. Wayne Waters took his own life instead.

Then, on 6 May, the psychopath claimed his third murder victim in less than seven months, when he executed an innocent twenty-three-year-old Moyross man, Robert Fitzgerald. In a cruel twist of irony the victim was a second cousin of Brian Fitzgerald, who had also been murdered by the cold-blooded Campion. Robert Fitzgerald's death was not connected to the shootings of the previous days or to his cousin's murder. He was not involved in the feud but he was friends with individuals associated with the Keane and Collopy mobs. Such tenuous connections were often the only motivation Murder Inc. needed to kill.

For Campion the feud provided a convenient excuse to settle a personal score. The two men had simply had a row over a woman and the dangerous hit man did not take kindly to being usurped in love. Fitzgerald left a house party in Moyross at around 3 a.m. and was on his way home through a local alleyway when Campion emerged from the shadows. Robert Fitzgerald turned to make a run for it and Campion shot him once in the back. Then, as his injured prey lay prostrate and helpless on the ground, Campion executed him with a single gunshot to the back of the head. At the time of the killing there were at least three armed Garda patrols on the streets of the troubled estate but the locals were so used to hearing gunshots in the night that they hadn't bothered calling the police. Despite a major investigation, no one was ever charged with Robert Fitzgerald's murder.

The intense, visceral feuding had sucked in at least twenty families since Murder Inc.'s infamous double-cross had

ABOVE LEFT: Kenneth Dundon Senior
ABOVE RIGHT: Wayne Dundon
RIGHT: John Dundon
BELOW LEFT: Ger Dundon
BELOW RIGHT: Dessie Dundon

ABOVE LEFT: Larry McCarthy Junior

ABOVE RIGHT: Christopher McCarthy

LEFT: Gareth Collins/Keogh

BELOW LEFT: Anthony 'Noddy' McCarthy

BELOW RIGHT: Jimmy Collins

ABOVE LEFT: Nathan Killeen

ABOVE RIGHT: Jim 'Chaser' O'Brien

RIGHT: Anthony Kelly

BELOW LEFT: Gary Campion

BELOW RIGHT: James Martin Cahill

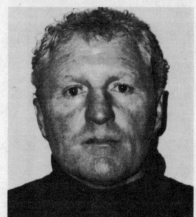

ABOVE LEFT: April Collins
ABOVE RIGHT: Annabel Dundon
LEFT: Ciara Killeen
BELOW LEFT: Anne Casey
BELOW RIGHT: Lisa Collins

Burned-out houses in Southill

Houses in Ballinacurra Weston, stronghold of the Dundon/McCarthy gang

Kieran 'Rashers' Ryan, son of Eddie Ryan

Mark Moloney, killed by Murder Inc.

Murder Inc. member, Paul Crawford

Murder Inc. member, 'Fat' John McCarthy

Eddie Ryan

Kieran Keane

'Fat' Frankie Ryan

Stephen 'Dougie' Moran

Martin 'Marlo' Hyland

Eamon 'The Don' Dunne

Declan 'Decie' Griffin

James Cronin

Hit man Barry Doyle

Michael 'Mikey' Kelly

Troy Jordan

Hassan Hassan

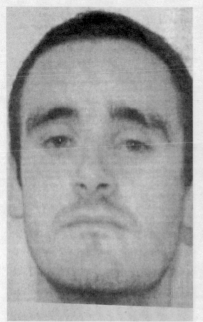

Vincent Collopy

Brian Collopy

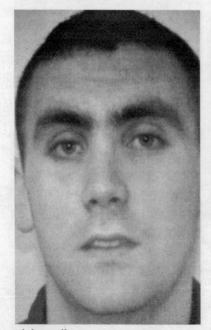

Philip Collopy

Johnny 'Pitchfork' McNamara

LEFT: Kieran Keane's widow, Sophie Keane

BELOW: Christy Keane confronts photographers at a gangland funeral

ABOVE LEFT: Chief Supt Dave Sheehan

ABOVE RIGHT: Chief Supt/Assist. Commissioner (Retired) Gerry Kelly

LEFT: Former Commissioner Fachtna Murphy

BELOW LEFT: Det. Supt Jim Browne

BELOW RIGHT: Former Commissioner Pat Byrne

ABOVE AND LEFT: Machine pistol and cache of grenades seized by Gardaí in Limerick

BELOW: Machine pistols and pistols with silencers seized from the mobs

Shane Geoghegan

Brian Fitzgerald

Sean Poland

Latvian mother Baiba Saulite

Roy Collins, shot dead by Murder Inc. in April 2009

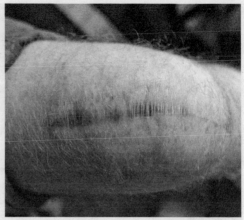

ABOVE LEFT: Barman Ryan Lee, shot and injured in December 2004

ABOVE RIGHT: The injury caused to Ryan Lee's leg

RIGHT: Author interviewing Ryan in 2005

BELOW: Brannigan's Pub – burned out by Murder Inc. in 2005

backfired. Spontaneous violent clashes between the two sides had become the norm across the streets of Limerick. The high-security operations that surrounded the appearances of warring gang members in the local courts complex were becoming a regular spectacle on the city's north side. Despite the heavy police presence, the steps of the court building on Merchant's Quay became a frequent flashpoint where the hate-filled mobs regularly attacked each other. The violent melees had become such a problem that they began to adversely affect the city's businesses, especially the tourist trade.

Two of the city's most popular visitor attractions – St Mary's Cathedral and King John's Castle – were adjacent to the courts complex. The tourists who came to visit the ancient city well versed in the arts of war often got to witness an unscheduled enactment of a more modern type of war to that recorded in its annals. Scores of the combatants from both sides were subsequently convicted of public order offences that had been committed at the courts. On 13 May 2003, Owen Treacy had recovered sufficiently from his wounds to break away from his Garda minders. He attacked supporters of the Ryans who were taunting him outside the building. Treacy had been attending the trial of Noel Price and Michael Stanners. The two Murder Inc. gang members were convicted and each jailed for twelve years for an arson attack on Treacy's father's home in 2001. Owen Treacy was charged with a public order offence and received a three-month suspended sentence. Judge Tom O'Donnell ordered the State's chief witness against Murder Inc. to stay away from the courts unless he was a defendant or was called to give evidence.

Two weeks later, on 27 May, the city was rocked by another

eruption of spontaneous street violence when the warring tribes had a vicious fight at the Supermac fast-food outlet on the Ennis Road. Around 5.30 p.m. a member of the Keane/ Collopy side spotted the Ryans there and immediately called for back-up. Within minutes reinforcements arrived from both sides and the car park became the scene of a pitched battle involving at least fifteen people. The mortal enemies bludgeoned each other with iron bars, baseball bats, golf clubs, pool cues, wheel braces and steering-wheel locks. A baby chair was even grabbed from the restaurant and used as a battering ram. The combatants' rage rendered them oblivious to the horrified audience of motorists in the slow-moving rush-hour traffic and to the families with young children in the restaurant and the play area next door. Among the spectators were members of the Garda sub-aqua unit, who were travelling past in a convoy of three jeeps. The burly police officers moved in to break up the fracas and nine men were arrested. Among them were Kieran Ryan, Philip and Raymond Collopy and Kieran Keane's younger brother Anthony. The thugs were charged with a variety of offences and remanded in custody.

By the summer of 2003 at least thirty of the serious players in both gangs were locked up. The number of Limerick gangsters on remand or serving sentences posed a major security challenge for the prison system, as the thugs brought their war on to the prison landings. On 3 May, Dessie Dundon was attacked and injured in Wheatfield Prison in Dublin. In Limerick, six members of his gang were suddenly shifted to other prisons as part of an emergency operation because the authorities had learned of a plot to kill them. Relatives of the warring thugs had even fought each other at the gates of the prison after scheduled visits. The warders in

Limerick jail, who had already endured a campaign of terror at the hands of the Dundon/McCarthys, had to ensure the opposing sides were segregated. The extended family backgrounds of new inmates were thoroughly checked so that the wrong people were not put together on the same landings, sparking an all-out riot. Such was the threat level that the use of razor blades in Limerick was banned and the State bought electric shavers for the prisoners instead. As the numbers of feuding criminals increased, almost every prison in the country acquired a 'Limerick wing'.

After the discovery of Kieran Keane's mutilated body in January, the Keane/Collopys had decided they wanted a spectacular act of revenge to even up the odds. In early June Gardaí learned that the gang had acquired a powerful car bomb from dissident Republicans. It was intended to blow up several members of the Dundon/McCarthy mob. The plan was to attach the device to a car owned by a woman who drove the gangsters around the city. The Keanes had plenty of form when it came to resorting to bombs. A device which had been attached to a car belonging to a Ryan gang member had failed to explode in 2001, and in February 2003 Gardaí had intercepted members of the gang transporting pipe bombs from Dublin. This time the Keanes hoped there would be no mistakes. They were wrong.

Detective Inspector Jim Browne was tipped off that a shed behind a bungalow in the countryside at Mungret, County Limerick was being used as a bomb-making factory by the gang and it was placed under surveillance. An undercover investigation had revealed a link between the factory and members of the Continuity IRA who, coincidentally, also had close links to Dougie Moran in Dublin. The various

Republican gangs had always been a shadowy background presence in organized crime in Limerick.

On 3 June, heavily armed ERU officers raided the property and found the under-car bomb, which was about to be delivered. Army bomb squad experts later described the device as being capable of killing up to four or five people and injuring many more. It had been made from high explosive and fitted with a mercury tilt switch and a magnet for attachment to a vehicle. The steel casing of the device was designed to deliver the maximum amount of flesh-shredding shrapnel upon ignition. A large amount of bomb-making equipment, a machine-gun, hundreds of rounds of ammunition, cocaine worth €30,000 and a cocaine packaging press were also recovered. It was a major coup for the Gardaí and doubtlessly averted an atrocity on the streets of Limerick.

Four men were arrested and later charged in connection with the haul. Thirty-six-year-old Declan 'Darby' Sheehy, a close criminal associate and friend of Kieran and Christy Keane, was found standing close to the device. He was one of the ringleaders of the gang since Kieran's demise and was facing charges arising from the riot at the fast-food outlet in May. Also arrested were fifty-eight-year-old Richard Smith and his thirty-year-old son, Sean, who were living in the rented house. They were originally from Brixton in London. The fourth man was thirty-one-year-old Michael Scanlan, who had close links with the Continuity IRA and the Keanes. While they were being questioned by Gardaí the Smiths revealed the involvement of several criminals and terrorists in the operation, but they refused to testify in court. In the meantime the impressive haul had not stopped the bloodshed.

John Ryan had been keeping his head down since the Kieran Keane murder. He had been forced to move his family after their home close to the Island Field had been the target of countless gun and arson attacks. He had become the public face of his clan and had singled himself out for revenge. The day after Keane's murder and the return of his missing nephews, he hinted at a motive for the killing when he spoke to reporters: 'If they [had only] left them [his nephews] go loose, or told us that they were dead. They told us nothing at all. They left us linger on the whole time, so we had to get revenge somewhere along the line.' In truth John Ryan had been centrally involved in the hoax kidnap plot to lure Keane to his death.

But on 7 July 2003 he dropped his guard when he went to help a friend lay a patio at the front of a house in Thomondgate, close to the Island Field. It wasn't long before his enemies' spies were on their mobile phones. As Ryan worked a motorbike pulled up along the kerb. The pillion passenger got off and shot the gangster three times in the leg and abdomen. The bike then sped off in the direction of St Mary's Park, the Keanes' stronghold. John Ryan died later in hospital. That evening it was the turn of the Keane/Collopys to have a party, and they phoned the Ryans to announce that the grotesque celebration was underway.

The two suspects for the attack were teenage members of the Keane/Collopy mob – aged sixteen and seventeen. The next generation of killers was already being blooded to ensure the war continued. Several members of the Keane family were arrested for questioning about the murder, including Kieran Keane's widow, Sophie, and their fourteen-year-old son Joseph. When Gardaí searched the teenager, they found a note in his clenched fist. It made for chilling reading and illustrated how vengeance and hate had become a family inheritance.

The handwritten note contained a list of names. At the top was written: 'People who set up and killed my father all will be dead by the time I am 32, now I am 14. That's a promise boys.' This was followed by the list of names headed by the word 'Scumbags'. The list included the names of the main players in the Dundon/McCarthy gang, including the five men then awaiting trial for his father's murder. It also contained the names of Larry McCarthy Junior, Anthony Kelly, Cowboy Hanley, Jim O'Brien, Keith Galvin and Kieran and Edward Ryan. The people who were in prison had a question mark beside their name, while those still at large had a tick. At the bottom of the note the teenager outlined his plan for vengeance:

> Date 17/5/03. Time exactly at 1.47 a.m. People with ? are locked up. The people with the tick will be got before the other six and all of them will be got before I am 32 because all of the people who are getting locked up will be out by then. They will be got by me or somebody else for my father, Kieran Keane's death.

The note was signed off and addressed to his mother with the words: 'I love you Mam.'

Four years later, eighteen-year-old Joseph Keane smirked and told his mother that he loved her as he was being led away. He was starting a six-year sentence for kicking an innocent teenager to death in a case of mistaken identity. Keane and his nineteen-year-old cousin, Richard Treacy, a younger brother of Owen Treacy, thought eighteen-year-old Darren Coughlan was aligned to the Dundon/McCarthys. Their victim, who had nothing to do with crime, was another innocent victim of the madness.

*

A few weeks after the John Ryan murder, Paul Coffey, the getaway driver in the Eddie Ryan hit, pleaded guilty to manslaughter in the Central Criminal Court. He was subsequently sentenced to fifteen years' imprisonment.

On 25 July, John Dundon was arrested by police in Manchester after they were tipped off about his whereabouts by Gardaí in Limerick. They had an extradition warrant for Dundon's return to face a charge of threatening to burn down a prison officer's home. A month later he was flown back under escort to Cork Airport, where he was arrested by Limerick detectives and placed in custody. In the end he only spent a few months in prison for the charge. In the interim the violence continued.

As the summer of 2003 came to a close one of the Dundons' victims attempted to even up the score. John Creamer, the cousin John Dundon had mown down in a hail of bullets, had been forced to flee Limerick after the murder attempt. He was given shelter by Michael Campbell McNamara, a member of the Keane mob. Creamer had little hesitation in accepting a contract to whack his cousin's partner-in-crime Anthony Kelly from the Keanes. On 21 August, Kelly was making tea in the kitchen of his plush mansion, Crag House, which was perched on a hill with a commanding view of Kilrush. At around 11 p.m. Creamer suddenly appeared at the window. He blamed Kelly for supplying the weapon used by John Dundon to shoot him in October 2001. He produced an automatic pistol and fired several shots through the window, hitting the godfather four times in the chest and arm.

Despite his injuries, Kelly managed to call the Gardaí and he was rushed to hospital. After emergency surgery, Anthony Kelly recovered from his wounds. A month later he was arrested by detectives investigating Brian Fitzgerald's murder. He admitted to detectives that he knew Philip Dean and that he was a friend of Larry McCarthy Junior. However, Kelly denied any involvement in the security manager's murder. He was released without charge while the investigations continued.

Eleven days before Kelly was shot there had been another setback for Murder Inc. As a direct result of the ongoing investigations in Limerick a major joint police operation involving Scotland Yard's anti-terrorism branch, the Lancashire Police and Gardaí had targeted the gang's English arms suppliers. Forensic tests on six weapons that had been seized by Gardaí over the previous twelve months found that they had been reactivated. The weapons included the one used to murder Brian Fitzgerald, the Uzi submachine-gun seized from James Cahill and the weapon found in the Keanes' bomb factory in Mungret. It was established that they were coming from the same source and Gardaí tracked them to the UK.

The Fitzgerald murder hunt team had established a direct link between the Dundon/McCarthys and Limerick ex-pat James Patrick Moloney, who was living in Bradford, West Yorkshire. Gardaí had also discovered that the weapons were being supplied to dissident terrorist gangs. The Limerick gang wars had progressed from being a local crime problem to a national one, and now they had escalated to become the focus of international attention. Shortly after the swoop on the shed in Mungret, in July detectives from Limerick travelled to London to brief the chiefs at the National Criminal Intelligence Service (NCIS) and Scotland Yard.

The Garda officers described the complex gangland tapestry of links between the Dundon/McCarthys, terrorists and other UK-based criminal gangs that had come to light through the admissions of Philip Dean. The UK security chiefs found it hard to believe that one Limerick outfit could be so well organized and dangerous and such a ferocious murder machine. The detectives described a huge international drug conspiracy and a low-intensity urban war, where every type of firepower was being used including AK47 assault rifles, machine-guns, grenades and bombs. The mob's connections to the dissident gangs that were mounting a terror campaign in Ulster were of particular interest to the UK security services. By the time the Garda officers flew back to Limerick, the NCIS and Scotland Yard chiefs were in no doubt for the need to shut down the weapon supply line to Limerick. As a result, the joint undercover surveillance operation was mounted.

Surveillance on James Moloney led police to the two members of the Morecambe Rifle and Pistol Club, Robert Naylor and James Greenwood, and their lucrative sideline in reactivating decommissioned weapons. On 10 August 2003, police arrested Moloney, Naylor and Greenwood after the gun enthusiasts had delivered three automatic weapons. Moloney told police that he had intended selling the weapons to 'people who might want to buy them'. In the follow-up investigation another forty reactivated weapons destined for the organized crime and terror gangs were seized and more arrests were made. The three men were subsequently convicted and jailed at the Old Bailey in November 2004. Moloney pleaded guilty and was sentenced to seven years, while Naylor and Greenwood were jailed for ten and nine years respectively. It had been another major victory for the forces of law and order. But the Dundons were still making their presence felt in the UK.

While their children were causing chaos back in Limerick, all was not well between Kenneth Dundon and his wife Anne, who were living in London. The alcoholic matriarch had fallen for fifty-year-old heroin addict Christopher Jacobs. They had met at the local dole office and began having an affair. On 8 October, in a blind drunken rage, Kenneth Dundon went to the junkie's flat in Hoxton, North London where his wife was also staying. Kenneth Senior was wearing a bala- clava and armed with a knife when he kicked in the door. He repeatedly stabbed Jacobs in the face and neck, inflicting appalling injuries. As he ran off his wife's lover choked to death on his own blood. Anne McCarthy witnessed the attack and later identified her husband as the killer. Dundon was arrested a few hours later but denied the allegations. He was released on police bail pending further investigations and promptly left for Limerick. A month later the British authorities issued a European arrest warrant for Kenneth Dundon and he featured on Scotland Yard's 'Most Wanted List'. The father of the most dangerous thugs in Ireland was an international fugitive.

A week later his sons Wayne and John were also making the news back at home. Their cousin Creamer's friend, twenty-three-year-old Michael Campbell McNamara, was an important member of the Keane/Collopy gang. He was also the boyfriend of Christy Keane's daughter. He had been involved in gun and arson attacks on the homes of the Dundons and McCarthys since the explosion of hostilities in January and was a suspect in a number of assassination attempts on his rivals. He had been questioned about John Ryan's murder. On one occasion Gardaí found a grenade in a car he had abandoned just before they pulled it over. They believed he had been en route to throw the bomb into one of the homes of Murder Inc. on Hyde Road. The Dundons decided Campbell McNamara had to die before he could do any further damage – and to send out a message.

But like the rest of the Keane/Collopy mob, Campbell McNamara had become extra vigilant and was always on his guard. He could only be lured into a trap by someone he trusted. John and Wayne Dundon paid a visit to Andrew Nolan, a friend of McNamara. The brothers made Nolan an offer he couldn't refuse – set up his friend or be killed. Like most of the people living in Limerick's working-class estates Nolan was terrified of Murder Inc. and he agreed to co-operate. On the night of Sunday, 19 October, Nolan called McNamara, offering to sell him a sawn-off shotgun for €700. The gangster knew his friend had been looking for a weapon for his own protection.

Later that night McNamara went to meet Nolan at the Carew Park Estate and walked into a death trap. The Dundon brothers and Gary Campion were waiting for him. They grabbed their victim and dragged him away to Barry's Field, an area of isolated waste ground nearby. There he was beaten and tortured over a number of hours. The Dundons wanted to use McNamara as bait to lure Brian Collopy, who was now the leader of their rival mob, into a trap. Collopy knew he was a marked man and had moved his family from their luxury home on the outskirts of the city back to the relative safety of St Mary's Park in the Island Field.

When McNamara phoned Collopy, the gang strongman instantly smelled a rat and refused to meet. In desperation the trapped criminal phoned again, but Collopy didn't pick up. The badly mutilated body of Michael Campbell McNamara was found the next day by a member of the public who was out walking. He was found lying face-up with his hands bound behind his back and his ankles and feet tied together. He had also been gagged to prevent his screams of agony leaking out. A post-mortem examination later revealed that the unlucky gangster had suffered an appalling death. It would be remembered as one of the most gruesome in the history of Limerick's gang wars. McNamara had been stabbed several times in quick succession, with the wounds in clusters in the back and chest. There was also evidence that he had been tortured and severely beaten in what was described by Gardaí as a medieval-style torture and death. A shotgun was fired at point-blank range into his pelvis and buttocks, mutilating his lower body. Then the young gang member was finished off when he was blasted with a shotgun at close range in the back of the head. It was an act of unparalleled savagery that shocked even Limerick's most hardened cops.

The Dundons had sent a clear message to their enemies that the Piranhas would continue to pursue them without mercy. Andrew Nolan, who initially fled the country, was subsequently jailed for four years after he pleaded guilty to a charge of reckless endangerment. He told Gardaí that he would rather do hard time in prison than testify against the savages. He said: 'Three men were waiting for him [Campbell McNamara] at the shop. I don't want to name them. I have kids. I don't mind for myself.'

News of Campbell McNamara's grisly end came at an opportune time for Murder Inc. The following morning the Central Criminal Court sat in Limerick for the keenly awaited Kieran Keane murder trial. It was one of the first cases to be heard outside Dublin. Murder Inc. had already tried to disrupt the justice process before proceedings began. There was an arson attack on the courts building on Merchant's

Quay. More chillingly, there had also been a fire-bomb attack at the home of one of the prosecution lawyers in the case a few days earlier. A ring of steel was put in place around the courts building in an intensive security operation. Garda snipers were posted on rooftops, a helicopter clattered overhead and a water unit patrolled the River Shannon to the rear of the complex. The building was swept for explosives and everyone entering was electronically scanned for weapons. The Gardaí were taking no chances.

The palpable sense of fear that pervaded the city quickly manifested itself. The court was unable to empanel a jury of 12 people from a panel of 529. Jurors presented medical certificates for myriad problems, but mainly for 'stress and anxiety' because of the seriousness of the case. Prospective jurors clearly felt that the gangs could get to them. Despite the determination of the judiciary to hold the trial in the city there was no choice but to transfer it to Dublin. The failure to hear the case in Limerick showed the world how the mobs were undermining the rule of law. The trial was set down to commence in Cloverhill Courthouse in Clondalkin, west Dublin, on Wednesday, 5 November.

Two days before it started the Limerick gangs were again in the national headlines after thwarting the legal system. On 3 November in Dublin the trial of Christy Keane's son Liam, for the 2001 murder of teenager Eric Leamy, collapsed. The six original witnesses to the murder had developed what Mr Justice Paul Carney described as 'collective amnesia'. The first witness to be called to testify began shouting at the judge that he had 'seen nothing, knew nothing and heard nothing' as he approached the witness box. Liam's father's lieutenants had ensured the witnesses knew what fate would befall them if they testified. As a result the trial fell apart and the DPP was left with no choice but to enter a *nolle prosequi* and drop the charge against the smirking teenager.

Mr Justice Carney could scarcely conceal his utter frustration at such a blatant attack on the fundamentals of law and order. 'The like of what has happened in this case has never, I can assure you, been encountered in this court before,' he declared, as he released the jury. But Liam Keane was jubilant. As he left the court building he turned and gave the two fingers to waiting cameramen. His face, a frightening mix of hostility and aggression, appeared on the front pages of the next morning's newspapers. The picture sent a chilling message to Irish society. A murderer was walking away a free man after his trial had collapsed amid an atmosphere of unmistakable fear and intimidation. The young thug had become a household name and his snarling picture became an image synonymous with the underworld's attitude to law and order. The Limerick crime crisis was again dominating the national agenda.

The disintegration of the Liam Keane trial, coming just two weeks after the failure to empanel a jury in his uncle's murder case, caused an unprecedented public outcry. Within hours of the collapse of the trial the Justice Minister, Michael McDowell, held a number of meetings with Garda management and personnel from the offices of the DPP in a bid to work out how to deal with the crisis. The gangland problem was seen to be spiralling out of control as other mob wars raged in Finglas and Crumlin in Dublin. As a direct result of the collapse of the Liam Keane trial, the Government enacted new legislation. It enabled the courts to accept as evidence witness statements made to the Gardaí which were later recanted in court.

Two days later the Kieran Keane trial finally got underway

in Dublin. There were no further disruptions after a jury was successfully empanelled. There was tight security in and around the court building. It had been chosen as the most secure option for the trial because prisoners could be brought to and from the court through a secure, underground tunnel linking it to Wheatfield Prison. The judge, Mr Justice Paul Carney, and prosecution counsel were provided with armed police escorts for the duration of the month-long trial. The seven men and five women of the jury were driven to the courts complex each day, under armed escort. Everyone entering the building walked through electronic scanning equipment.

Throughout the trial, the five killers – James McCarthy, Christopher 'Smokey' Costelloe, Dessie Dundon, Anthony 'Noddy' McCarthy and David 'Frog Eyes' Stanners – appeared confident and cocky, smiling and waving to family and friends in the court. They sneered across at members of the Keane family, including the murdered man's widow, Sophie. The five gang members sat in a row beside each other, behind their five individual defence teams. Each defendant denied all the charges against them.

Five days after the trial commenced the Dundons and their accomplices launched a new plan to derail the legal process. They attempted to kidnap Christy Keane's wife, Margaret. Three men, believed to be John and Wayne Dundon and their henchman Gary Campion, tried to grab the gangster's wife when she got out of a taxi at her home at around 2 a.m. A car was waiting close by to take Keane and her kidnappers away. However, she began screaming and fought off the attackers, which brought her friends to the rescue. The three thugs, who were wearing balaclavas and never spoke, then ran off. Gardaí believed that the mob had intended to hold Margaret Keane hostage to convince Owen Treacy to suffer the same amnesia that had struck the witnesses in her son's trial. Detectives who knew the Dundon/McCarthys best reckoned that the gangster's wife would not have returned alive. Following the incident members of the Keane/Collopy mob kept a constant guard over Margaret Keane and her home.

The incident had not shaken Owen Treacy. He proved to be a reliable and strong witness. On 7 November Treacy took the witness stand, flanked by two close-protection officers from the ERU. Over the next eight days he was subjected to intense cross-examination by the five individual defence teams representing the accused men. He was not intimidated by the stares and threats being directed at him by the people who had tried to kill him. He showed no fear and refused an option to sit out of their view, and responded to the taunts and threats with gestures of his own.

As Treacy continued to give evidence under cross-examination, on 13 November John Dundon approached the victim's wife, Donna, in the back of the Cloverhill courtroom. In a loud voice he snarled into her face: 'I swear on my baby's life that when this is over I am going to kill Owen Treacy.' Dundon didn't seem to mind that his threats were witnessed by several Gardaí, as well as by the Keane and Treacy families. Detectives immediately arrested the loud-mouthed gangster. Two days later, he was charged with threatening to kill Owen Treacy. Dundon's big mouth had given Limerick an unexpected reprieve as he was remanded in custody and refused bail. Making loud threats would become an occupational hazard for the Dundon brothers. It earned the gang the less complimentary nickname of the 'Dumdum/McCarthys'.

On the evening of Saturday, 20 December, after two days and nights of deliberations, the jury unanimously found the five Murder Inc. members guilty of murder, assault, attempted murder and false imprisonment. Mr Justice Carney sentenced all five men to mandatory life sentences for murder and deferred sentencing on the remaining charges until 3 February 2004.

The verdict was a major relief for the Gardaí in Limerick. In the weeks of the trial a number of officers had been attacked and threatened by thugs supporting the killers. As a result armed officers had been deployed to escort unarmed uniformed Gardaí as they patrolled the flashpoints. This was the first time in the history of the Irish criminal underworld that the largely unarmed Gardaí had been forced to take such precautions.

Following the verdict, Kieran Keane's widow took the stand in order to tell the court how the murder had affected her and her family. 'They are animals,' she said of the five men who had just been convicted. 'My life stood still and my life was finished the day they took my husband's life.' She was then asked by prosecuting counsel what her husband had done to deserve such a death. Before she could reply, one of his killers shouted: 'He sold drugs and killed people. He killed Eddie Ryan.'

As the five men were led away in handcuffs to a convoy of prison vans, Noddy McCarthy shouted at Treacy and the Keanes: 'For every action there's a reaction – remember that. You'll be looking over your shoulder for the rest of your life, boy.'

8. War and Peace

Apart from an absence of empathy or remorse in their psyche, the savages in Murder Inc. were also notoriously perfidious. Everything the treacherous Piranhas said or did was wrapped in a web of deceit and duplicity. As one former associate bluntly put it, 'the fuckers couldn't even lie straight in their beds'. The only time the leaders of the mob were in any way sincere was when they issued threats of the gravest, terminal kind. People who suffered the wrath of the Dundons and their vile cousins learned that lesson the hard way. Nobody questioned the veracity of their words when they vowed to kill someone. Wayne Dundon summed it up when he warned an adversary: 'You will be going in a body bag and you know our threats are serious.' When Noddy McCarthy warned Owen Treacy that he would be looking over his shoulder for the rest of his days, his gangland victim knew that the convicted killer was delivering an emphatic message. In the weeks and months following the convictions for the Keane murder, the Dundon/McCarthys stepped up their plans for more vengeful bloodshed.

The feuding between the clans had settled into the equivalent of a low-intensity urban war. In a rare interview with the RTÉ *Prime Time* programme in January 2006, Brian Collopy was uncharacteristically candid as he described the hatred between the two sides. 'It was kill on sight. If we got a phone call, we'd try to get one of them; if they got a phone call, they'd try to get one of us. It was blind madness. It was life or death, them or us,' he said. And there was plenty of evidence to back up his admission. The violence had claimed eight lives between November 2000 and the end of 2003. There had been several attempted murders, and dozens had been injured in the 150 shooting incidents directly associated with the 'blind madness'. Several houses had also been firebombed and indiscriminately raked with bullets.

Nationally 2003 had been the bloodiest year yet recorded since organized crime first emerged in Ireland on the back of the Northern Troubles in 1969. The feuds were still raging in Finglas and Crumlin in Dublin and there were twenty gangland murders in the country that year, a quarter of which occurred in Limerick. Murder Inc. and their henchmen had been directly responsible for four of those killings, while the Keane/Collopys had carried out the other one. With the inclusion of Declan Griffin's killing in Dublin, which was ordered by Dougie Moran, the Piranhas could lay claim to 25 per cent of the national gangland death toll.

Detectives investigating a number of assassinations in Dublin and Cork also suspected that the hit men had been supplied by the Dundon/McCarthys. The mob had suddenly emerged as a new brutal force. A secret Garda intelligence report drawn up in 2003 identified seventeen 'highly organized' criminal gangs operating in the country. The Dundon/McCarthy mob, which had subsumed the Ryans, was classified as the most dangerous in Ireland. They were Public Enemy Number One.

Preventing anarchy in the ancient city required the most intensive police operation in the history of law enforcement in Ireland. By the beginning of 2004, over thirty gang members were in custody and in excess of 250 weapons had been seized over the previous two years. In December 2003 Gardaí had made the chilling discovery that the gangs were equipping themselves for a more sinister type of assassination when they seized a number of long-range sniper rifles. The man leading the offensive against the mobs, Chief Superintendent Gerry Kelly, described the use of such weapons as a worrying development: 'Whatever chance one has of controlling and solving attacks involving handguns where people have to get close up to their victims, there is no chance of controlling attacks with long-range weapons.' But the implacable Garda operations had saved many lives. Local wags joked that Limerick Gardaí had decommissioned more weapons than General John de Chastelain, who supervised the destruction of IRA weapons as part of the peace process in Northern Ireland.

A week after the Dundons murdered Michael Campbell McNamara, Chief Superintendent Kelly ordered yet another emergency security operation and called in armed reinforcements from Cork and Dublin. His officers had received credible intelligence that several murder contracts had been ordered on members of the three main feuding gangs in the city. Kelly told this writer at the time: 'It is not an exaggeration to say the place is awash with blood money being offered to carry out murders. The target for one killing is also the client ordering another. It is a thriving market for would-be assassins. It requires a huge effort to prevent as many of these as is possible but we can't be everywhere all the time.'

The feuding gangs had clearly not heeded the words of the priest officiating at the funeral of the man the Dundons had so horrifically mutilated. Fr Donough O'Malley, who had presided at other gangland funerals, spoke for the entire community when he directed his words to the dead man's criminal associates and their enemies. 'Now is the time to stop being unkind, selfish, fighting, vengeful. I ask you in the name of God to stop fighting, stop killing, you can do it, you will do it with God's help,' he pleaded. One of the criminals in the church sniggered and was heard to say: 'The only help God can give us is a few Glock automatics, or he could whack the Dundons for us ... we'd thank him for that.' In the meantime the war continued.

Between 1 December 2003 and 10 January 2004 there were thirteen shooting incidents associated with the feuds. The shootings continued over Christmas and were concentrated in the stronghold of the Dundon/McCarthys, who were involved in a separate, additional feud with another local family. A house belonging to a Murder Inc. member was shot at on New Year's Day and another was burned down. Dougie Moran, who drove a custom-built bullet- and bomb-proof BMW jeep, ordered two more vehicles for his cousins in Limerick at a cost of over €150,000, paid in cash. On 8 January, the Dundons' twenty-year-old cousin Christopher McCarthy was arrested with twenty-three-year-old Gary Kirby after a drive-by shooting in which three houses on the south side were attacked in the same incident. Five children were in one of the houses when it was raked with bullets and buckshot. Luckily no one was hurt in the attack.

McCarthy and Kirby both had long criminal records, including convictions for violence and threats to kill. They were charged with the possession of firearms with intent to endanger life. At a bail hearing in the District Court, McCarthy claimed he feared for his safety and said he wore a bullet-proof vest twenty-four hours a day – even in bed. The Murder Inc. thug casually lied through his teeth as he portrayed himself as an unwitting participant in the feud. 'I was dragged into the feud after the other family called me names.

I wear a bullet-proof vest since my mother's house was shot in three years ago,' he bluntly told the court. Gardaí objected to bail on the grounds that Christopher McCarthy was heavily involved in the feuds and would commit other serious crimes if released. The gunmen were remanded in custody.

A few months later two more Murder Inc. gunmen, twenty-one-year-old Gareth Collins and David 'Skull' McCormack, aged nineteen, also found themselves on the wrong side of the prison walls. Collins, who sometimes used the name Keogh, was a brother of Ger Dundon's partner, April. His father, Jimmy, was a senior member of the Dundon mob. Gardaí caught the two gunmen in possession of firearms when their car was stopped by armed detectives in the village of Bruree, County Limerick. Gardaí believed they were on their way to do either a robbery or carry out a hit. Objecting to bail, Detective Garda Ronan McDonagh claimed Collins was a 'close associate' of the gang 'waging a war on the streets of Limerick'. Bail was refused. In a bid to quell the violence, the courts in the city had adopted a less liberal approach to bail when compared with the rest of the country. If gang members were remanded in custody, the crime rate tended to drop.

Gary Kirby didn't need to worry about his temporary loss of freedom for long. A month after his arrest the career criminal was jailed for life for the murder of one of Murder Inc.'s enemies – Trevor McNamara – in 2002. During the trial evidence was heard that the victim's skull had been smashed in with a pick-axe handle, before he was stabbed ten times in the neck and body. Kirby had claimed he was defending himself and that he feared he was going to be stabbed by the victim. As he was led away, Kirby roared 'scumbags' at Gardaí and spat at people in the public gallery.

Seconds later a mass brawl broke out in the hallway of the courthouse between relatives of the accused and the deceased.

Christopher McCarthy's incarceration in January prevented his involvement in a number of hits that Murder Inc. started planning in the last few months of 2003. Informants from within the Dundon/McCarthy mob had reported back to their Garda handlers that Wayne Dundon had ordered the deaths of Owen Treacy and nineteen-year-old Liam Keane. Weapons and a stolen motorbike were stored at a derelict house in Moyross in preparation for the two jobs. Treacy was under armed police protection and would prove difficult to get at, but Dundon, the informants said, was still prepared to send a hit team after him. It didn't matter to him if the cops got hit in the crossfire. All he cared about was the point the mob would make by eliminating the high-profile 'rat'. It would also be an embarrassment for the police, an added benefit.

In January, despite describing himself as a humble bread-van driver, Treacy splashed out on a brand-new, top-of-the-range BMW worth over €50,000 to replace the one he had previously owned. Dundon told his associates that he wanted it blown up. Gardaí stepped up security around the gangster and waited for the Dundon/McCarthys to make their move.

Wayne Dundon, however, decided to sort out Christy Keane's son Liam first. Following the forced abandonment of his murder trial in the Central Criminal Court, the teenager had become the public face of the family business. As he walked free amid a national furore, the parents of his victim Eric Leamy were left emotionally distraught, filled with a sense of dread and despair knowing that they would have to encounter the sneering criminal on the street. The result of the trial had also been greeted with dismay by the ordinary decent people living in the estates that the vicious thug claimed as his turf. Once again the gangs had shown that they could beat the system.

Dundon reckoned that taking out such a dangerous, high-profile gangster would be a huge publicity coup. The Piranhas would show the world that mob law was more effective than the laws of civic society. And it would seriously demoralize the opposition. But it was also a matter of kill or be killed. Like his murdered uncle before him, the hate-filled, chaotic young thug could not restrain himself from attacking and threatening his enemies at every possible opportunity. After his release the teenaged Keane made no secret of his desire to spill the blood of anyone with the name Dundon, McCarthy or Ryan – and he had the capacity and firepower to do it. As a result it earned him the top slot on the Dundon/McCarthys 'to be done' list. Liam Keane was a dead man walking.

The night after Keane's acquittal, extra armed patrols were deployed on the streets where he lived and a police helicopter kept vigil overhead. Gardaí were primed and ready, expecting the Dundon/McCarthys to make a move against their enemy, who was now the best-known mobster in Limerick. Members of the extended Keane/Collopy gang and their allies had also sent out their own patrols to ensure the safety of their boss's brutal boy.

On 5 November 2003, two days after ducking the murder charge, Keane had received a three-month suspended sentence in Limerick District Court for a public order offence committed a few weeks earlier in October. He had been

arrested for being drunk and disorderly the night after Campbell McNamara's funeral. He had carried the coffin of his
murdered pal earlier that day and openly scoffed at the priest's
exhortations for peace. Getting a suspended sentence in his
second successful joust with justice hardened his arrogance
and the young Keane believed he was untouchable. Instead
of keeping his head down, he made no secret of his victory
and swaggered around the city in a bullet-proof vest looking
for trouble.

On 26 November, Gardaí again arrested Keane outside
the city's courts complex for threatening a member of the
opposing faction. The Dundons were getting ready to move
in, but just before they got to him Liam Keane was jailed for
four months, on 6 January 2004, for the public order incident
at the courts. Two weeks later, Limerick District Court also
granted a Garda application to activate the three-month suspended sentence imposed on 5 November. Although he
didn't know it, Keane's bad behaviour – and the Gardaí – had
helped him escape an assassin's bullet.

Meanwhile the relentless Garda investigations scored
more victories over the mobsters. On 24 January, the Gardaí
finally located Murder Inc.'s assassins' storage depot in Moyross. They recovered a cache of two automatic pistols, two
sawn-off shotguns and a high-powered motorbike. On 29
January, Keane gang member Michael Scanlan was jailed for
nine years for possession of a bomb at Mungret in June 2003.
It had been intended for use against the Dundon/McCa-
rthys. In February, Richard Smith was jailed for five years
while his son Sean got twelve years. Sean Smith admitted to
Gardaí that he was to be paid €10,000 to deliver the bomb.
Keane acolyte Darby Sheehy was acquitted by a jury. Detective Sergeant Tom O'Connor told Scanlan's trial that the

bomb was intended to 'put the feud on a more violent and bloody plain'.

On Tuesday, 3 February 2004, Mr Justice Paul Carney sat in the Central Criminal Court in Limerick for the much-anticipated sequel to the dramatic Kieran Keane murder trial. The judge was determined to sentence the five killers on the outstanding charges of false imprisonment and attempted murder in the city that they had terrorized. He wanted to send an unequivocal message to the warring gangs that they could not thwart the justice system.

Major security operations, reminiscent of the Mafia show trials in Italy, had become a regular spectacle in Limerick. But that day the security was even tighter than before. Almost 100 uniformed officers, backed by heavily armed colleagues, were on duty for the ninety-minute hearing. The hoodlums were accompanied by over twenty prison officers wearing body armour. They were brought to court in a convoy of police and prison vehicles under the watchful eye of a Garda helicopter.

The convicted men were now serving life sentences and there was little for them to lose if they orchestrated a riot or an attempted breakout. There was an equal risk that a sniper might try to shoot Owen Treacy or some other member of his assembled gang. Both sides had been shown to have access to sniper rifles, bombs, high-powered weapons and professional assassins – the police were taking no chances. Garda sharp-shooters, equipped with assault rifles, watched from nearby rooftops. On the ground below, their colleagues came equipped in case a riot broke out at the courts complex – the by now familiar flashpoint for the tribes.

The atmosphere in Merchant's Quay was tense as scores of supporters and family members from both sides of the bloodbath turned up to jeer and threaten each other. Wayne Dundon and his entourage wore specially printed T-shirts with the words 'Keanes are rats' emblazoned across them. The criminals paraded in front of the large number of press photographers present, making sure they got a good shot. In the crowded courtroom sixty Gardaí stood between both sides and surrounded the Murder Inc. men sitting in the dock. Owen Treacy and the rest of the Keane family were under guard in the public gallery as they awaited Mr Justice Carney's arrival.

The hoodlums, three of whom had cartoon nicknames – 'Noddy', 'Frog Eyes' and 'Smokey' – that belied their status as cold-blooded killers, acted like a bunch of children on a day trip. They laughed and waved to supporters while shouting threats at the man whose botched murder had led to their convictions. Either the sobering reality of their life sentences hadn't sunk in yet, or the 'macho men' were putting on an unrepentant face for the world.

Before sentence was passed, Superintendent Gerry Mahon, the officer-in-charge of the investigation, summarized the background to the feud. 'This feud started in the summer of 2000 when two families who were previously close associates had a disagreement, which ultimately led in November 2000 to a murder taking place in the Moose Bar in Cathedral Place. Three further murders have occurred, all directly related to this particular feud,' he said, as the five killers joked and laughed. Seemingly oblivious to the childish display from the bench below, Superintendent Mahon listed the astonishing catalogue of serious crimes which had accompanied the murder spree: assaults, stabbings, possession and use of explosives, the possession and use of high-powered weapons, intimidation and criminal damage.

'The prime motivation in this feud is the sheer and absolute hate each side has for each other. It is a hate that has not diminished to this day. The motivation and the objective of this particular gang was to murder both Kieran Keane and Owen Treacy and lure two other people into the trap, and I believe two other murders would have occurred had they been successful,' the investigator continued. 'The motivation was to eliminate those who stood in their way and those perceived to be their enemies with the objective of totally dominating Limerick City.' As Superintendent Mahon gave his grim assessment the five men just giggled.

Mr Justice Carney then sentenced David Stanners, Christopher Costelloe, Dessie Dundon and James and Anthony McCarthy to fifteen years each on the count of attempted murder and a further seven years each for the false imprisonment of Owen Treacy and Kieran Keane. The sentences were to run concurrently. As they heard their fate, the five men whooped with laughter, cheered and shouted threats at the Treacys and Keanes. But Mr Justice Carney had a stark warning for the ebullient thugs and their clans: 'Life sentences have already been imposed on each of the accused in this case. I wanted to say primarily to the friends and supporters of the accused on the outside that each of these men will die in prison unless there is intervention in their cases by the Parole Board. The Parole Board is entirely independent, but it seems unlikely to intervene while the feud is a live issue. This should be borne in mind by the friends and supporters of the accused outside and the accused themselves.'

As the five men left the court for the last time it appeared the judge's warning had been completely ignored. Their supporters cheered them on, as if they were war heroes. In the background both sides hurled insults and death threats at each other. Owen Treacy shouted abuse at his enemies as he left the court under armed guard. But as the warring thugs dispersed, under the watchful eye of an army of police officers, it appeared that reality was finally dawning on the relations of the guilty men, and angry recriminations were exchanged. One of them was heard to say of Frog Eyes Stanners: 'If that fuckin' bollocks had done it right then we wouldn't have this shite goin' on and the lads would be out. He made a complete fuckin' mess of it.'

After the hearing Chief Superintendent Gerry Kelly said he hoped the feuding clans would take notice of the judge's warning. He commented: 'This definitely draws a line in the sand and I hope that the families involved will take notice of this and the feuding will stop with this generation.' He revealed that the local Gardaí had established lines of communication with the various warring families and had been trying to persuade them to stop killing and harming each other. But he said he was still of the belief that his officers were at risk from the gangs: 'An unarmed Garda in a car at night is a high risk and that is why they must be accompanied by an armed escort.'

A week after the Keane killers were sentenced, the Dundons were back in the limelight. This time it was their father, Kenneth Dundon, who was making the headlines. He made Irish criminal justice history when on 11 February 2004 he became the first Irishman to be arrested under a European Arrest Warrant. He was facing a charge of killing his wife's lover in London. The first member of the family to make it onto Scotland Yard's 'Most Wanted List' was arrested by Gardaí in Limerick. He was remanded in custody, where he joined two of his sons, Dessie and John, and several other friends and relations. Dundon Senior subsequently fought the British extradition order all the way to the Supreme Court but was sent back to face trial at the Old Bailey in September 2005. A year later, he pleaded guilty to the lesser charge of manslaughter and was jailed for a relatively lenient six years.

Despite the personal setbacks and the loss of so many gang members, Wayne Dundon was determined to prove that nowhere was safe for his rivals. On the morning of 20 February the psychopath made his point. Two nail bombs were thrown across the perimeter wall of Limerick Prison into the exercise yard used by members of the Keane/Collopy gang. An Army bomb squad carried out controlled explosions on both devices, which were described as being viable but crude. They comprised two six-inch metal containers, made up of nails, powder and fuses. The discovery prompted a complete lock-down of the slammer as warders received a tip-off that a firearm had also been smuggled inside. No weapon was found but security at the prison was beefed up as staff expressed real concerns for their safety. The prison now had to be protected from attack on both sides of its walls. The Limerick mobs had set another precedent.

The Keane/Collopys wasted no time taking retaliatory action. At 5.00 p.m. that evening a member of Murder Inc. had a lucky escape as he sat in his car queuing at a McDonald's Drive-thru in Dooradoyle, a Limerick suburb. Two men on a motorbike drove up alongside and the pillion passenger fired two shots into the car, missing the target. In the busy restaurant parents and their children dived for cover. Four associates of the Keane/Collopy gang were arrested an hour later for questioning about the incident but there was insufficient evidence to charge them. As the tit-for-tat exchanges continued, the city's Gardaí also found themselves in the firing line.

In May 2004 there were more gun attacks on Gardaí patrolling the troubled Moyross Estate, home to the McCarthy family and considered Murder Inc. territory. A police van on patrol in the area was shot at but no one was injured. A week later three Gardaí who had located a stolen car in the same area narrowly escaped injury when a masked gunman blasted their patrol car with a shotgun. None of the unarmed officers was injured, although the rear of the squad car was peppered with shotgun pellets. The indiscriminate nature of the attacks was a source of deep concern for police chiefs. They had lost their colleague, Jerry McCabe, eight years earlier when he was gunned down by an IRA gang and they dreaded more fatalities. In a follow-up investigation, six teenagers were arrested for questioning and a firearm was seized.

In early April Wayne Dundon and his cousin Christopher McCarthy, who had obtained bail on the firearms possession charge, spotted Brian Collopy and another associate in a car. When Collopy noticed the dangerous thugs in his rear-view mirror he sped off, with Dundon and his cousin in hot pursuit. The Murder Inc. pair called for reinforcements and they were joined in the abduction attempt by associates in another car and a jeep. Collopy drove to Mayorstone Garda Station and ran inside, seeking refuge. He identified his would-be assailants and Gardaí later arrested the cousins and three others. All five men were found to be wearing bullet-proof vests, which the Gardaí seized. On 8 April the cocky thugs went to the District Court to apply for the return of their essential apparel.

During the hearing Dundon told Judge Tom O'Donnell that he needed the body armour because there had been an attempt on his life in February. He even stood up to show the judge that he was wearing another protective vest. 'They [the other gang] are trying to kill me and the guards don't care. It's a serious matter for me, being shot,' Dundon informed the judge in an aggressive tone. Objecting to the return of the vests, Detective Inspector Jim Browne said Dundon was the brains behind the gang and his officers had received information that the gang were going to kick off more 'operations' when the body armour was restored. Judge O'Donnell refused to return the items and Dundon immediately lodged an appeal.

On 29 June, the nine men charged in connection with the riot at Supermac's on the Ennis Road were convicted after a thirteen-day trial. The belligerents were jailed for a total of thirty-eight years between them. 'Kidnap' victim Kieran Ryan and three members of the extended McCarthy family were jailed for six years each. Another of their associates, David Sheehan, was jailed for five years and three months. Twenty-four-year-old killer Philip Collopy, who had escaped the Keane murder trap in 2003, was jailed for two years after he pleaded guilty to the unlawful possession of a weapon. Declan 'Darby' Sheehy got three years while Raymond Collopy and Kieran Keane's younger brother Anthony were also jailed for terms of two years each.

The legal bill to the State for the lengthy trial was in the neighbourhood of €600,000. The Keane murder trial had run up legal costs of another €1 million plus. Apart from the human cost in shattered lives, the war was weighing heavily on the taxpayer as the overall bill for maintaining law and order in Limerick was running into millions. After passing sentence Judge Carroll Moran, who had gained an unrivalled knowledge presiding over the most serious crime trials in the city, described the ongoing feud: 'This problem has evolved over the past three to four years as an extremely serious problem and in fact it is the most serious problem in the city and it has to stop. I would be open to the most serious criticism and well-justified criticism if I did other than try to bring an end to this mindless violence. It's going nowhere.'

The judge wasn't the only one to realize the damage being caused by the tribal warfare. Pragmatists in both gangs could see it was having a detrimental effect on their respective drug operations. The violence was attracting huge media, political and police attention. A rigorous 'stop and search' policy by the Gardaí, as well as increased patrols and checkpoints, were seriously disrupting the movement of drug shipments. The constant police activity was also turning up good quality intelligence. In 2003 Gardaí in the city had seized narcotics worth over €3 million and several of the gang's dealers were before the courts. At the same time the Criminal Assets Bureau had begun focusing on the finances and assets of the gang members. In June 2003, the Garda National Drug Unit had intercepted a truck in Dublin transporting €13 million worth of heroin and hashish. It was destined for Limerick for onward distribution throughout the Midwest region. Gardaí had seized another €3.5 million worth of cocaine, heroin and ecstasy in Dublin that December, which they believed was also destined for the Limerick mobs.

The police attention was worrying the businessmen behind Murder Inc., especially Jim 'Chaser' O'Brien and Anthony Kelly. They argued that there should be a halt to the violence because it was causing too much disruption to the trade and focusing unnecessary attention on their international connections. O'Brien had built a huge drug-trafficking operation since fleeing Ireland after the Fitzgerald and Keane murders.

Operating between bases in Spain, Holland and Belgium, he organized large-scale drug- and gun-smuggling routes between the Continent, the UK and Ireland. Larry McCarthy Junior, who was living between Spain and the UK, was also heavily involved. While the gangland violence was raging, behind the scenes Murder Inc. had seized control of a large slice of the multi-million Euro drug trade in the Midwest. They were also involved in a complex network with other major Irish drug gangs in Dublin and Cork, the UK and the Continent.

Dubliner Martin 'Marlo' Hyland from Cabra, who was then classified by Gardaí as the underworld's most powerful crime boss, had formed a close association with Murder Inc. An ambitious gangster who controlled a multi-million Euro drug distribution racket, Hyland was one of the first Irish criminals to realize the importance of being allied to the infamous Dundon/McCarthys. By 2004, Marlo was in the process of trying to amalgamate several of Ireland's criminal organizations to create a glorified crime corporation, similar to the Mafia in Italy and the USA. With the mobs working together, under one umbrella, they could pool resources to buy larger drug shipments at cheaper prices. The Gardaí and the prosecution service feared that such an alliance would be a potent force with the capacity to undermine the State. Luckily the temperamental egos of the gang bosses meant Hyland's plan never became a reality.

The Dundon/McCarthys also forged a deadly alliance with a gang headed by Crumlin hoodlum 'Fat' Freddie Thompson. The Thompson mob was embroiled in a ferocious gang war with some of their former associates, led by killer Brian Rattigan. Over the space of ten years the Crumlin/Drimnagh feud claimed the lives of twelve men. It ranked second only to the Limerick war in the depravity stakes. Through Fat Freddie, the Dundons also allied themselves to another drug gang from Dublin's north inner-city. The Rattigan gang, meanwhile, formed an alliance with the Keane/Collopys, who in turn were partners with Tallaght godfather Troy Jordan. The groupings became apparent to Gardaí who ran surveillance operations on the gangsters' meetings.

Gardaí in Dublin suspected that the Limerick mobs had been supplying guns and killers to their new associates. Forensic evidence showed that at least seven firearms seized from the Dundon/McCarthys in Limerick had been used in shootings and assassinations in Dublin. Another example of the connections between the Limerick and Dublin mobs was discovered after a notorious Finglas criminal, Declan Curran, was arrested for murder. The deranged twenty-four-year-old psychopath, who had already killed three people, was wearing body armour in bed when detectives lifted him. A follow-up investigation later traced the bullet-proof vest to a batch of five which had been purchased in the UK by a soldier in the Irish Army. The soldier, who had never come to the authority's attention before, was associated with members of the Keane family. The fact that a trusted soldier was connected to the mob was a worrying discovery. It illustrated how deep the tentacles of organized crime had spread into all aspects of society.

Chaser O'Brien and his partners-in-crime had become so big that they found themselves the focus of a number of international police investigations. The first major blow to the organization came with the seizure of ecstasy and cocaine valued at over €1.8 million in County Tipperary in September 2003. Two of O'Brien's closest associates, twenty-eight-year-old Cecil Kinsella and twenty-seven-year-old Christopher

Maguire, were arrested when the Garda National Drug Unit searched Maguire's home on 5 September. The haul included 162,500 ecstasy tablets and one kilo of uncut cocaine. Kinsella had also been caught with an automatic pistol, equipped with a silencer. The two drug dealers absconded when they got bail and joined O'Brien in Holland. O'Brien later sent the two fugitives to the UK to run operations there with Larry McCarthy Junior.

In 2004, O'Brien and his international associates became the prime target of a multi-jurisdictional police operation involving the Gardaí and their colleagues in Holland, Belgium and the UK. The operations were codenamed 'Sword' in Ireland, 'Slue' in the UK, 'Pub' in Holland and 'Lotje' in Belgium. The investigations confirmed that O'Brien was central to an extensive international criminal organization with links to gangs all over Europe. He ran his operation from Antwerp in conjunction with two criminals from Belgium and Holland. Over the next year the police would gradually move in on the former Limerick barman and his associates.

It was against this backdrop that, just weeks after trying to abduct him, Wayne Dundon began sounding out Brian Collopy about a potential peace deal. Bizarrely, considering Dundon's well-earned reputation for treachery and the fact that he had tried to murder Collopy on at least two occasions, the drug boss said he was interested. The continuing police operations had also cost the Keanes and Collopys millions of Euro in seized drugs. The previous November the Criminal Assets Bureau had also seized Brian Collopy's luxury home at Fedamore on the outskirts of the city. The CAB then hit him with a tax bill for over €500,000, made up of taxes, penalties and a bill for fraudulently claimed social welfare payments. The house was to be put on the market to settle the account. Collopy was not a proponent of the use of indiscriminate violence and he understood the value of not attracting unnecessary attention from the police. He and his associates had been stunned when the Dundons and McCarthys suddenly turned from friends to murderous foes the night they took Kieran Keane. The fact that Murder Inc. had twice tried to lure him to his death convinced Brian Collopy that a truce was the only option if he wanted to stay alive.

Pleas for an end to the violence had been ringing in the mobsters' ears for months. Gardaí had tried to convince the combatants of the folly of the feuds and a number of public representatives had offered to broker peace. The politician most trusted by all sides was Willie O'Dea, who in the spring of 2004 was the Junior Minister for Justice in the Fianna Fáil-led Government. O'Dea, who had been a staunch supporter of the Garda operations in the city, had already spoken out against the warring gangs. He described them as 'among the most violent, ruthless and brutal to be found anywhere in the world'. In March 2004 O'Dea was contacted by Wayne Dundon, who said he was prepared to sit down with the Keanes and Collopys and talk peace. It was a move totally out of character for the self-serving psychopath. But it was motivated by a growing realization that if the cops kept up their campaign, then most of the Dundon/McCarthy gang would end up behind bars – which was bad for business. Brian Collopy also contacted the minister with the same proposal. The unexpected development left the politician flabbergasted.

A peace summit of sorts was organized by O'Dea in the boardroom of a city hotel that evening. Dundon arrived with four other gang members, and along with the McCarthys and Ryans they sat on one side of the conference table. Sitting opposite was Brian Collopy with his brothers. The Keanes had refused to take part. When Christy Keane was informed of the plan he went ballistic with rage. The manner of his brother's betrayal and execution, and the near death of his nephew, were crimes that could never be forgiven. No amount of blood could pay those debts. As far as he was concerned, the idea of even contemplating peace with the Piranhas was unconscionable. The Dundon/McCarthys were also utterly treacherous individuals and Keane believed that trusting them to keep to any agreement would be the height of naivety. Anyone familiar with the Dundon/McCarthys' track record knew that 'peace' would only be a means to a nastier end.

Keane ordered his clan and loyal lieutenants to snub any meetings, and told Brian Collopy that their friendship was over if he did a deal with the devil. Collopy later commented: 'I asked one of the Keanes to go to the meeting as a representative. But word had been sent out from prison that there should be no representative from the Keanes at the meeting.'

Willie O'Dea also said his only regret about trying to negotiate peace was that the Keanes weren't there. The empty chairs at the boardroom table were the first psychological victory for the manipulative Dundon – his enemies were weaker if divided.

Willie O'Dea and the Mayor of Limerick, Dick Sadlier, sat at the head of the table and chaired the surreal meeting. O'Dea told the thugs that he had informed the Gardaí that the meeting was taking place and that he would be reporting back to them. Over a number of hours the two sides came to a tentative arrangement to stop trying to kill each other. Wayne Dundon and Brian Collopy stood up and shook hands across the table. O'Dea would later recall that he was very uncomfortable, but had decided to go ahead with the meeting. 'These are the most treacherous individuals you could meet and while I really could not trust a word they said, a lot of decent people had approached me and asked me to do something,' he explained to this writer some years later. 'I made sure that everything was above board because I had told the Gardaí and I let the gangsters know that this would not be like a Mikey Kelly peace deal, the criminal investigations would continue no matter what.' O'Dea said that he had found Dundon to be a 'particularly devious and manipulative individual'.

Christy Keane got word of the peace deal within an hour and was apoplectic. When he cooled down the godfather decided to teach his former protégés a salutary lesson about not doing deals with the enemy. He turned to his cell mate on the E1 Wing of Portlaoise Maximum Security Prison, which housed the hardest men in the criminal underworld. John Daly from Finglas was an extremely volatile and violent criminal who had been involved in drugs, armed robbery and murder since his teens. The fact that, aged twenty-three, he was serving his time for armed robbery on the 'Godfather's landing' with the likes of Keane and John Gilligan was tacit recognition of his credentials as a big-time villain. Daly had originally been part of the notorious Westies gang, whose leaders, Stephen Sugg and Shane Coates, had been murdered in Spain a few months earlier. He was a member of a group of young thugs who had been responsible for at least four murders and several attempted killings back in Finglas. He was also an associate of Marlo Hyland, who in turn was in bed with Murder Inc. The gangland neighbourhood was a complicated place.

At Keane's request, Daly organized his friends on the outside to arrange a surprise for Brian Collopy. In July 2004 the Collopys arranged a deal to buy a consignment of cocaine and heroin from Daly's associates for €45,000. It would fetch four times that much on the streets. When the Limerick hoods turned up to collect the shipment in Finglas they were suddenly surrounded by Daly's pals, including Declan Curran. A number of shots were fired in the air and the Collopys were ordered to hand over the money. They were advised to 'fuck off' back to Limerick before they got hurt. The Collopys could do nothing without the help of Christy Keane's allies in Dublin – the people who had organized the surprise party.

Before they got home Christy Keane let the Collopys know he had set them up as punishment for talking peace with the hated enemy. The incident caused a bitter rift in the Keane/Collopy camp, which was exactly what the Dundon/McCarthys wanted. On 19 August 2004 Gardaí prevented the outbreak of a shooting war between the former partners when they arrested two men on their way to attack Christy Keane's home. It was a worrying development for the police, whose hard work had helped ensure there had been no murders so far that year. If the feuding mutated into yet another form the consequences could be catastrophic. However, after a time, the two gangs effectively kissed and made up and went their separate ways.

In the meantime the Garda offensive continued, with drug and gun seizures taking place almost on a weekly basis. In August pipe bombs, guns and ammunition were found in a search of the Keanes' stronghold in the Island Field. In

October, detectives seized two handguns and a large amount of cocaine when they searched a house in Murder Inc.'s Ballinacurra Weston domain. A few days later another search in the same area uncovered a large quantity of commercial explosives that the gang had acquired for a new bomb. Five days later, two weapons and 500 rounds of ammunition were discovered in Moyross. There was also success on the legal front – and vindication for Mr Justice Carney who had encountered considerable opposition when he moved the Central Criminal Court to Limerick. By the autumn of 2004 the backlog of murder and rape trials had been cleared with guilty verdicts returned in at least fifteen cases. Thirteen people had been convicted of murder and another three of manslaughter. After the final trial the judge announced that 'the cupboard is now empty'. But despite these victories, the shooting incidents continued.

Liam Keane was still on Wayne Dundon's hit list. On 25 October the young thug found himself in the sights of a would-be assassin when a gunman on a motorbike fired several shots in his direction. Keane was standing outside a shop at around 7 p.m. when the hit man drove up and fired one shot. As the hoodlum ran for cover the motorbike returned and the gunman fired more shots at his target. The godfather's son was uninjured in the gun attack, the fourth in the city in less than ten days.

Wayne Dundon had also renewed his interest in real estate. The temperamental hoodlum waged a campaign of intimidation aimed at driving families from their homes in Ballinacurra Weston. It was similar to the Dundons' earlier experiment in social engineering. He wanted a Nazi-style *Lebensraum* for members of the gang whom the council had evicted from other estates because of anti-social behaviour.

Dundon and his henchmen approached a family who had put their parents' home up for sale. He told them that if they didn't accept a bid from the gang – which was way below the market value of the property – then they would not be selling the house to anyone. When the owners refused, the house was fire-bombed and daubed with graffiti declaring 'The Keanes are scum'. Dundon also forced other families to move out and sell their houses to his family for as little as €10,000.

In November 2004 Michael Murray, the outspoken State Solicitor, described the proliferation of gang violence as a clear sign that a mini-mafia had emerged in the city. He argued that it was folly to contend that the crime levels were merely down to inter-family feuds, and warned that the real motivation was organized crime. He said at the time: 'The authorities really haven't woken up to this, that there is this problem to be tackled. People who think this is not organized crime are living in cloud-cuckoo-land.' There had been a dramatic increase in the number of recorded shooting incidents during the year, which rose to sixty-one compared to thirty-nine in 2003.

In the meantime Wayne Dundon was enjoying his status as the boss. To the frustration of the police, he had proved hard to catch because he protected himself behind lines of flunkies and foot soldiers. As business prospered after the 'peace deal' he'd brokered, Dundon considered himself untouchable. But then he walked himself into a world of trouble when he turned the lives of a completely innocent family into a nightmare of unimaginable evil.

9. An Innocent Family

The grainy image from the security camera portrays three people – a young girl, a woman and a man – talking at the front door of the pub. Then a fourth person, another, much bigger man, steps into the frame and appears to join the conversation. He becomes animated and makes a gesture with his hand at the other man before leaving with the girl. To the uninformed viewer it appears to be nothing more than a run-of-the-mill interaction between a barman and some customers. But for a Limerick family the footage is a real-life horror movie. It is a chilling record of the exact moment when they came face-to-face with the terrifying malevolence of Murder Inc.

The time code in the corner of the footage will be for ever etched in the minds of the Collins family. For this was the moment, at 9.25 p.m. on 19 December 2004, that an evil force invaded their peaceful existence and unleashed a catastrophic chain of events. The apparently innocuous scene would turn their blissful lives into a living hell of fear and immeasurable grief. It would lead to an unprecedented, sustained assault on a completely innocent family that resulted in a shooting, an arson attack, a contract murder, intimidation, closed businesses, near penury, post-traumatic stress, police protection and, finally, forced emigration as part of a witness relocation programme. This was the moment the Collins family first encountered a violent savage called Wayne Dundon.

Steve Collins from Ballyfermot in Dublin had just qualified as a young electrician when he was sent to do a job in
Limerick in 1973 – and he ended up staying for good. The
reason for this unforeseen decision was that he fell in love
with a local girl called Carmel Lee. Less than a year later, in
January 1974, the smitten couple were married and they
settled in Limerick City. They had four children: Roy the eldest, Paul, Steve Junior and daughter Leeann, who was the
youngest. For several years Steve had a thriving electrical
contracting business, but then he decided to change direction and moved into the pub trade. In 1990 he bought the
Steering Wheel pub at Roxboro Shopping Centre in the heart
of the Southill working-class estate – a short distance from
Ballinacurra Weston. In 1992 the family moved to live in
Blackpool in the UK, where Steve ran a night-club while
continuing to own the pub in Limerick. As his sons came of
age they followed their dad into the trade.

In 1999 the family adopted Carmel's thirteen-year-old
nephew Ryan Lee after he had been tragically orphaned following the death of his father. Ryan was the son of Carmel's
brother Vincent, who had lived in Halifax. As a three-year-
old he'd witnessed his mother dying from a sudden brain
haemorrhage. In 1999 tragedy struck again when Ryan's
father, who had been suffering from a long-term illness, fell
sick during a holiday in Limerick and died. 'Ryan was very
close to us and the poor lad had a huge amount of tragedy in
his life so it was natural that we would rear him after his dad
died. He was a fabulous kid and we all loved him very much.
He has always been my fifth child,' Steve would later recall.

The same year Steve bought Brannigan's Pub in Mulgrave
Street, Limerick and in 2000 the family moved back to
live permanently in the city. Roy remained in Blackpool

where he ran another night-club before he too returned to Limerick in 2002. The Collinses were a model family – decent, happy and loving – who worked hard to bring up their children. In happier times Steve regularly brought the boys to watch Manchester United playing at Old Trafford, and summer breaks included cruising on Ireland's waterways. In business Steve had a reputation as an honest, hard-working entrepreneur. He and his family had no enemies – until a cold winter's night in 2004.

On Sunday, 19 December, Brannigan's, which had become one of the most popular watering holes in the city, was full in the build-up to Christmas week. Eighteen-year-old Ryan Lee, who was an apprentice electrician, was helping his adopted dad in the pub to earn some extra money. Around 9.20 p.m. he took a break from behind the bar and went to the front door for some air. As he stood outside a car driven by Wayne Dundon pulled up to the kerb. His wife, Anne Casey, and Dundon's fourteen-year-old sister Annabel got out and walked to the door.

Strict new laws had recently been enacted making it illegal for children under eighteen to be in a pub after 9 p.m. Ryan could see that Dundon's sister was under age and asked her for ID. Annabel protested, claiming that she was over eighteen, but she could not produce any identification. The women demanded entry and the young barman told Anne Casey she was welcome but he had no other choice but to refuse the child. Ryan, who was an inoffensive young man, gently repeated that it was against the law and Steve could lose his licence if the police arrived. But the Dundons and their ilk had no respect for laws. As the argument continued, Wayne Dundon appeared at Ryan's side to find out what was wrong.

Ryan Lee said later: 'Dundon came up to me and asked me in an aggressive tone: "What's the problem?" I told him that it was late and that I would need to see the young girl's ID before she could be let in because it was the law. Dundon got angrier and said: "It's her first night out, give her a fucking break." I replied that I couldn't because it was way too late for an under-age person to be on the premises. I would need ID to prove that she was over eighteen years of age.'

This was not what Wayne Dundon wanted to hear and his mood darkened. Ryan continued: 'He stepped up close to my face and put his finger in the shape of a gun and said: "Fuck you, you're dead." He was really big and intimidating. Up close you can see the evil burning in his eyes. I thought that he was going to hit me there and then but he didn't. He said to his wife: "Are you staying?" Then he grabbed his sister by the hand and took her back to his car. He kept staring back at me, even when he got into the car. He watched me for a short while and turned the car on the road and sped off so hard that the tyres spun on the road.'

Anne Casey went into the pub to join her friends. Exactly twenty-four minutes later, at 9.49 p.m., the pub's CCTV cameras recorded a motorbike arriving outside with two men on board. Wayne Dundon, the pillion passenger, was wearing a crash helmet when he got off the bike. He walked quickly through to the lounge and went inside the bar counter. As he stalked up the length of the counter, he looked closely at each startled staff member. Then he went into the front bar where he spotted the subject of his murderous rage: Ryan Lee was pulling pints for the locals. Dundon stood behind his victim and produced a large, long-barrelled handgun. He took aim and fired a single shot from close range, hitting the eighteen-year-old in the side of his left knee. The bullet travelled through Ryan's kneecap and out the other side, shattering it in the process. The bullet lodged itself in the floor.

'I was standing at the taps about to pull a pint and, out of the corner of my eye, I noticed a guy standing behind the counter with a motorbike helmet,' Ryan remembered. 'I half turned to look at him to find out what was going on. I could see that he was wearing a balaclava under the helmet. I could see his eyes . . . they were pure evil. I didn't see the gun at first. Then I heard the bang and felt a burning sensation in my left knee. I spun around and remember looking into this girl's eyes across the counter. She looked shocked. I grabbed my knee and then fell down. I knew I had been hit. It was a weird feeling.'

Dundon tried to leave through the front door of the bar counter, but it was locked. Then he turned to go back out the way he'd come in. As he stepped over his victim, who was lying on the ground in shock and pain, Dundon decided to finish him off. The crazed gangster fired another shot into the barman. This time the bullet hit Ryan's right hip, travelled through his groin and lodged in his left leg. In the confusion that followed Dundon lowered the weapon and walked quickly back out through the lounge.

Steve Collins heard the bangs and the screams of shocked customers. He followed the gunman outside as he ran to the waiting motorbike. Steve grabbed Dundon as he got on the bike and tried to pull him off. The killer turned and fired a single shot, which missed the publican's head by millimetres. 'The blast from the gun was deafening but I heard the whistle of the bullet going past my ear. I felt the force of the bullet,' Steve recalled. The bullet was later found imbedded in the pub wall. The bike sped off into the night and disappeared as Gardaí raced to the scene. In less than ninety seconds the incident was over – but the Collinses' troubles were only beginning.

Ryan Lee was rushed to hospital where he underwent emergency surgery to save his knee. He remained in hospital for two weeks and had to spend Christmas away from his family. The teenager was unable to walk for several months and underwent further operations to rebuild his knee.

The attack was more evidence of the casual, blood-curdling barbarity that was an intrinsic part of the Murder Inc. psyche. Dundon obviously assumed that he would get away with it – but he was wrong. Like most other citizens in Limerick, Ryan Lee could recognize the city's most feared gangster. There was also clear CCTV footage to back him up.

Steve Collins had known Brian Fitzgerald and was all too aware of the fate that lay in store for those who incurred the wrath of the Dundons. He knew in his heart that once the mob had come into their lives they would never leave. Steve was faced with an appalling dilemma. If he did nothing, Murder Inc. would smell fear and make their lives a hell. If they made a complaint to the Gardaí they would remain a target – but at least there was a chance of making Dundon pay for his indiscriminate savagery. The Collins family were damned either way, but Steve hoped that the police would protect them. The Gardaí had identified Dundon from the security footage shortly after the shooting. Ryan and Steve agreed to make an official complaint and were deter-mined not to back down. It was a decision which would have devastating consequences, but one that the family never regretted.

'This sudden act of violence terrified the family because

we had never known something like this before. It was some-thing that you read about in the papers,' Steve explained. 'We took the decision together as a family that we had no other choice but go all the way with this. And once a complaint was made against them they were going to come after us no mat-ter, even if we withdrew the charge. They had done it to Brian Fitzgerald; he withdrew his complaint and they still murdered him. That is the type of animal you are dealing with, so we didn't really have a choice.'

His adopted son, who would be the State's main witness, shared his dad's beliefs. Ryan told this writer: 'Dundon wanted to kill me and there was no way I was going to let that go. I knew that these people were terrorists but I had to go ahead and give evidence against him in court or else he would get a lot worse. But I was scared. I have never been in trouble in my life.'

The officers leading the investigation, Detective Inspector Jim Browne and Detective Sergeant Eamon O'Neill, were already heavily involved in the counter-offensive against Murder Inc. Browne was the officer-in-charge of Brian Fitzgerald's allegations against Larry McCarthy Junior and John Dundon. He and his colleagues had been deeply affected by the security manager's murder and felt in some way that they had let him down. They were determined that the cycle would not be repeated with the Collinses.

Dundon's uncontrollable temper had given the police an opportunity to put the most dangerous hoodlum on their beat away for a long stretch behind bars. There wasn't suffi-cient evidence to charge the thug with the actual shooting, though, because the bike and gun had not been recovered. Dundon, who was forensically aware, had also gone to ground after the incident so the Gardaí would be unlikely to find evidence linking him to the outrage. But there was ample evidence to sustain a charge of threatening to kill Ryan Lee, which carried a maximum sentence of ten years.

Two days later, on 21 December, Gardaí caught up with Wayne Dundon and he was arrested for questioning about the shooting and the threat to kill. Under interrogation in Henry Street Station the following morning, Dundon suddenly attacked two detectives in a blind rage. In full view of the camera recording the interview, the mobster pummelled Detective Garda Arthur Ryan and his colleague, Detective Garda Brendan Casey, in a flurry of punches, injuring both of them. For the second time in as many days Dundon had played the starring role in a real-life horror movie. Before the mobster was restrained by other Gardaí he smashed Detective Garda Ryan's jaw in several places. The officer, who had been one of the detectives on the trail of Murder Inc., was so badly injured that he was unable to return to work for over a year. He was the second officer to be seriously injured by Wayne Dundon since his arrival in Limerick.

Later the same day Dundon was brought before the local District Court, where he was charged with threatening to kill Ryan Lee and assaulting the two Gardaí. Detective Garda Ronan McDonagh objected to bail on the grounds that Dundon had access to firearms and posed a serious threat to his victims. There was also a risk that the accused might abscond to the UK or the Continent, where he had connections. The gang boss spent Christmas behind bars with his brothers John and Dessie, his father and several of his cousins and associates, and Limerick enjoyed a peaceful festive season.

The New Year did not start well for Murder Inc. and it would not prove to be a particularly prosperous one. The gangsters did get plenty of day trips from prison – to appear in court. On 11 January 2005, twenty-two-year-old John Dundon was jailed for four-and-a-half years by the Circuit Criminal Court in Dublin, after he pleaded guilty to the charge of threatening to kill Owen Treacy during the Kieran Keane murder trial. The court heard that Dundon had made the threat to Treacy's wife Donna. The psychopath's counsel said his client had been under considerable stress at the time of the offence because his brother and cousins were on trial for the murder. 'In the course of this trial, he lost his head and said something monumentally stupid,' counsel said truthfully. Monumental stupidity was a Dundon trait.

Judge Yvonne Murphy said it was a very serious offence to threaten the wife of a witness. She said the criminal justice system depended on witnesses giving evidence and that Dundon's actions were 'an offence against public justice'. The sentence was backdated to the date of the threats, 13 November 2003, when he had been taken into custody and refused bail.

On 25 January the smirking thug was back before a judge, this time in Limerick Circuit Criminal Court. He received another twenty months for threatening to burn down the home of a prison officer on 21 August 2001. John Dundon had pleaded guilty to the offence in October 2004, but sentencing had been adjourned on condition that Dundon be of good behaviour for one year. Judge Carroll Moran had given the thug an opportunity to resile from his wicked ways. But there was only one way of life for John Dundon. Six weeks after that court appearance the loudmouthed thug had threatened Donna Treacy in front of a large gathering of police. Judge Moran said he had to take this into account, together with the fact that he had given Dundon a chance.

The sentence was set to run consecutively with the four-and-a-half-year sentence.

On 18 February, Wayne Dundon also got a day trip from prison when he appeared in Limerick Circuit Court. He was appealing the earlier decision of the District Court, when his application to have his bullet-proof vest returned was denied. Opposing the appeal State Solicitor Michael Murray put it to Dundon that he and his associates had been 'on active service', pursuing Brian Collopy, and that they were all members of the Dundon/McCarthy crime gang. Wayne Dundon denied knowing that his hated foe had sought refuge in a Garda station or that he was a member of any gang. He said he used the body armour because he had been shot at.

The gangster became angry and excitable in the witness box, behaviour which normally signalled an imminent emotional explosion. When Dundon was riled he tended to jabber incoherently. His counsel repeatedly asked the gangster to speak slowly because Judge Terence O'Sullivan had difficulty understanding his 'Limerick accent'. Delivering his decision, the judge said he had not been 'terribly impressed' by Dundon's evidence and would be foolish to accept it. As he dismissed the application Wayne Dundon erupted.

He sprang from the bench where he was flanked by prison warders and dropped his trousers. Before they could restrain him, Dundon bent over, slapped his bare buttocks and shouted to the judge: 'See that, your honour – that's what the Dundons think of you and the Gardaí – fuck you, your honour.' With virtual steam spewing from his ears, Dundon stormed out of the court surrounded by a phalanx of cops and warders who led him back to the holding cells.

There was a stunned silence in the courtroom after he left. Judge O'Sullivan announced a brief adjournment to consider what he was going to do about Dundon's bizarre display of contempt. When he returned the judge remarked that he didn't want to make 'a large issue' of the matter but he had to deal with the 'discourtesy' shown to the court. Michael Murray said the Gardaí intended to prepare a file for the DPP with a view to having the thug charged. However, Judge O'Sullivan said he was only dealing with the matter of contempt in a court of law, where respect was expected. 'I accept that people do tend to get over-excited in a law case, although I haven't seen that level of excitement before,' he said euphemistically. Dundon's counsel said his client was under a lot of strain and wished to apologize. 'He's under no illusions now that his conduct was grossly unacceptable and he wishes to purge his contempt,' he said. The judge accepted the apology and said he was prepared to let the matter rest.

In the meantime, the members of Murder Inc. behind bars continued to operate a lucrative drug trade despite the many setbacks and seizures. The prison became the hub of the gang's operations, co-ordinated by the Dundons with the use of mobile phones. Mobile phone technology had revolutionized organized crime, making it possible for gangsters to continue running their empires from the comfort of their cells. Murder Inc.'s lieutenants and family members used regular visits to keep the mobsters briefed about what was happening on the outside. Orders and instructions were sent back with them. Nothing happened in Limerick that the gangsters didn't know about. One former gang member recalled: 'Just because they weren't here didn't mean they weren't in control. They knew everything that was going on and if they had a problem with you there were lots of the lads prepared to whack you for them.'

Outside the prison walls the drug-trafficking operation

was being co-ordinated between the gang in Limerick, Dougie Moran in Dublin, Larry McCarthy Junior in the UK and Chaser O'Brien in Belgium. They networked through their various gangland allies, including the Marlo Hyland and the Freddie Thompson gangs in Dublin. The uneasy truce with the Collopys was still in place, and with Murder Inc. members accounting for most of the over thirty key Limerick gangsters in prison, there was a lull in hostilities in the spring of 2005.

Wayne Dundon had other things on his mind, namely how to deal with the more pressing problem of Ryan Lee and Steve Collins. The trial had been set down for hearing on 19 April and time was running out.

The two important State witnesses had been placed under armed protection by Gardaí. The detectives wanted to avoid a repeat of the fate meted out to Brian Fitzgerald two years earlier. But the armed guards didn't prevent Dundon's henchmen from making every effort to dissuade Ryan Lee from testifying in court.

Steve Collins had expected the intimidation to begin shortly after Dundon's arrest – and unfortunately he was right. The insidious mob first tried subtle warnings. It was a scenario that bore chilling similarities to the experiences of the murdered night-club security manager. It was the first part of the Piranhas' well-rehearsed intimidation routine.

Steve recalled: 'People were being told to come up to us advising us that it would be a good idea not to proceed with the case.' Extended family members and friends of the victim were also approached to warn them of the dire consequences if they went ahead with the case. Larry McCarthy Junior approached one of Steve's employees with a message for Steve offering him €30,000 to drop the case in the run-up to the trial. 'I knew that McCarthy would be coming back looking for the money plus interest if I ever stooped to take his dirty money – I sent him a message saying no thanks,' Steve Collins told this writer.

The pressure was soon ratcheted up. The first strike on the family was a failed arson attack on Brannigan's. Steve received a phone call in case there was any confusion about the message being sent. 'This voice on the phone told me: "In the interests of your family don't go near the steps [the court] or there will be bloodshed." Then there were cars pulling up outside the pub and revving their engines and all that sort of thing, but we were determined to stick to our decision to proceed with the case.'

The night before Wayne Dundon's trial a letter addressed to Steve Collins was dropped in at the home of Ryan Lee's girlfriend. The chilling message it carried was unambiguous. It read: 'Steve, if you think it's over think again. Look at all the people that are dead. Look, if you want to call it quits you know what to do. If not, we will attack you, your staff and your businesses . . . it's up to you.' Time would show that Wayne Dundon meant every word.

The following morning Steve gave the letter to the Gardaí who were escorting him and Ryan to court. They were determined to go ahead.

As the case started, the mob's menacing dark shadow extended over the Circuit Criminal Court. A gang member in the body of the court recognized a male juror as he was being sworn in to hear the case. He went outside and made a phone call. Minutes later the juror's son and his son's girlfriend each received phone calls informing them that he was on the jury in Wayne Dundon's trial. The implied message was that the juror should deliver a 'not guilty' verdict and also convince the rest of the panel to come in with the same one. The juror's frightened son and the son's girlfriend rang him about the menacing calls – and pleaded with him to get off the jury.

Twenty minutes before the trial was about to begin, the juror approached the Garda who was escorting the jury panel. He seemed scared and didn't know what to do. The officer brought the incident to the attention of Judge Carroll Moran who called the juror to hear his concerns. The man said his family members had been contacted by someone 'in the body of the courtroom' who informed them he had been selected for the jury. Judge Moran asked the juror if he would be happy to remain on the jury, to which he replied: 'If it came to it I would but I would be concerned for my son.' Dundon's defence counsel said his client, who was in custody, had 'no knowledge' of any phone calls. The judge was concerned at the intimidating approach and discharged the entire jury. The following morning a new jury was empanelled – Dundon's efforts to scupper the trial had failed.

As the trial began on 20 April 2005, Ryan Lee and Steve Collins were surprised to be told that they could not refer to the shooting incident at Brannigan's in their direct testimony. This was because Dundon was appearing on a charge of threatening to kill or cause serious harm. Although there were ample grounds to suspect that Wayne Dundon was the actual shooter, there was no evidence to charge him with that offence. Any mention of the incident could prejudice the jury and the existing charge would be dropped.

During the two-day hearing Dundon wore earphones and listened to music. Steve Collins would later recall how the hoodlum stared at him and tapped his watch, 'indicating what I thought was "your time will come"'. Dundon sneered across the courtroom at his victim whenever the jury wasn't looking. But it didn't deter Ryan Lee who hobbled to the witness box on crutches and told the court what had happened. Together with the CCTV footage, it was an open-and-shut case. On the evening of the second day the jury returned a unanimous guilty verdict against Wayne Dundon, and he was remanded in custody while the judge considered what sentence to impose.

A week later Dundon was back in the same court on charges of assaulting the two Garda detectives; he pleaded guilty. During a subsequent sentencing hearing for that offence and for the attack on Ryan Lee, the court was told that Ryan and his family were still under Garda protection and were in fear of their lives. Dundon's counsel objected to the admissibility of evidence concerning that case, which he claimed was 'extraneous' material being entered by the prosecution to influence the judge's decision. He said the evidence would 'lure my Lordship' into grave error. Prosecution counsel argued that the 'surrounding circumstances' of the case were highly relevant as the 'grave and serious threat' against the Collins family continued. 'It continues up to this day to overhang the injured party and he continues to believe the threat is there,' the prosecution counsel said. The court was also shown the video footage of Dundon's savage assault on the two detectives.

On 12 May Dundon was brought again to the Circuit Criminal Court to hear his fate. In keeping with the mob's attitude to the judiciary he listened to music on his earphones throughout, utterly disinterested in what was being said about him. Detective Sergeant Eamon O'Neill gave evidence of Dundon's previous criminal record, and also read out the threatening letter which had been sent to Steve Collins before the commencement of the trial. The experienced detective, who had been a police officer in the city for over twelve years, described the gangster as 'one of the most violent criminals I have ever come across during my time in Limerick City'.

Before passing sentence, the judge said that it would be to 'disregard common sense' to say that the shooting had nothing to do with the threat. 'The shooting was indicative of the context in which the threat was made. It was indicative of the significance attached to the threat and the manner in which it was to be interpreted by the victim,' said Judge Moran, who had the distinction of jailing most of Limerick's most dangerous criminals. But the judge said he was not sentencing Wayne Dundon for anything that he had not been convicted of. He also pointed out that in mitigation there was little said in favour of the hoodlum, except that he was married and had one child, with another on the way. He sentenced Dundon to the maximum ten years possible for the threat to kill. He also imposed two concurrent three-year sentences for the assaults on the detectives. Dundon appeared nonchalant as he was led away to a prison van.

The brutal twenty-seven-year-old thug might have seemed unconcerned as he left the courtroom, but it didn't take long for the reality of spending at least seven years in prison to dawn on him. His wife gave birth to their second child three days later. In his cell in Cork Prison, where a wing had been allocated to Murder Inc., Dundon showed his true feelings about the court result. He was sharing a cell with Gareth Collins who was doing a five-year stretch for possession of a firearm. Nine years later, when Collins broke the mob's code of *omertà*, the gangster told a court how Dundon was 'cracking up'. He said he overheard Dundon on the phone to his wife Anne, shortly after he was sentenced, crying with rage and telling her: 'I swear, I swear, they're not getting away with it.' Dundon was fuming and wallowing in self-pity when he got off the phone. The remorseless psychopath did not believe that he had been the author of his own destiny. His wife was home alone looking after his two kids and in his warped mind Dundon blamed his innocent victims for her plight. Collins claimed in court that Dundon said Anne wanted him to 'make sure I kill one of them for this'. He quoted his boss as saying: 'Look what they [the Collinses] are after doing to us, they're after tearing the family apart.' Wayne Dundon decided that Steve Collins and his family would never find peace.

As Dundon was brought back to prison, Steve Collins and Ryan Lee went for a few drinks to celebrate with the Garda investigation team. 'People who we never met before were coming up and shaking hands and congratulating us because they were delighted that Dundon was behind bars,' said Ryan later. 'For weeks we were getting messages of goodwill from people all over Limerick. It was incredible to think that one individual in particular could cause so much fear and anxiety among people.'

The jailing of the gangland savage received extensive coverage in the national media, confirming his well-earned reputation as one of the most dangerous criminals in Ireland. The day after he was jailed, Dundon's favourite hit man, Gary Campion, also received a two-year sentence for threatening to kill a warder in Limerick Prison. On 13 May the killer pleaded guilty to making the threats while serving a sentence for a variety of offences including road traffic offences, possession of an offensive weapon, assault and threatening to kill. During the incident a year earlier

Campion had threatened to kill prison officer John Ryan while he was being restrained from attacking another inmate. 'I've shot people in this town for €10,000 and I'd have no difficulty spending €20,000 to have you blown away. If it's the last thing I do, I'll get you and your family. I know your family. I will have ye all blown away,' Campion screamed repeatedly at Ryan. The hit man also shouted at the prison officer: 'Ryan, you still have to go out that Dublin Road every evening,' indicating that he knew where the warder lived. When Ryan dismissed the threats Campion said that he had shot people for less and 'it wouldn't be my first time'. No one doubted that he was telling the truth.

Back on the streets of Limerick there was a huge sense of relief that the worst of the Murder Inc. rabble was locked up. But it didn't mean that the violence ended when the prison gates slammed behind them. Within a week of Dundon's sentencing, and while still observing their truce with the Collopys, Murder Inc. carried out bomb attacks on two houses as part of the feuding. In one incident young children had a lucky escape when a grenade exploded after it was thrown through the front window of their home.

While the gang boss's incarceration brought relief to the lives of some, Wayne Dundon had no intention of forgetting the family who had stood up to him. A month later he sent a message to Steve Collins and Ryan Lee to remind them that Murder Inc. would never forgive such outrageous temerity. At around 4 a.m. on the morning of 16 June, Brannigan's Bar was extensively damaged in a fire which gutted the premises. Steve Collins was devastated, and worse was to follow. The insurance company refused to recoup his losses until the pub was rebuilt. He spent a considerable amount of money on plans to construct shop units and apartments beside the new pub but planning permission was turned down. Next the banks suddenly stopped lending, preventing Steve from rebuilding. The once-thriving business would never reopen and it dealt a huge financial blow to Steve and his family. It was one from which they would never recover – and all because a psychopath's teenage sister wasn't allowed inside to have a drink.

10. Breaking the Silence

The prospect of a second devastating trial now hung over the heads of Murder Inc. They were seriously concerned about the prospect of their former courier Philip Dean making it safely to his seat in the witness stand. He had enough knowledge of the mob's operations to put the leadership away for guns, drug and murder offences in one fell swoop. The Piranhas would have to do everything in their power to ensure that that didn't happen.

The Dundon/McCarthys had realized within a few months of Dean's arrest in January 2003 that the courier had given the police extensive information about their criminal activities, and especially about their individual roles in the Brian Fitzgerald murder. When Gardaí put the traitor's allegations to gang members while they were being questioned about the murder, Dean became a confirmed rat. It was clear that he had become a massive liability and there was only one way to resolve the problem – kill the snout.

But that would prove to be difficult. An initial attempt to silence the gun runner failed. They had tried to intimidate him by attacking the home where his partner and children lived in Birmingham. The day after the fire-bomb attack the British police took the family into their Witness Protection Programme. In Ireland, Dean was segregated from the rest of the prison population and three prison officers were assigned to protect him around the clock. The Dundon/McCarthys and their assorted associates still managed to relay threats to him through a network of contacts within the prison system. Such was the threat level that Dean's food was specially prepared in case he was poisoned. The gang's hit man James Cahill would later admit that a special form of odourless and highly potent rat poison had been smuggled into the prison for that purpose.

The overweight, repulsive killer also revealed that the gang plotted to assassinate Dean when he was brought to court from prison. A female gang member was sent to monitor the movements of his escort in the hope that the mob could shoot Dean en route. Consideration was given to using a rocket launcher to blow up the prison van transporting him. The security services knew that Murder Inc., above any other gang in the country, had the ability and willingness to carry out such a spectacular attack because they had no fear of the consequences.

Gardaí in Limerick had meanwhile compiled a huge investigation file around the admissions and statements of Philip Dean. Officers had spent hundreds of hours painstakingly corroborating every piece of information the courier had offered up. Dean had proved to be a reliable witness. His assistance had already helped smash an important international arms-smuggling racket and also had led to the conviction of a number of significant players, including the hit man James Martin Cahill for possession of a firearm. But then disaster struck.

Philip Dean was due for release from prison in the spring of 2005. But as his release date approached the existential threat and the enormity of testifying against the mob finally got to him. Despite the fact that both he and his young family were in the WPP, and he had been assured of a new life abroad, he told Chief Superintendent Gerry Kelly's officers that he could not go through with the trial. When Dean left prison, he and his family abandoned the WPP. The Gardaí had no power to compel him to testify. Some sources have since claimed to this writer that Dean was unhappy about the arrangements being made by the WPP for his life after prison. Others believe the mob made him an offer he could not refuse. Whatever the reason, his refusal to go ahead with his testimony was a demoralizing setback for the Gardaí. But a few months after his departure there was an unexpected breakthrough.

James Cahill was an unbalanced, dysfunctional heroin addict with serious psychiatric issues. Basically, he was as mad as he was bad. Sitting in his prison cell in Portlaoise Prison he had become increasingly edgy and paranoid. He knew from the allegations put to him by the police that he could very likely face a murder charge, and the killer didn't know that Dean had decided to withdraw his evidence. Everyone was watching nervously to see what the cops did next. Cahill had been privy to the various plots hatched by Murder Inc. to get rid of the State witness. He also began to hear screaming voices in his head while in solitary confinement. The assassin would later describe what he was hearing. 'I was coming down the stairs in Portlaoise and I was getting some heroin off the lads and the voices were saying "he's on camera",' he told the Central Criminal Court. He said the voices called him a paedophile and a supergrass, and sometimes seemed to be coming out of the television, answering him back and asking him questions. Cahill was heading for a meltdown.

In his paranoid state of mind he believed that Murder Inc. would see him as a potential weak link and try to get rid of him. The hit man's fears were not unfounded, considering the mindset of his bosses. If they wanted, they could easily have Cahill dealt with. He was also afraid that he would be killed by prison officers or by 'politicals' – members of Republican terror gangs who were also held in Portlaoise. The killer withdrew to his cell and pondered the prospect of watching his back on the prison wing for at least another two and a half years before he was eligible for parole. Eventually he was overwhelmed by his fears and phoned the Gardaí in Limerick.

The Brian Fitzgerald murder investigation team at Mayorstone Garda Station first received the call in May 2005, just as they were celebrating the conviction of Wayne Dundon. They could scarcely believe it when their prime suspect invited them to visit him. 'They are going to kill me,' were the first words he blurted out to the detectives when they met him in prison. Cahill was agitated and very nervous. To their astonishment he said he was prepared to make a full confession and also to testify against the rest of the murder gang. But before he named names he wanted a transfer to a more secure facility.

'I shot him and no one else. I want to get this out of my system. I want to get this out in the open,' Cahill insisted. Then he named everyone involved in the plot – the Dundon brothers, Chaser O'Brien, Gary Campion, Anthony Kelly, Dougie Moran and Larry McCarthy Junior. He described attending a meeting to plot the murder of Brian Fitzgerald and being told by McCarthy Junior that the bouncer had made a statement against him. He said the gang leader offered him €10,000 for the hit, in two payments of €5,000 each. Cahill claimed that Kelly showed him how to use the murder weapon and alleged that he was told: 'Put one in that cunt's head.' Cahill then described in detail how he pointed the gun at the back of Brian Fitzgerald's head and turned away as he pulled the trigger.

Cahill had also been involved in moving drugs and guns for the gang with Philip Dean. 'The main work the gang was involved in was in bringing in drugs and guns into this country. Money was their god, it was all for the money. They made thousands and thousands of Euros out of the drugs. I know, I was part of all of that,' the hit man told the police.

Over the following weeks, Cahill made a number of statements in which he outlined in detail everything he knew about the murder of the night-club security manager. Cahill said he wanted to be taken into the WPP but was prepared to plead guilty to the murder, without any preconditions. He wanted to clear his conscience. The WPP was not an option because Cahill was facing a life sentence, and there could not be any consideration given to immunity from prosecution. In the interim he was segregated in prison for his own protection.

The admissions were an astonishing development and offered a tantalizing opportunity to solve the murder. The detectives involved in the case already had a huge amount of evidence gathered that corroborated a lot of what the hit man had to say. There were a number of urgent meetings with the DPP to discuss the dramatic development. On the same day that Steve Collins's pub was destroyed by fire, 16 June 2005, James Martin Cahill was formally charged with the murder of Brian Fitzgerald.

In September, Cahill made another statement to Gardaí in which he claimed that John Gilligan and the hit man Patrick 'Dutchie' Holland had asked him for the Book of Evidence in his case to give to 'people in Limerick'. Holland was serving a sentence for drug trafficking and was the hit man hired by Gilligan to murder journalist Veronica Guerin in 1996. Cahill was assigned a number of prison officers for close protection, but in his paranoia he believed that the warders were also going to kill him, and he threw boiling water over one of them.

In the meantime there was more trouble on Murder Inc.'s horizon. The ongoing multi-jurisdictional investigation into the activities of Jim 'Chaser' O'Brien and his associates had caused serious disruption to the gang's drug-trafficking business. It hadn't stopped their operation completely, as compromised routes were quickly replaced by others, but the seizures were costing the Dundon/McCarthys a lot of money. Between September 2003 and October 2004 the various investigations had resulted in the large-scale capture of firearms, cocaine, ecstasy, heroin, hashish and illegal cigarettes in Ireland, the UK, Holland and Belgium. The busts were valued in excess of €20 million and included a 1.2-tonne haul of cannabis seized in County Kildare. Twenty-five individuals, most of them of Irish and English nationality, had been arrested.

As part of the investigation O'Brien's Tipperary associates, Cecil Kinsella and Christopher Maguire, were tracked down in the UK and extradited back to Ireland to face drug and firearms charges. In July 2005 Kinsella was jailed for ten years for drug trafficking and possession of a firearm. Maguire got six years for the same offences. That same month Larry McCarthy Junior was also netted in the international police trawl. The police had the Limerick crime boss under surveillance in London after discovering his involvement in another weapons-smuggling operation. McCarthy hadn't wasted any time finding a new source for buying guns after the police had swooped on the gun enthusiasts in Morecambe two years earlier.

A flat in Hackney was being used by the crime boss as a glorified gun warehouse, in conjunction with a number of other English gangsters. When police raided the flat they arrested McCarthy Junior. He was supervising the sale of a Mac 11 Ingram machine pistol to an associate. Four months earlier, on 17 March, an eighteen-year-old with learning difficulties was arrested while transporting an identical weapon to Limerick. Patrick Dowling was typical of the type of individual the Dundon/McCarthys used to do their dirty work. He suffered from ADHD and was homeless as a consequence of his anti-social behaviour. Dowling was paid a paltry sum to collect the weapon and deliver it to the gang. When Gardaí stopped the taxi he was travelling in they also found 150 rounds of ammunition and a silencer in the bag containing the deadly weapon. The firearm had been part of a batch supplied by Larry McCarthy Junior.

During the arrest operation in London, over 1,200 rounds of ammunition were also seized, including deadly 'dum-dum' bullets that were being loaded with gunpowder in a bullet press by McCarthy's associates. The leader of Ireland's most dangerous gang was charged and held in custody pending his trial. It was another major body blow to the mob back in Ireland.

In June 2006 Larry McCarthy Junior was convicted at Southwark Crown Court of conspiracy to possess a firearm with intent to endanger life and conspiracy to possess a prohibited weapon. Three other people were also convicted in connection with the gun raid. At the request of the UK authorities, two Limerick detectives, Paddy O'Callaghan and Gerry Cleary, gave evidence of the gangster's previous convictions at his sentencing hearing. The officers also described his involvement in Murder Inc., which infuriated the thug. McCarthy was jailed for eleven years. Sometime later, evidence was uncovered that McCarthy was in the advanced stages of planning a prison break. Two separate keys were found in a search of his prison cell. As a result he was transferred to Belmarsh Maximum Security Prison in London, where he was classified as a Category A prisoner.

On 6 October 2005, in another operation connected to the international investigation, the Garda National Drug Unit seized cocaine and heroin worth over €1 million when they searched a truck and a shed in Carrabeg, County Louth. One of the men arrested was truck driver Kieran Boylan, a convicted drug dealer and associate of Chaser O'Brien's. It later emerged that he had been working as a double agent for a separate Garda unit. As a result of the drug bust, Boylan found himself the focus of a major national controversy which centred on serious allegations of collusion between him and certain Garda officers. Another drug-trafficking charge against him had been dropped by the State in unexplained circumstances. It was claimed that the double agent was an off-the-books informant who had continued to be a drug trafficker with the full knowledge of certain police officers. In return for giving him a free hand, Boylan allegedly set up his own customers to be busted by Gardaí. The controversy became known as the Boylan affair and led to an acrimonious public row between the Gardaí and their oversight body, the Garda Síochána Ombudsman Commission (GSOC). GSOC spent four years investigating the collusion allegations and submitted a file to the DPP. The State prosecutor subsequently decided that none of the officers involved in the Boylan affair had a case to answer.

On 27 October 2005, Chaser O'Brien finally ran out of road. He was arrested by the Belgian Federal Police following a lengthy surveillance operation by Belgian and Dutch cops. He was detained on charges pertaining to membership of a criminal organization. At the same time, his two main partners-in-crime were also arrested. A cache of machine-guns and pistols was seized at a premises controlled by fifty-two-year-old Redgy Tygat, a Belgian national. Across the border in Holland, Dutch national Edwin Kanters was also lifted. When the police raided Kanters's home they discovered a major ecstasy factory. The criminal was in the process of packing a consignment of 300,000 ecstasy tablets that were destined for O'Brien's Irish associates. The arrest of the high-living farmer's son was another critical blow to Murder Inc. O'Brien was held in custody until his trial in 2007, when he was jailed for three years for membership of an organized crime gang and five years each for firearms and drug offences. When judged against Belgium's more relaxed sentencing policy, Chaser had received a significant sentence.

The day after O'Brien's arrest, Murder Inc. ended a fourteen-month lull in gangland killings when twenty-five-year-old David 'Sid' Nunan was lured to his death and shot in the back. The hard man from Southill, who had fifty previous convictions, was a foot soldier in the Murder Inc. mob. He operated with twenty-year-old 'Fat' Frankie Ryan from Moyross, who was a trusted member of the gang's inner-circle. The two hoods were heavily involved in the drug operation and had also carried out several feud-related shootings.

Nunan had been released from prison four days earlier, on 24 October, after serving a two-year sentence for possession of firearms. While he was inside the gangster was involved in a row with a Dublin gang after he gave one of their members a serious beating – and they wanted revenge. Unfortunately for Nunan his victim's mob had a close alliance with the Dundon/McCarthys. When the Dundons were asked to kill their own man they were happy to oblige. The likes of Nunan were dispensable and easily replaced. And it would be seen as a big favour which would have to be reciprocated. Fat Frankie got a call from prison and he agreed to do the job, even though Nunan was supposedly his friend – it wasn't personal, just business.

Nunan suspected nothing when he accompanied Ryan to the village of Parteen in County Clare on the pretext of burgling a private house. As the pair walked towards the house at the end of a secluded laneway in the early hours of 28 October, Ryan pulled a gun and shot his friend a number of times in the back at close range. Before the hood's body was found the Dundons were informed that the job was done. The cold-blooded execution bolstered Murder Inc.'s fearsome reputation in the underworld. Fat Frankie was arrested in the follow-up investigation and Gardaí were confident that they had enough evidence to charge him with murder.

A week before Nunan's killing, the last of the Dundon brothers still at large, eighteen-year-old Ger, joined the rest of his clan behind bars. In April 2004 the youngest sibling in Murder Inc. was given a three-year sentence for the possession of €30,000 worth of cocaine and a firearm when he was fifteen. The sentence had been suspended on condition that he stayed out of trouble for three years. But the Dundon boys were incapable of rehabilitation. By October 2005 Ger

Dundon had been arrested three times for public order offences and the sentence was activated.

Over fifty criminals involved in the feuds were behind bars by the end of 2005 as a result of the relentless Garda action. The majority of the criminals inside were from Murder Inc., reflecting the fact that they were by far the most active gang in the city. There were almost as many members of the crime clan behind bars as there were free to cause havoc around Limerick.

A few weeks after the arrest of Chaser O'Brien, on 24 November 2005 the worst fears of his partners-in-crime were realized when James Cahill pleaded guilty to the murder of Brian Fitzgerald at the Central Criminal Court. There was tight security as Cahill was led into the court from an armoured prison van. After the killer confirmed his guilty plea, Detective Sergeant Seamus Nolan from Henry Street Garda Station described the events on the night of 29 November 2002 when the security manager was executed.

The murder victim's widow, Alice, sobbed in the witness box as she described the devastation visited on her and her children by Murder Inc. 'Brian was only one man in the world but he was all the world to me. Brian wasn't just my husband, he was my best friend. He was a major part of my life. We grew up together,' she said. 'We had planned for a future with my two sons, a future that we won't see now,' she continued. After the murder, she had been forced to leave her job of seventeen years because she was medically unfit to continue. She was left to rear her young family on a widow's pension of €180 a week. Her little boys feared that if she went to work like their dad she would not come home again.

'There are days when I can't open my front door because

of regular flashbacks. I can smell the smoke of the gunfire and the loud bangs I will never forget. I feel I will never again be safe or happy. I have not spent one night in my home alone,' she added.

Through his counsel Cahill apologized to the Fitzgerald family for the appalling suffering he had caused them. Taking the witness stand, the hit man told Mr Justice Paul Carney: 'I am willing to say that I will testify if a further case is coming.' In a pleading voice the killer asked that all the evidence and transcripts be kept on file in case he was unable to testify. 'I feel my life is in danger in prison, not just from prisoners but from prison officers because of what I feel in this case,' he said. 'What I am trying to say is that I will testify against people. That's why I feel my life is in danger.'

Mr Justice Carney sentenced Cahill to a mandatory life sentence for the murder and remarked: 'I think I understand what the accused is saying.' As Cahill was being led away in handcuffs, surrounded by armed detectives and prison officers, he turned and shouted: 'Ask him [Judge Carney] to bring the killers to justice.' The plump, balding killer was a pathetic sight as he was led to the waiting prison van. He looked agitated and scared and shouted to reporters: 'I am going to be murdered in my cell tonight or in the next few days. Watch.'

Cahill's name was added to Murder Inc.'s growing hit list. The mob was being squeezed from all sides and it appeared that their days were numbered. But it didn't stop a sudden surge in assaults and gun attacks on the streets of Limerick.

On 4 November 2005 Kieran Keane's son Joseph, his cousin Richard Treacy and friend Shane Kelly beat another teenager to death in an act of indiscriminate, gratuitous violence. Eighteen-year-old apprentice electrician Darren Coughlan had never been in trouble in his life when the young gang members spotted him. His bloodline was enough to make him a target of their blind hatred. He was a cousin of David 'Frog Eyes' Stanners, one of the Dundon/McCarthy mob jailed for the murder of Keane's father and the serious injury of Richard Treacy's brother Owen.

The thugs chased their victim across open ground, and when he fell they laid into him in a flurry of fists and boots. Darren Coughlan suffered severe head injuries in the mindless attack and died three days later in hospital. Philip Healy, the dead teenager's friend who had witnessed the attack, became a prisoner in his home when it was discovered that he intended to give evidence against the killers. His family were given police protection and security cameras were installed on their modest home. Steel shutters were erected over the windows to stave off gunshots and petrol bombs. Such was the level of intimidation from the Keanes, other family members were forced to leave their homes. Healy refused to retract his evidence and Keane, Treacy and Kelly subsequently pleaded guilty to manslaughter and were jailed for six- and seven-year terms.

After months of relative calm the mob war again erupted on the streets in the latter quarter of 2005. Between October and December there were fifty shooting incidents in the city. Most of them were linked to the various feuds and brought the total number to eighty-three for the year. It was an increase of twenty-two shooting incidents over the previous year, and over double the figure of thirty-nine recorded in 2003. Just over a quarter of the 313 shootings recorded across the State in 2005 happened in Limerick. The shooting rate was dramatically higher in the Treaty City than in Dublin, where there were 145 such incidents among a population at least thirteen times larger. On 29 November Christy Keane's brother Seanie was shot four times when he answered the front door of his home in the Island Field. His injuries were not life-threatening. The attack was not thought by Gardaí to be connected with the feuds. On 22 December a car was rammed into the front gate of Sophie Keane's house and set alight.

There appeared to be no end in sight to the madness.

11. Boy Soldiers

Anthony 'Noddy' McCarthy used national television to send a chilling reminder from his prison cell that the war was far from over. 'The feud hasn't gone away,' he bluntly warned. 'They say that since they locked up me and my family the problem has gone away. But since then there's been over forty attempted murders in Limerick; there's been shootings, petrol-bombings, everything. The problem is far from gone away.' The killer was keeping a score sheet. The controversial interview was broadcast in January 2006 as part of an RTÉ *Prime Time* programme that focused on the worst gang war in Irish criminal history, and the putative 'peace pact' between Wayne Dundon and Brian Collopy.

McCarthy's main concern was that more of his lot were in prison than their rivals. And that, said the twenty-four-year-old, had fuelled 'a vacuum of hatred and a desire for revenge' in the feud. The killer sounded like the spokesman for a political revolutionary movement pursuing a noble cause. Noddy implied that the disproportionate number of his family and associates in prison was down to the prejudices of the police. In other words, the Dundon/McCarthys were as much victims as villains. He didn't reference the fact that he and his clansmen had been found guilty of horrific crimes. 'This is one of the reasons why the problem is not going away,' he said defiantly. Another reason why the 'problem' was not going away was the ready supply of young recruits, some as young as ten, who were willing to carry out the mob's dirty work at home.

Long before the emergence of organized crime in Limerick, the badly planned local authority estates were hopeless ghettoes and breeding grounds for delinquency. The worst-affected estates had the lowest rates of educational achievement and the highest levels of unemployment per head of population in the country. It was fertile ground for the gangs. From the outbreak of the gang wars in 2000 the strife-ridden estates acted as a conveyor belt, churning out canon-fodder for the two sides. The vulnerable children were growing up in a world where the culture of the gun prevailed and violence was the norm. Anti-social behaviour had reached epidemic proportions as whole communities were held to ransom. Gardaí and the emergency services regularly found themselves under attack as mini-riots erupted with disturbing regularity across the city. Homes were being pelted with petrol bombs in sporadic, indiscriminate acts of vandalism.

The huge Moyross Estate in particular, home to the Dundons' cousins the McCarthys, was turned into a veritable war zone as feud-related shootings and chronic vandalism escalated dramatically. Residents were left in no doubt that it was Murder Inc. turf. In a three-month period alone, between September and November 2006 there were almost thirty shooting incidents. That period accounted for almost a third of the total shootings which took place during the whole year. Gangs of marauding youths went on the rampage, regularly ambushing Gardaí in petrol-bomb attacks. That same year, five families in St Mary's Park, stronghold of the Keane/Collopys, were forced to bolt from their homes as a result of arson and gun attacks. Parents who could afford to move had fled like refugees from the worst-affected estates across the city to protect their children from the toxic hate.

The gangland feuding exacerbated already chronic social problems by attaching a sense of glamour and excitement to the stultifying drab ghettoes. The relatively new phenomenon of heroin addiction also added to the misery – and created plenty of young strung-out junkies willing to do anything for a fix. Socially marginalized, out-of-control kids from broken homes, children who knew only disorder in their lives, were eager to impress the glamorous gangsters they so admired. The gun-toting thugs with their bling lifestyle and flash cars were the role models of a new generation of impressionable, feral children. For the vast majority of the young people in Limerick, the home of Munster rugby, their heroes were the burly men in the red jerseys who fought with honour in Thomond Park. But in the sub-culture of the troubled estates it was the young men in bullet-proof vests doing drive-by shootings that many of the children wanted to emulate.

One of the most disturbing aspects of the Limerick feuds was that children were deliberately deployed on the frontline and suffered the brunt of the senseless violence. The phenomenon was unique to the city's underworld. The mobs were unconcerned about shooting children or exploiting them to do their dirty work. A nineteen-year-old Murder Inc. gunman was unequivocal on the subject, when he was quizzed by Gardaí after being arrested for firearms offences. Alan Kelly was asked was he not concerned that children might get caught in the crossfire. 'I wouldn't give a fuck if a child was shot in the middle of the road . . . I've nothin' to lose . . . I don't give a fuck about anyone,' scoffed the hard man, who was ten when he first witnessed a shooting. To drive home the point he signed his statement, 'AK47'. Kelly was rewarded with a four-year prison sentence.

The Limerick gang wars blighted the lives of hundreds of young children. They were the collateral damage of the mindless mayhem. Kids whose families weren't involved in the feuds were exposed to the running gun battles and assaults taking place on the streets where they lived. Children of the families directly involved in the feuds had witnessed the murders and attempted murders of parents and relatives. They had been exposed to arson attacks and drive-by shootings at their homes in the dead of night. Proportionately more children in Limerick had suffered injury from bullets than anywhere else in the country.

Post-traumatic stress among youngsters was also commonplace. It was manifested in behavioural difficulties, which led to drug abuse, alcoholism and crime. Through their violence, the Limerick gangs killed the innocence of many children – it was a much more frightening tally than the death roll of the mob's actual enemies. In one incident in 2006, gunmen opened fire on two men as they played football with their sons, who were aged eight and twelve. Gardaí said it was miraculous neither of the children was hit but they were left profoundly traumatized. A number of months later, a five-year-old boy was shot and injured when the Keanes tried to assassinate his uncle, a member of Murder Inc., in a drive-by shooting. And these are just two examples of the hundreds of incidents involving children which pepper the story of Limerick's feuds like buckshot.

On the estates in the gang's strongholds, play for many young boys involved mock gun battles, imitating the actions of their elders. Some of these lads had progressed to playing with real guns by the time they were fifteen and sixteen. Children as young as five were caught transporting guns and ammunition. In one incident in 2006, two teenagers, aged sixteen and seventeen, were arrested with handguns on their way to do a shooting. In another, a fifteen-year-old was detained after shots were fired at unarmed Gardaí, and a thirteen-year-old was caught after he opened fire on the home of an old-age pensioner. Elsewhere a fourteen-year-old shot himself by accident while 'practising' with a handgun. At the trial of another fifteen-year-old boy, who was charged with holding a handgun for Murder Inc., the city's juvenile court was told he had no choice but to do their bidding. The child had been warned that his head would be 'blown off' if he didn't mind the weapon, which forensics showed had been used in several shootings.

In another case a fourteen-year-old boy, who had fired a sawn-off shotgun into a house, told Gardaí he'd done so because he 'felt like it'. The kid, who was wearing a bullet-proof vest when he was arrested, even bragged about pulling the trigger. 'I usually shoot with my left hand,' he gloated. There were more children appearing in Limerick's juvenile courts on firearms offences than anywhere else in Ireland. The warring mobs, who had earned the city's unenvied designation as Europe's murder capital, had achieved another disreputable record. The situation was analogous to the use of children in conflicts in Sierra Leone and the Congo on the African continent.

A boy soldier's coming-of-age was marked by his first arrest for a serious offence. It was not unusual for the recorded video tapes of the youth's interview with the Gardaí to be played for the rest of the gang. A preposterous legal provision allowed the tapes of an interview to be handed over to a suspect. Gang bosses across the country took full advantage of the arrangement and watched the tapes to ascertain if an individual had said too much. In Limerick the performances of the youngsters were carefully analysed, and advice was given about dealing with the cops. If the kid kept his mouth shut there was a celebration to mark his manhood. It was the gangland equivalent of a bar mitzvah and ensured the new generation were loyal foot soldiers.

Local Superintendent Frank O'Brien described how the gangs sacrificed the innocent for their own malevolent purposes. 'Unscrupulous individuals at the high end of the feud-related activity are targeting children and grooming them. These are vulnerable young people who believe this criminality gives them status as hard men,' he said, following the trial of a teenage gunman. The evil was akin to paedophilia and it was spreading like a contagion. Apart from the police, the first professionals to notice the effects were teachers.

Delegates at one of the annual teacher union conferences in April 2006 were visibly shocked when a colleague from Limerick described her job as being 'absolute hell on earth'. In a voice frayed with emotion she said: 'Where I teach, I meet students every day who have come from housing estates where there would have been drive-by shootings the previous night. And they talk casually about going and bringing out their sawn-off shotguns,' she said. It was against this chaotic backdrop that one of the most sickening acts of violence against young children ever witnessed in Ireland occurred five months later.

On Sunday, 10 September 2006, a barbaric attack on two young children finally made the world sit up and take notice. Sister and brother, six-year-old Millie and four-year-old

Gavin Murray from Moyross, suffered horrific burns when a petrol bomb was thrown through the window of their mother's car. The burning petrol turned the children into human fireballs, causing devastating injuries. Millie and Gavin had been sitting in the back seat behind their mother, Sheila, who was driving. The children suffered up to 30 per cent burns to their upper bodies and were hospitalized for several months. Such was the extent of Gavin's injuries that his right ear effectively melted away after he was pulled from the burning car. He had to be sedated each time nurses cleaned and re-bandaged his raw, weeping wounds. The children were left in agony as they underwent extensive skin grafts and had ongoing treatment for years. They also had to wear protective clothing.

The motive for the mind-numbing attack was almost beyond comprehension – the children's mother had refused to give two local thugs, seventeen-year-old Jonathan O'Donoghue and sixteen-year-old Robert Sheehan, a lift. They wanted to go to court to see their associates who had been arrested during two nights of rioting in the estate that had come to be known as Little Beirut. When Sheila Murray said no, O'Donoghue, Sheehan and their seventeen-year-old friend John Mitchell decided to punish her. They hurriedly made a petrol bomb and threw it into the open car window as she drove by. At their subsequent sentencing hearing, where the trio received between two and eight years each, Judge Carroll Moran described the attack as one of 'anarchic nihilism'.

The crime caused universal revulsion and stunned disbelief across a nation that took Millie and Gavin to their hearts. The appalling act placed the spiralling crisis on the national agenda. It finally forced the State to realize that Limerick was in the midst of a social emergency which could no longer be ignored. The Government commissioned the Fitzgerald Report, which in 2007 recommended a huge regeneration programme be implemented to reverse the years of neglect and social exclusion. The plan envisioned demolishing most of Moyross and building new, smaller estates in the area, with proper amenities and an emphasis on creating a sense of community. It was then intended to spread regeneration to Southill, Ballinacurra Weston and St Mary's Park. The process is still ongoing, but it was dramatically slowed down as a result of the economic crash.

While the attack on Sheila Murray and her children wasn't directly related to the ongoing feuds, the corrosive influence of the crime gangs was blamed for creating the environment that made casual acts of brutality the norm. Now it was no longer just the Gardaí and the courts on the gangsters' backs. With wider Government involvement, the innocent people the mobs had terrorized for so long were given a new sense of optimism. They began to believe that they would be released from the shackles of hopelessness and despair they were living in. An essential aspect of the State's response was a clampdown on anti-social behaviour by the city's council, in conjunction with the Gardaí. Residents in the new estates would require a certificate of eligibility before being housed and stricter eviction rules were applied. The attack on Millie and Gavin had inadvertently put a halt on Murder Inc.'s intimidating version of social planning. As part of the regeneration policy, extra Garda resources were allocated for community policing, to break down barriers and create an atmosphere of mutual trust. An additional 100 Gardaí were also transferred to the city. In 2010 Limerick's Community

Policing Unit received a 'Rehab People of the Year' special award, 'for their courage, ingenuity and outstanding dedication to the citizens of Limerick in working to make the community safer'.

The months leading up to the petrol bombing had seen a dramatic escalation in gang-related violence, especially in Moyross. The shooting rate in the area was up by over 145 per cent on the previous year. At the same time Gardaí were making scores of arrests and seizing large amounts of weaponry. The average age of a typical gunman was between seventeen and eighteen years of age. But for each potential killer taken off the streets there was a ready replacement. And most of the violence was being co-ordinated from prison by the Dundons and the McCarthys. Noddy McCarthy wasn't lying when he said the 'problem' was far from over.

In a typical example of the siege mentality, Richard 'Happy' Kelly, a seventeen-year-old tearaway who suffered with a cognitive disorder, was abducted and murdered by members of Murder Inc. in April 2006. The young car thief had mistakenly stolen a vehicle belonging to the mob that contained a consignment of drugs. The tragic teenager was blissfully unaware of this when he burned the car after a night's joy-riding. His killers would not tolerate such disrespect. Kelly's skeletal remains were found in November 2007 by fishermen tending their nets in a lake in County Clare. No one was ever charged with the murder. In gangland there were no places of detention for unruly kids who didn't do what they were told.

The Keane gang meanwhile had no intention of giving up on their quest for revenge. With the Dundons and several of the McCarthys in prison, 'Fat' Frankie Ryan was keeping the operation running. On 10 May 2006, nineteen-year-old Aidan Kelly, an associate of Murder Inc., died when he was shot five times in an ambush by the Keane/Collopys. He had accompanied Ryan and Christopher McCarthy to a laneway in Blackwater, County Clare, to pick up a firearm. The Keanes had set a trap for Ryan but Kelly, an expectant father, walked into it first. The gang, including Johnny 'Pitchfork' McNamara, then opened fire on Fat Frankie and McCarthy, who escaped by jumping over a ditch.

In keeping with his penchant for treachery, Wayne Dundon predictably decided to renege on his peace deal with Brian Collopy and began planning his rival's demise. John Dundon was sharing a cell in Mountjoy Prison with Hassan Hassan, a Lebanese crime boss. He was serving time for car theft and the abduction of his two sons. Hassan controlled a gang made up of hoods from the Middle East and North Africa who ran several criminal rackets in Ireland and the UK. Through his connections in Lebanon, Hassan was also involved in large-scale drug importations and the sale of illegal firearms.

The Lebanese criminal had forged links with a number of Irish gangs, including Marlo Hyland and his associates in west Dublin. He ran a sophisticated multi-million Euro car 'ringing' scam, in which high-powered cars were stolen to order by other criminals. The cars were fitted with the registration plates and chassis numbers of similar cars that had been written off in crashes. The vehicles were then shipped out of the country to the UK and Eastern Europe. Similarly, cars pilfered in the UK were smuggled to Ireland as part of the scam. The gang also dealt in valuable parts stripped from stolen vehicles.

In June 2006 John Dundon asked Hassan to supply a hit man to kill Brian Collopy. The plan was that the criminal would be lured into a trap by one of Hassan's people on the outside. The vigilant godfather was likely to drop his guard because he was unaware of the connection between the Lebanese criminal and Murder Inc. Collopy also naively believed his peace pact with the Dundons was still intact. Luckily for him, the Gardaí had informants in Hassan's group and were tipped off about the plot.

On 14 June, thirty-six-year-old Egyptian national Ibrihme Hassan travelled to Limerick with another foreign national at the behest of their boss. At the same time a major Garda operation swung into action as surveillance officers shadowed the hit team. In Limerick the ERU was on standby to make an arrest. Hassan, who was a heroin addict, met with a member of Murder Inc. and took possession of a semi-automatic .38 pistol, equipped with a silencer. He and his accomplice drove to Lord Edward Street in the city centre. They parked the car and left the weapon in the glove compartment.

The would-be assassins got into a second car to go and find Collopy. As they did so they were arrested. One of the officers involved in the swoop was Detective Garda Arthur Ryan, who had only recently returned to work following the injuries inflicted on him by Wayne Dundon. When Gardaí seized the weapon it was cocked and ready for use, with a round up the breech. The Egyptian later claimed that he had been ordered to bring the weapon back to Dublin for a criminal gang. Gardaí knew the true story but there was no way of proving it. Ibrihme Hassan subsequently pleaded guilty and was jailed for five years.

In the meantime the tit-for-tat attacks continued and so

did the Garda efforts to stop them. The then Justice Minister, Michael McDowell, secured €21 million in an extra budget allocation to fund Operation Anvil. The money was to fund intelligence-led operations against organized crime across the country. In Limerick it enabled the deployment of four extra static armed units to patrol three of the worst-hit estates on a constant basis.

Operation Anvil was soon showing results. On 29 June more than fifty officers took part in dawn raids on several locations across the city. They seized over €1 million worth of cocaine and heroin, over 1,000 rounds of ammunition, seven handguns and six stun guns, all of which belonged to the Keane/Collopy mob. A day later three rifles and a box of ammunition were found in a search of St Mary's Park.

Despite the increased police activity the two gangs continued to target each other. Two members of Murder Inc. were shot at in a hail of bullets during a drive-by shooting in July. A grenade was thrown through the window of a house belonging to a grandmother of the Dundon/McCarthys. Five days later, shots were fired through her front windows when she was asleep. The homes of Wayne and John Dundon were fire-bombed on the same night. A sixteen-year-old youth who was related to John Dundon through marriage was shot in the leg in another drive-by. Five hours later the home of Eddie Ryan's nephew, 'Fat' John McCarthy, was also raked with gunfire. Four years earlier the house had been sprayed with bullets by a teenager armed with an AK47 assault rifle. The homes of the widows of Eddie Ryan and Kieran Keane were also targeted. Shots were fired into Ryan's home while Sophie Keane's car was peppered with bullets.

As the madness escalated the Dundons' old enemy Johnny 'Pitchfork' McNamara had a lucky escape on 23 August when twenty shots were fired at him from a machine-gun. Five days later one of his associates was also fired upon by the pillion passenger on a motorbike. The same night a sixteen-year-old girl was injured when she was hit by a ricocheting bullet when a bunch of teenagers were doing some target practice in Ballinacurra Weston. On the other side of the city, a fifteen-year-old boy accidently shot himself in the leg when the gun he was playing with discharged. Another fifteen-year-old youth was arrested for three different drive-by shootings and charged with possession of a firearm with intent to endanger life. It was in the midst of this chaos that the Murray children were seriously injured.

Frankie Ryan continued to co-ordinate the mayhem and act as an enforcer for his gang of cut-throats. He also kept the Gardaí occupied as he became their number one Murder Inc. target. Ryan had been arrested for questioning in connection with the murders of David Nunan and Aidan Kelly. Gardaí believed that they had enough evidence to charge him with the Nunan killing and a file was being prepared for the DPP. But the Keane/Collopy side still wanted the dangerous thug dead. Before Fat Frankie could be brought to justice, mob law got to him first.

Gary Campion was released from prison on 15 September 2006. The return of the contract killer to his stomping ground of Moyross was the last thing the Gardaí or the besieged community needed. With the escalation in feud-related warfare Campion would have plenty to keep him busy. Frankie Ryan for one was glad to see the return of his old friend. Two days later he arranged to meet Campion to discuss his next assignment – murdering members of the Collopy and Keane clans. Despite Campion's fearsome reputation as a cold-blooded killer, Ryan trusted him as a 'made guy' in Murder Inc. It was a fatal mistake.

While he was inside, Campion had secretly agreed to switch his allegiances to the Keane/Collopy mob. He had befriended Christy Keane while sharing a landing with him in Portlaoise. His loyalty was a sellable commodity, and the Keane/Collopy mob had made a more attractive financial bid for his services. To the heartless killer it was always business. And it wasn't the first time that he had agreed to work for Murder Inc.'s hated enemies. Campion had previously accepted a contract from Philip Collopy to shoot several people attending a birthday party in the city. The plan was that the killer would barge into the celebration with a Glock automatic supplied by Collopy and blast everyone in sight. Luckily, on that occasion the Gardaí had been tipped off about the hit and averted a massacre when they seized the gun.

Campion's older brother Noel, who had been released in July, had already openly switched sides from Murder Inc. He had begun to organize his own drug rackets in conjunction with the gang from the Island Field. After his release Noel had gone on a gun holiday in Florida to brush up on his shooting skills, which he knew would be of great assistance in his new business venture.

Shortly before 10.45 p.m. on 17 September, Frankie Ryan picked up Gary Campion outside the house in Delmege Park where he lived with his partner and their two children. It was a short distance from where Millie and Gavin Murray had been horrifically injured a week earlier. The young gangster had been spinning around the area in his Toyota Camry with eighteen-year-old Erol Ibrahim who was sitting in the front seat. Campion jumped into the back, behind Fat Frankie. The atmosphere was friendly and the pair began chatting.

Campion asked his friend: 'What's the story so Frankie, any birds lately?' Frankie began to answer: 'Naa, fuck all birds now, Gar—' At that moment Campion calmly shot Ryan once in the back of the head with a handgun. As he slouched forward with his foot still on the accelerator, the Murder Inc. man's blood splashed across Ibrahim. Campion leaned in between the two front seats, using his free hand to steer the car to a stop on the side of the road about 270 metres from where the ill-fated journey had begun. It didn't bother the assassin that he had carried out the shooting so close to home.

Campion jumped out and opened the front passenger door where Ibrahim was frozen in shock. The hit man leaned over him and calmly took aim, firing a second round into Ryan's head to ensure he was dead. Ibrahim fell onto the road and begged for his life. For a moment Campion considered whacking Ibrahim but decided to spare him. Gardaí and local criminals would later describe the decision as completely out of character for the merciless hoodlum. Before he ran off he warned Ibrahim: 'If anyone rats on me, they're dead.'

Gardaí quickly established that Gary Campion was their prime suspect and began searching for him. Erol Ibrahim, who was deeply traumatized by the incident, only told cops what he knew after he was arrested for questioning. On 23 September detectives from Limerick found the safe house where Campion was hiding in Mitchelstown, County Cork. A team of armed officers, led by Detective Inspector Declan Mulcahy and Detective Sergeant Paddy O'Callaghan, burst into the house around 4.35 a.m. Campion jumped naked from his bed and instinctively attempted to jump through the closed upstairs bedroom window. He violently resisted arrest but was eventually wrestled to the ground and hand-cuffed by the detectives. 'Who ratted me out?' he demanded.

As the Gardaí drove him back to Limerick for questioning the killer launched into a bizarre, blood-curdling rant. 'If you left me out longer I'd have killed more people, fucking scumbags is all they are,' he steamed with venom. 'I'll clean up Moyross, not ye; I have lots more to kill.' Then he turned his attention to Detective Sergeant O'Callaghan and sneered: 'The next time I see you, you'll suck my cock, you fucking will. If I leave you anything to suck with . . . . fuckin' rats.'

The following evening Gary Campion was formally charged with Frankie Ryan's murder and returned to prison after just eight days of freedom. The one-man killing machine, who had claimed four lives and the suicide of a fifth, was segregated inside for his own protection – for good reason. His former pals in Murder Inc., specialists in the art of the double-cross, were stunned by his treachery. The Dundons immediately issued orders to avenge their friend, and that included killing any member of Campion's family who could be found.

Inevitably the murder dragged Limerick and Moyross back into the national media limelight. It clearly illustrated that the gangs were indifferent to the furore following the burning of two little children a week earlier. It also sparked a new spate of cyclical violence. In one incident, later compared in court to an 'old-style gangster film out of Chicago', Murder Inc. members tried to kill two men from the Keane gang in a high-speed shoot out. Two days after the Ryan murder, the hoodlums spotted Seanie Keane and Willie Moran in a Hiace van on the road to Bruff in rural County

Limerick. The Murder Inc. men drove up behind the van and one of them leaned out the side window and began shooting at it. The Keane mobsters had a lucky escape and drove to a Garda station for shelter. One of the shooters, twenty-year-old Paul Reddan, was later convicted of firearms offences and jailed for five years.

Even though most of his pals were locked up, Murder Inc. were there in spirit for the funeral of 'Fat' Frankie Ryan. A friend of the dead man had been asked to read a poem from the altar which had been written by the mob in prison. It was a barely disguised public declaration that there would be more justice of the 'eye for an eye' variety. It read:

> God above in heaven, why did his life end?
> Why did you let them take my friend?
> All we know now is a fight to the end.
> We have written this letter but have no address,
> Frankie, my brother, we are all left in a mess,
> We don't know what to say, but we all know what to do.
> Everything we do, we will think of you.

It was signed by Noddy and Christopher McCarthy, Gareth Collins, Wayne, Dessie and John Dundon and Frog Eyes Stanners. The jailed mobsters also sent a special floral wreath, 'Frankie, love, the Dundon Boys'. As a mark of respect for their fallen hero some members of the mob had his name tattooed on their chests alongside Glock automatics. That was how they remembered the dead.

The Dundon boys were busy planning revenge for their friend, and there was also the pressing matter of trying to shut James Cahill up permanently. On 17 October 2006, Anthony Kelly was the first man to be arrested and charged with the murder of Brian Fitzgerald. After he'd been shot by

John Creamer, and when he realized that Cahill was prepared to testify against him, Kelly had decided to leave Ireland permanently. He relocated to Morocco, the birthplace of the hashish trade, where he had a home and plenty of friends. He was arrested when he returned to Kilrush to quietly arrange the sale of his Irish house.

Two weeks later Kelly applied for bail to the Dublin High Court. The Gardaí were determined that he would not be released from custody and launched a strenuous objection to bail. Detective Sergeant Seamus Nolan told the court that Kelly and an associate, Larry McCarthy Junior, had recruited Cahill for the murder of Brian Fitzgerald. He said Cahill was prepared to give evidence against the accused. He also revealed that Philip Dean had been placed in the WPP because of fears for his safety, after he had given police a substantial amount of information.

Detective Sergeant Nolan told the court that there was a fear that Kelly would leave the jurisdiction and would take serious steps to make sure Cahill did not appear to give evidence against him. 'They [Cahill and Dean] are even more at risk of being murdered now that he has been charged,' the officer said. The detective said the accused had tried to sell his home and that Kelly's furniture firms were a cover for a massive drugs and firearms importation business. He accused Kelly of being one of the country's biggest drugs importers.

When it was put to Detective Sergeant Nolan, by Kelly's counsel, that Anthony Kelly's sister had offered a substantial €75,000 bond to secure his bail, the detective replied candidly: 'I would object to €75 million. He drives a car which is worth in excess of €100,000 and has substantial interests in Morocco, Europe and China. I believe he is closely linked with criminals in this area. I believe Mr Kelly should not be granted bail. I do not think any assurance would ensure that he will turn up at court,' the detective said. In an acknowledgement of the power of the mob concerned he admitted that nowhere was safe from their reach. 'I believe there is a substantial and real risk witnesses will be murdered, even within the confines of prison.' Bail was denied.

Around the same time, John Dundon's cell mate, Hassan Hassan, needed a return favour. The Lebanese gang boss had sworn revenge on his estranged twenty-eight-year-old wife, Baiba Saulite, from Latvia. Hassan had abducted the couple's two infant sons in December 2004 and had taken them to live in Syria with his sister. Through her solicitor, John Hennessy, Baiba had fought a year-long legal battle to have her children returned. Baiba Saulite was one of the first clients in Hennessy's newly opened law practice in Swords, County Dublin. Hennessy also kept up the pressure on the Gardaí to take action against the Lebanese car thief, who was subsequently charged with abduction. In the process Hassan developed a deep hatred for the solicitor. Hennessy's first case would almost cost him his life.

In the early hours of 27 February 2006, there had been an attempt to kill the solicitor when petrol was poured through the front letterbox of his home and then set alight. The hallway was engulfed in flames but the lawyer had managed to escape. Despite the attack, Hennessy testified against Hassan in the Circuit Criminal Court in Naas where the gangster was on trial for running a car theft racket. As a mitigating factor against imprisonment Hassan had deliberately misled the court, claiming he was the children's sole guardian.

Hennessy's evidence scuppered the ruse and Hassan was jailed for four years.

On 11 October 2006 detectives from Swords Garda Station called to see John Hennessy. They had just received detailed intelligence, through the Crime and Security Branch, that a Moroccan asylum seeker had been hired by Hassan Hassan to kill the lawyer. John Dundon had organized the handgun and a silencer to be used in the assassination. The hit was foiled when an informant in the gang tipped off his Garda handlers. The asylum seeker was then arrested on a separate matter by officers from the Garda National Immigration Bureau.

Hennessy was kept under observation by armed and uniformed Garda units for two weeks until the Crime and Security Branch were satisfied the plot had been thwarted. At the same time Baiba was also being threatened and intimidated by her former husband. When her car was petrol-bombed outside her home in Kinsealy she moved to live in a house near Swords, but the mobsters found her again. Baiba told her friends that she was living in fear of Hassan Hassan and talked of leaving Ireland for good with her children and of returning to Latvia.

Her suspicions were warranted. Two other members of the Lebanese gang were keeping the terrified woman under surveillance, waiting for the right moment to make their move. The non-nationals decided that they couldn't go ahead with the crime when they saw her with her little boys. It would also later emerge that another man had refused to take the murder contract because the fee he was offered was too low – €10,000. Hassan Hassan again turned to his ruthless cell mate for help with his problem. John Dundon took out his mobile phone and called his friend Martin 'Marlo' Hyland.

As a gang boss Hyland had some scruples, and he would have been horrified at a request to murder an innocent young mother-of-two. Dundon didn't say who the target was – just that he needed a gun and a car for a job in Limerick. The request came at a time when the embattled Dublin godfather badly needed friends – particularly powerful friends in the drugs and murder business. Hyland's empire was imploding as a result of a major Garda investigation, codenamed Operation Oak, which had been launched by the National Bureau of Criminal Investigation in November 2005. The operation had been a spectacular success for the police – and a disaster for Hyland. As he found his world crumbling around him, Marlo was anxious to ingratiate himself with as many heavy-hitters as possible. The ruthless Dundons were valuable allies.

The Piranhas had been the first people to be hit in Operation Oak when two female couriers were arrested with €300,000 of cocaine in Limerick train station. Twenty-eight-year-old Mary Crawford and a friend, twenty-five-year-old Pamela Hedderman, had returned home on the Dublin train after collecting the drugs from Marlo's gang. Crawford's brother Paul, from Southill, was a key member of the Murder Inc. gang and had been responsible for many of the drug deals between their mob and 'Fat' Freddie Thompson's outfit in Dublin. The cops wanted the Dundon/McCarthy gang to think the bust was the result of the local Gardaí getting lucky. A week later Operation Oak had notched up a much bigger success. This time they busted two of Marlo's associates transporting a tonne of hashish, with a street value of €7 million, on the Swords Road on Dublin's north side.

By the time Dundon picked up his phone, the Gardaí were tearing Hyland's empire apart, brick-by-brick. Over €20 million worth of heroin, cocaine and cannabis and an arsenal of sixteen firearms and ammunition had been seized over the previous year. And while Hyland had managed to evade arrest, his gang members bore the brunt of the gang-busting operation. By the autumn of 2006 a total of forty-one people associated with the gang, including his closest lieutenants, had been arrested. Twenty-six of them were facing serious criminal charges for drug trafficking, attempted armed robbery, money laundering and possession of firearms. The Criminal Assets Bureau had also opened a second front and officers were moving to seize Marlo's ill-gotten gains.

As the situation deteriorated Marlo became more isolated. Members of the gang, who were facing serious charges, fell out with the godfather, blaming him for their predicament. He was either a Jonah who brought them bad luck or, worse, Hyland was an informant. The gang boss had also become deeply suspicious of those around him because no matter what he seemed to do, the police knew about it first. He was under pressure too from one of Europe's most powerful international crime syndicates, led by ex-pat Irish gangster Christy Kinahan. The 'Dapper Don' was demanding payment for the drug shipments the police had intercepted. Hyland also owed Murder Inc. money and John Dundon had just called in the debt. The godfather had no choice but to organize the gun and car on his behalf.

John Dundon had been in touch with notorious hit man Paddy Doyle from north inner-city Dublin. Doyle was a member of 'Fat' Freddie Thompson's gang, who were still involved in the bitter Crumlin/Drimnagh feud, which claimed at least twelve lives over ten years. The Dundons were particularly impressed with Doyle's credentials as a killer as he was the prime suspect for three gangland murders that had been committed over a forty-eight-hour period in November 2005. The first two victims, Darren Geoghegan and Gavin Byrne, were members of Doyle's gang – Geoghegan had been his best friend. But just like the company policy in Murder Inc. the killings weren't personal – just business. Doyle shot his two pals in the back of the head after he got into the back seat of the car they were driving. Gardaí believe he dispatched the pair as part of an internal row over money. The third victim was Noel Roche, a member of the Rattigan gang in Drimnagh, whom Doyle shot in Clontarf two days later. After the murder spree the killer fled to the Costa del Sol. When Dundon called, Doyle was happy to help and recruited two young hit men from Cabra to do the job.

A high-powered BMW was stolen by Marlo Hyland's men and stored in an underground car park they used to stash getaway cars, drugs and guns. One of the hit men went to meet John Dundon's sister Annabel and her boyfriend, Joe Hehir, on the Naas Road in Dublin. Hehir was also a member of Murder Inc. Dundon had been given a map of the Holywell Estate with the location of Baiba Saulite's home marked on it and he also had her photograph. He passed the documents to one of his henchmen during a prison visit and Hehir was then given an envelope and told to deliver it with his girlfriend. It also contained a piece of paper with directions on how to get to the house from the M1 motorway, which bypasses Swords.

On the afternoon of 17 November, John Dundon phoned Marlo from his prison cell to arrange collection of a firearm. Hyland asked the Limerick hood where the 'piece of graft' – the shooting – was to take place. Dundon said it was in Limerick. Garda intelligence sources would later learn that Hyland asked Troy Jordan in County Kildare to supply him with a 'clean' Magnum revolver. The weapon was part of a cache Jordan was holding for him. Hyland phoned Jordan and arranged for the collection of the 'silver thing' later that evening. Jordan had no idea what the weapon was going to be used for; all he knew was that it was to go to Limerick.

On the evening of Sunday, 19 November, a pizza delivery man arrived at Baiba's door. She said she hadn't ordered one and he left. Minutes later Hassan Hassan received a phone call in prison informing him that the victim was at home. Dundon then called Paddy Doyle, who gave the hit men in Cabra the go-ahead. Shortly before 9.45 p.m. Baiba appeared at the front door of her new home to share a cigarette with a friend. She didn't like smoking in the house in case it affected her two little boys, whom she had just put to bed.

As she stood at the door a man wearing a scarf and base-ball hat suddenly ran up to her. He pulled the Magnum revolver from his jacket and shot the young mother at close range. Baiba was hit twice in the chest and once in the shoulder. The impact of the bullets pushed her backwards into the hallway. She collapsed on her back, gasping for breath as blood flowed in a torrent around her body. The bullets had caused devastating injuries to Baiba's lungs. The defenceless young woman choked to death on her own blood. Her killer sprinted to the stolen BMW and made his escape. It was abandoned and set alight a short distance away.

When Gardaí arrived at the scene they bundled the victim's two boys in blankets and took them out of the house, protecting their innocent eyes from the horrific sight of their lifeless mother on the ground. With no family members in the country, the children were immediately taken into care. Within an hour armed police had also taken John Hennessy out of his home, fearing that he was next on the hit list. He would spend the next seven years under full-time police protection. The murder was another shocking new low in the story of organized crime in Ireland. The fact that an innocent woman could be so callously gunned down was greeted with universal shock and outrage.

Gangland violence was spiralling out of control. The murder brought to twenty the number of gun murders so far in 2006 – seventeen of them classified as gangland killings. The assassination of innocent people was becoming a disturbing new trend. It had begun in Limerick with the Murder Inc. executions of Brian Fitzgerald and Sean Poland. The Dundons and their clan had firmly established their place in the hierarchy of evil – and set an example for others. In March 2006 another innocent woman, Donna Cleary, was shot dead when a drugged-up criminal indiscriminately fired shots into a house party. And the fact that organized crime had planned to murder an officer of the court sent shock waves through the legal profession.

The level of public revulsion and anger at the mother-of-two's murder could be gauged through Joe Duffy's *Liveline* phone-in programme. Over the following days, thousands of callers flooded the show's phone lines to express their anger, shock and disgust. Hundreds of people later attended a memorial service for Baiba held in a local church in Swords. The Taoiseach of the day and the country's most senior politicians felt compelled to add their voices to the chorus of condemnation.

At a press conference three days later, the officer-in-charge of the investigation, Detective Inspector Walter O'Sullivan, made an impassioned plea for help in tracking down the killers. Rarely had a senior cop been so passionate and forthright in his comments: 'This was a truly horrific crime. A young woman gunned down in the prime of her life, the mother of two children. I would appeal to all persons who enjoy life, who love life, and all that life has to offer, to come forward. There are no words left to describe this crime.'

When Hassan Hassan applied for compassionate temporary release from prison to attend his wife's funeral the Gardaí strenuously objected. Detective Inspector O'Sullivan dispelled any lingering doubts the court might have harboured, declaring: 'I am extremely concerned for his [John Hennessy's] life and the persons associated with his office. I fear, from privileged information in my possession, that if Hassan Hassan is released on bail that he will commit more serious offences that, according to the information I have, include murder, assault, intimidation and interference with witnesses.'

The lives of Baiba's two innocent children, five-year-old Ali-Alexandra and three-year-old Mohammed Rami, were irreparably damaged. The traumatized and confused little boys suddenly found themselves without their mother and remained in foster care for a number of years.

Although Gardaí had good quality intelligence about the organization of the murder and who was behind it, neither Hassan nor John Dundon was ever charged. A number of gangland witnesses said they were too scared to testify. Within a few hours of Baiba Saulite's death Gardaí had raided the cell occupied by the Murder Inc. boss and his Lebanese friend, but they found nothing. Just over two weeks later, John Dundon was again taken from his cell by Gardaí – to be charged with murder.

On 5 December, along with his brother Dessie and Gary Campion, the three killers were taken from prison and charged with the murder of Brian Fitzgerald. Campion suddenly found himself sharing the dock with his former pals who now wanted him dead in revenge for Fat Frankie's murder. Prison officers and Gardaí had to keep them apart to prevent a row breaking out in the court. There was a ring of steel around Limerick District Court when the trio were brought for the brief hearing, in a convoy of prison vans escorted by ERU jeeps. Two weeks later the Supreme Court also rejected an appeal by Anthony Kelly, seeking to overturn the High Court's refusal to grant him bail for the murder charge.

The Saulite murder caused consternation in Marlo Hyland's gang. When word leaked out on the street and in the media that the godfather was involved, his reputation was left in tatters. Secret Garda phone intercepts recorded Troy Jordan angrily berating Hyland for indirectly involving him in the horror. He said he wouldn't have handed over the weapon if he knew its true purpose. Hyland claimed he believed Dundon when he said the weapon was for use in Limerick. Jordan later confirmed this story when he was arrested by Gardaí for questioning in connection with the murder. The Cabra godfather was deeply concerned about being connected with the outrageous crime. There were still some criminals who disapproved of such a murder. Killing other hoods was one thing – murdering a defenceless woman was completely different. This was a crime no gangster would want his name attached to.

At the same time the increasingly volatile and paranoid Hyland tried to assassinate one of his business associates, Michael 'Roly' Cronin. It presented Eamon Dunne, one of Hyland's closest lieutenants, with the opportunity he had been waiting for. The dangerously ambitious gangster convinced Hyland's two most loyal hit men that it was time to get rid of their boss. The psychopaths didn't need much persuading: both of them were facing long jail sentences for drug trafficking after being caught during Operation Oak. Hyland was informed by Gardaí that his life was in danger.

At 9.19 a.m. on the morning of 12 December 2006, the two hit men walked into the house in Finglas where Marlo was staying with his niece and her family. Hyland was asleep upstairs and a young trainee plumber called Anthony Campbell was downstairs fixing a radiator. One of the killers held the twenty-year-old while his accomplice, who was armed with a .45 semi-automatic pistol, crept upstairs. The lieutenant shot Hyland three times in the head as he lay face down, asleep. Another four rounds were fired into Marlo's back. Downstairs the cold-blooded killers briefly considered what to do with the terrified young plumber. The gunman lifted his gun and shot him in the head, killing him instantly. He was the second innocent person to be gunned down without mercy in a few weeks. Crime had become the number one concern of the Irish public.

The Dundons weren't overly concerned about the death of their former ally. That was the way it was in gangland – life was cheaper than a kilo of hash. When Dunne emerged as the new boss, and earned the nickname 'The Don', Murder Inc. had no problem doing business with him. The mob still needed a steady supply of product to keep up with demand at home.

Back in Limerick the Keane mob had stepped up their efforts to whack Murder Inc. drug dealer Paul Crawford from Southill. On 2 November, seventeen bullets were fired into Crawford's family home in a drive-by shooting. The front room was peppered, with the indiscriminate rounds narrowly missing children who were watching TV. The next day the occupant of a stolen car pointed a sawn-off shotgun at the gangster as he walked along the road. The gun failed to fire and the gang drove off at speed. They were later captured by the ERU in a high-speed chase. A fifteen-year-old boy was among four arrested. Two days later, the killers showed their determination when they made another attempt on Crawford's life.

The drug dealer was standing in front of the family home with his five-year-old nephew, Jordan, when a hit man opened fire with a machine-gun. The child was shot in the right thigh and later had to undergo an operation. At the time Crawford admitted to *Irish Independent* reporter Barry Duggan that he was the target. 'They came in here to get me; to finish me off. They wanted me dead and shot my nephew. There is a hit out on me. They want me dead,' he said. Yet again, the shooting of an innocent child made national media headlines. The Irish public were being bombarded every day with news of the latest mindless gangland atrocity.

The would-be assassins, who had already made at least three attempts on Crawford's life, were not concerned that they had shot a child. On 18 December they struck again and this time shot dead their target's innocent brother, Noel, in a case of mistaken identity. Noel was a father-of-six who had no involvement in crime. He was celebrating his fortieth birthday and was standing outside the family home when his killers struck. Paul Crawford was upstairs when the hit men arrived. Within hours he was making his own threats.

Gardaí investigating the murder were searching a house in Southill when the Murder Inc. man arrived and vowed to kill the woman who lived there. He pointed to her house and the houses on either side. 'That will be done tonight, children and all, that one as well and that one too. My brother Noel is dead, ye are all dead too,' the grief-stricken thug warned.

Paul Crawford was charged with making the threat and was jailed for nine months. In August 2007 he was jailed for two years for breaching an exclusion order banning him from Southill because his presence there was a catalyst for violence. Limerick City Council had obtained the order in the District Court in June 2007 when he was released from prison. Gardaí told the court that Crawford was using his parents' home, where his brother was murdered, as an HQ for the Dundon/McCarthy mob. They revealed that there had been a 'dramatic drop' in the number of incidents between 18 December 2006 and 17 June 2007, when Crawford was in custody.

If anyone had been keeping a score sheet, the Crawford murder brought to nine the number of deaths directly connected to the feud between Murder Inc., the Keanes and the Collopys. When the other killings carried out by the Dundon/McCarthys and their henchmen were added in, including those of Brian Fitzgerald, Sean Poland, Declan Griffin and Baiba Saulite, the death toll attributable to the Limerick mob was fifteen people in less than six years. Despite the growing number of arrests for firearms offences and the seizure of seventy-six weapons, the shootings still continued unabated. In 2006 the city had the highest number yet recorded of reported shooting incidents: a total of ninety-seven, an increase of fourteen on the previous year. Limerick again accounted for a quarter of all reported incidents where firearms were illegally discharged in the Irish Republic. The victim of one of those incidents was gang boss Brian Collopy, who was shot and injured in an attempted hit on 20 December. The gangster was struck twice in the ankle and the thigh but recovered.

The murder of Noel Crawford was further proof that the city had spawned a generation of child killers. The shooter was seventeen-year-old Jonathan Fitzgerald and his accomplice was fifteen-year-old Michael O'Callaghan. Fitzgerald was subsequently jailed for life. O'Callaghan's sentencing hearing was told that his father had been stabbed to death when the boy was just three. His mother was an alcoholic and he had grown up in a 'dysfunctional family'. The teenager had been involved in crime since childhood and was shot when he was fourteen. He had also shot another man, for which he received a suspended sentence. O'Callaghan got seven years for his involvement in Crawford's killing. Two more young lives had been destroyed amid the chaos.

12. Arming for War

The number one priority for the Dundon/McCarthys was to silence James Martin Cahill. When the four defendants in the Brian Fitzgerald murder trial received the Books of Evidence they could see from his statements that there was potentially a strong case to put them all away for life. But getting to their former hit man was proving difficult; he was segregated in solitary confinement and under constant guard. Hassan Hassan had organized for a powerful type of odourless rat poison to be smuggled into the prison and put into Cahill's food by a trustee. The mob had tried to do the same with Philip Dean. But the prison service found the poison and arrangements were made to prepare the hit man's food separately under close scrutiny. The only way to get the job done was to have him shot or blown up on the outside.

From the comfort of their prison cells they set about organizing one of the most audacious conspiracies in gangland history. The conspirators hatched an arms smuggling plot worthy of an international terrorist group. Wayne Dundon decided to buy an awesome arsenal of weapons, including assault rifles and rocket launchers. The weapons would be used to literally blow Cahill away as he was brought to court in a prison van. He was being held in Portlaoise Prison and a rocket attack could be mounted anywhere along the motorway journey to Dublin. There was no concern for, or even thought given to, the fact that prison officers, police and innocent bystanders could also be killed in such a full-blown terrorist attack. Consequences were never a consideration. Dundon also planned to use the powerful weapons in a new offensive to wipe out Murder Inc.'s enemies in Limerick. He was preparing to launch an all-out urban war, the likes of which had not been seen since the darkest days of the Northern Ireland Troubles.

Wheatfield Prison in Clondalkin, west Dublin, where most of Murder Inc.'s members were held, had become the mob's de facto corporate HQ. The Limerick hoodlums shared the same wing and, because of their fearsome reputations, had the run of the place. Warders, whose colleagues in Limerick had been subjected to an appalling campaign of intimidation and attacks by the gang, were not prepared to incur the gang's wrath. It simply wasn't worth it. The situation was even worse for the rest of the inmates, who were bullied and terrorized by the Dundon/McCarthys.

The Dundons and their cousins controlled the drug trade in the prison and the equally lucrative sale of mobile phones. Every inmate in Wheatfield had to show 'respect' to their brutal overlords. The prison management had adopted an unofficial laissez-faire approach to the Murder Inc. thugs, in return for no trouble. Wayne and John Dundon would spend their days on the phone issuing orders and threats to their minions in Limerick. They planned and co-ordinated shootings through their network of mostly teenage lackeys on the streets of Moyross, Southill and Ballinacurra Weston.

Unlike other prisoners they weren't obliged to take part in educational programmes or work details. They could also freely move between landings, which the other inmates couldn't do. The Dundon/McCarthys didn't even have to queue with the other lags when they wanted a meeting with the prison governor. Instead they could forego the tedium of waiting in line and lounge in their cells making phone calls. When their turn came, the staff summoned them over the tannoy system. Life inside wasn't too tough on Murder Inc.

One former inmate described to this writer some years ago what life was like in the Murder Inc.-controlled slammer. 'Everyone was terrified of the Dundons. If you didn't do what they told you then you were beaten or sliced up. A lot of us just wanted to do our time and then get out but they made life absolute hell. They were absolute animals,' he recalled. 'If we didn't bring drugs and phones in for them then they threatened to get our families on the outside and everyone knew that they didn't make idle threats. Some guys were driven to the point of suicide by those bastards and a lot of us applied for transfers to other prisons just to get some peace. People just have no idea what it was like . . . they were pure evil scum,' the former lag added with a shake of his head.

For Wayne Dundon it was a logical progression to move from organizing drug deals, shootings and murders to masterminding one of the biggest international arms deals ever co-ordinated by an Irish criminal gang. With Chaser O'Brien, Larry McCarthy Junior, Anthony Kelly and at least fifteen of the gang's other main players locked up, Dundon had to rely on his minions to source the munitions. Two gang associates, twenty-seven-year-old Glen Geasley from Ballincollig in Cork and twenty-one-year-old Sean Callinan from Tullamore, were instructed to make contact with the UK gang McCarthy Junior had been dealing with before his arrest in London. The Turkish mob concerned had extensive Eastern European connections specializing in the supply of all types of military-spec armaments.

In February 2007, Geasley met with the Turkish gang's contact in London who put him in touch with another man to discuss a deal. On 22 February he was introduced to an Englishman called 'George', who then brought Geasley to meet two other men, 'Raj' and 'John'. In keeping with the cloak-and-dagger nature of the deal, the meeting took place in an old Victorian warehouse, under railway arches in a backstreet. Both sides were wary of each other in case it was a set-up. Before discussions began, all parties took off their outer clothes to show that they were not wearing wires or firearms.

Geasley told his contacts that he was representing Wayne Dundon who was a 'major criminal godfather' behind bars in an Irish prison. He said Dundon was the 'decision man' and wanted the weapons 'for a war in Limerick between Wayne's people and their enemies'. One of the dealers showed Geasley a laptop with a selection of pictures of the different types of hardware they had available. It was accompanied with a price list. The Murder Inc. man was given a mobile phone number to ring and Geasley said he would get back to them. He returned to Ireland where he reported directly to Dundon on a visit to prison. Wayne Dundon was happy that they had made contact with the right people. But in the shadows the Gardaí were even happier – the Piranhas had taken the bait.

Through the years of relentless pressure the Gardaí had established a network of informants within the gang. The secretive Crime and Security Section in Garda HQ in the Phoenix Park, Dublin, had also been listening in on some of the phone calls being made by the Dundons. Luckily, they had learned of the plot as soon as it was hatched. Needless to say, criminals acquiring such firepower would be an extremely grave development. The Dundon/McCarthys would have to be stopped. In London the security services had also planted agents in the arms gang McCarthy had been dealing with. A number of high-level conferences were held between the Gardaí and the UK's Serious Organized Crime Agency (SOCA). It was decided that both sides would work together to set up one of the most sophisticated undercover stings ever witnessed in Irish crime fighting. For the second time Murder Inc. was at the centre of a major international police investigation. The unfolding drama, codenamed Operation Beam, was co-ordinated by Detective Chief Superintendent Tony Quilter.

'George' and the two shady arms dealers Geasley met in a London backstreet were all specialist undercover SOCA agents. Their first meeting in the warehouse had been recorded in perfect sound and vision. In order to establish proof that Wayne Dundon was in charge of the conspiracy 'John' informed Geasley that they needed confirmation that he was, as he claimed, acting for the Dundons. After all, 'John' had been told that Dundon was the decision man and the 'arms dealers' needed assurance that they would be paid. It was arranged for the secret agent to visit Wheatfield Prison.

On 5 April 2007, 'John' was instructed by Geasley to visit another inmate, Thomas Flood, in Wheatfield. He was also told to wear a T-shirt with 'Old Navy' printed on it. This term would become 'John's' identification code in their future dealings. When the SOCA agent arrived, John Dundon was in the visitor's cubicle next to Flood. The agent handed over a copy of the *Irish Independent* which contained inserts from the *London Life* magazine, including an advert for mobile phones. The mobile number on the advert was 'John's' contact number for further discussions on a deal. Dundon picked up the newspaper and nodded to the under-cover agent as he went back to his cell.

A few days later the SOCA agents were contacted again by Geasley with a shopping list for an awesome arsenal of firepower. The inventory included twenty-four weapons, including two Russian-built RPG-7 rocket launchers, five Russian AK47 assault rifles, five American AR-15 assault rifles, two Uzi submachine-guns, ten semi-automatic pistols and a large quantity of assorted high-velocity ammunition. There was enough ordnance on the list to equip a conven-tional military unit for war. The SOCA 'arms dealers' agreed to sell the cache for £45,000 (€60,000) in cash. The condition of sale was that the money would be paid up-front on deliv-ery. The transfer of the merchandise would take place in Cork on 20 April 2007.

'Raj' contacted Geasley on 20 April to say he had arrived in the Rochestown Park Hotel in Cork and that he wanted the cash before the shipment could be handed over. When Geasley arrived at the hotel he phoned Dessie Dundon on his mobile phone in prison. Dundon told his front man to get two sample weapons to test fire before the cash was paid. The agent refused, insisting on the full payment up front. To prove that the arsenal had arrived in Ireland, 'Raj' showed Geasley a mobile phone picture of the RPG-7 rocket launch-ers with that day's *Evening Herald* newspaper in the forefront. (The weapons in the picture had been seized from the Provi-sional IRA by the Gardaí during the Troubles. They had been dusted off and taken out of storage for the sting operation.) Back in their prison cells the Dundons were excited that everything was going to plan. Dessie told Geasley to agree to the conditions.

Later that day £45,000, in used British and Northern Ireland bank notes, was delivered in a Tommy Hilfiger sports bag to Geasley by a woman. He handed it over to 'Raj'. At the same time 'John' was twenty minutes away at the Ibis Hotel on the main Cork to Waterford Road. He was waiting in a van with the weapons from Garda HQ. Geasley directed Sean Callinan to pick up the arsenal from the undercover officer.

When 'John' was showing Callinan the weapons the ERU moved in and he was arrested. Simultaneously Geasley was also arrested and the cash was seized. In Wheatfield Prison, Gardaí searched the Dundon brothers' cells and three mobile phones were seized. Murder Inc. had been dealt a humiliating blow.

While it was a huge victory for law enforcement, the plot demonstrated the nihilism of the Dundon/McCarthy machine. It was a sobering reminder that they would never give up. Their message was the same as the IRA's had been after the Brighton Bomb in 1984 when they blew up the Conservative Party Conference. 'We have to be lucky once . . . you have to be lucky all the time.'

In February 2008, Geasley and Callinan pleaded guilty to a charge of conspiring with others to possess weaponry. Detective Chief Superintendent Quilter told the court: 'Geasley represented himself as an agent of a criminal organization based in this country, running their empire from Irish prisons.' Judge Patrick Moran said he dreaded to think of the consequences if the extraordinary police operation had not foiled the arms plot. Geasley was jailed for twelve years, with the final five suspended, while Callinan was jailed for six, with the final three suspended. There was much speculation at the time that the pair had benefited from a secret plea-bargain arrangement with the State, in return for pleading guilty. But it was also accepted that both men were working on the orders of the Dundons. At the time of writing, Murder Inc.'s gun-running plot is still officially an open case. Gardaí say they hope to bring others, 'higher up in the organization', before the courts.

Despite the failure of Murder Inc.'s plan to replenish its arsenal, there was no reprieve for the Treaty City. Shootings, arson and grenade attacks continued at the same depressing levels as in previous years. Six days after their international arms plot was rumbled the Dundon/McCarthys notched up another killing.

Since the murder of 'Fat' Frankie Ryan the Dundons had sworn vengeance on their former lieutenant Gary Campion for his act of supreme treachery. But there was no way of getting access to the killer. He was languishing in prison as a co-accused with John and Dessie Dundon for the murder of Brian Fitzgerald. The next obvious target was Gary's equally dangerous older brother Noel, who had already moved away from Murder Inc. and was muscling in on their territory with his own rackets.

In March 2007 there had been two attempts on Noel Campion's life and his home in Moyross was peppered with bullets in a drive-by shooting. In retaliation, the drug dealer had fire-bombed the family homes of murder victims Frankie Ryan and Aidan Kelly. Around 10.40 a.m. on 26 April Campion was the pillion passenger on a motorbike headed from Moyross to the courts complex in the city centre. He was due to appear on a minor road traffic offence and had decided not to wear his bullet-proof vest. As the bike drew up to lights at the junction of Inglewood Terrace, Treaty Terrace and High Road, a gunman stepped out of a phone booth. As the killer opened fire the motorbike driver collided with a car and was thrown through the car's windscreen. Campion was hit three times as he tried to run. He collapsed and died on the ground nearby. If he had worn his customary body armour he would have survived the attack.

News that Noel Campion had been assassinated in vengeance for their beloved Fat Frankie was celebrated by the Murder Inc. crew in Wheatfield Prison and Ballinacurra Weston. The Dundons phoned their co-defendant Gary Campion to share the good news that they had killed his brother. That night there was a drunken street party and the Dundon/McCarthy entourage lit a bonfire. Even the children joined in, chanting: 'Whack, whack, Noely got it in the back.'

Two months later the killers of Kieran Keane were confident of winning an appeal against their convictions and were planning to walk free. In Ballinacurra Weston bonfires were built again and huge amounts of alcohol were bought for the anticipated homecoming party for the 'heroes'. Painted banners, bunting and flags were prepared to celebrate the return of the five men. More than 100 T-shirts with slogans supporting the Dundon/McCarthy gang were also specially printed as a souvenir of the momentous occasion.

On 25 July, however, their hopes were dashed and the party was cancelled. The Court of Criminal Appeal rejected all grounds of the men's appeal. The gangsters in the dock, who had laughed and joked when they were originally sentenced, showed their true colours when they heard the news.

They shouted abuse and spat at the judges and the prosecution's legal team. In a fit of temper, two of them threw their copies of the heavy 105-page judgment across the courtroom at the judges' bench.

Their relatives and supporters also screamed abuse at the judges and members of the media in court. As Gardaí moved to quell the disturbance the judges, Mr Justice Kearns presiding, Ms Justice Elizabeth Dunne and Mr Justice Brian McGovern, were escorted from the bench. Limerick State Solicitor Michael Murray welcomed the court's decision. 'It is a very significant result and vindicates the good police work of the Gardaí in Limerick who headed the investigation,' he said. 'I hope it will go down to those involved in the feud that the long arm of the law will eventually prevail and that they will realize the futility of pursuing the violent agenda.'

The decision was good news for the Gardaí and the ordinary decent citizens of the city. The people in the worst-affected estates were experiencing war fatigue as, more than four years after the murder of Kieran Keane, the violence showed no sign of ending. Not even the infamous sieges of Limerick in the seventeenth century had lasted as long. If the five killers had been released there would have been chaos.

There was also relief in the Keane stronghold where there was good reason to celebrate. Kieran Keane's dangerous nephew Liam took the partying too far. He was arrested that night for being drunk and disorderly and for threatening and abusive behaviour. Liam Keane told the judge he was celebrating the failed appeal by his uncle's killers. The judge gave the heroin addict a three-month sentence to sober up.

The reaction from Murder Inc.'s supporters was predictable. Over the next month there were fifteen shooting incidents in Southill and Moyross alone. Two men were shot and injured in separate incidents. In Limerick Prison up to twenty members of Murder Inc. caused thousands of Euros' worth of damage during an orchestrated mini-riot on the D2 Wing. Televisions on shelves and hanging on wall-brackets were removed and smashed by the inmates. Then on 19 August a sniper using a high-velocity rifle fired four shots at an unmarked Garda patrol car in Southill. The officers escaped injury, but it was a sinister development.

The backlash from the police was instant. The deliberate shooting of Gardaí threatened all-out anarchy and could not be tolerated in any civilized society. A force of fifty officers, backed up by a helicopter, armed support and a dog unit, raided forty houses in Southill. The swoop resulted in the seizure of two handguns, a rifle and a sawn-off shotgun. Such large-scale search operations had become a regular event as cops tried to keep a lid on the boiling cauldron.

Over seventy firearms were seized in 2007, while a similar number had been taken off the streets the previous year. A record 103 shooting incidents were reported in Limerick that year, compared to 97 in 2006. The figures confirmed the city's continuing reign as the gun capital of Ireland. By comparison, Dublin had 123 such incidents. It illustrated the scale of what Noddy McCarthy had euphemistically referred to as 'the problem'. A total of forty-one people were convicted of firearms offences in 2007, reflecting the enormous workload on local Gardaí. The ancient city 'well versed in the arts of war' had consolidated its reputation as being the most violent municipality in Western Europe.

On 8 October 2007, twenty-five-year-old Gareth Grant was shot dead by twenty-one-year-old Greg Crawford. The two men were from the St Mary's Park area that had been the scene of scores of shooting incidents associated with the various feuds. Crawford, who was facing a charge for firearms offences at the time, was subsequently convicted of the murder, which was related to a separate feud. A month later another innocent young man, nineteen-year-old Jeffrey Hannan, was savagely beaten to death with a hatchet near his home in Southill. The suspect was an eighteen-year-old foot soldier in Murder Inc. called Stephen O'Sullivan.

The teenage O'Sullivan was typical of the young recruit favoured by Wayne Dundon and his clan. He was a violent, uneducated drug abuser from a dysfunctional home. His forty-three-year-old father, Eddie Casey, a Murder Inc. member, had over seventy criminal convictions. In June 2006 Casey had been jailed for eleven years for the rape of a young student in Galway. The twenty-three-year-old victim was grabbed off the street as she walked alone through the city centre. He dragged the terrified young woman to a grassy area and threatened to stab her before raping her. O'Sullivan's uncle, Ray Casey, was once described by Gardaí as being one of the 'most violent criminals in Limerick'. In 2002 he was jailed for life for kicking a barman to death. He robbed his innocent victim before dumping his body in a skip.

Coming from such a background, it was easy to see why Stephen O'Sullivan hero-worshipped Wayne Dundon. The teenager had no problem enthusiastically carrying out shootings and beatings at his idol's behest. A Garda said of him: 'O'Sullivan idolized Dundon and would have done anything for him and the gang. He was given cash and coke for doing jobs and was involved in a number of shootings.'

On 15 October 2007, Anthony Kelly, Gary Campion and John and Dessie Dundon stood trial for the murder of Brian

Fitzgerald before Mr Justice Peter Charleton in the Central Criminal Court. All four pleaded not guilty. Arrangements were made to ensure that Campion and the Dundons arrived in court separately and were kept apart. Like the Keane murder trial, the hearing was also held under tight security in Cloverhill, which had become the favoured venue for dangerous gang-related cases. The jury of twelve men sworn to hear the case were told that the trial could last up to ten weeks. In his opening address, Senior Counsel for the State, Denis Vaughan Buckley, told the jury that the main prosecution witness was James Martin Cahill, who had pleaded guilty to committing the murder and who claimed that the four accused had taken part in the planning and execution of the offence.

The trial heard evidence from Alice Fitzgerald, who recalled the events of the night her husband was murdered. Neighbours also told of being woken by the shouts for help and gunshots. One neighbour said she heard someone shouting out 'Oh God no', followed by two or three shots, then a gap of around thirty seconds, before another two or three shots sounded. Another woman said she heard Brian Fitzgerald crying out: 'Help me, I'm being shot at.'

On the ninth day of the trial, the hit man took the witness stand. Over the following six days he made some bizarre revelations that made him sound like he had gone mad. In his direct evidence Cahill said that before the murder Anthony Kelly gave him a gun and a clip full of bullets and showed him how to use it. He said he was asked by Larry McCarthy Junior, referred to in court as 'Mr A', to shoot someone who had 'made a statement against him'. Cahill said he was offered €10,000 and agreed to do it for that amount.

The killer said he had travelled to Dublin with McCarthy

Junior to arrange the motorbike which was to be used in the attack. He described how, after several meetings with the gang members, he was driven to Kelly's house, where Kelly provided him with a gun and showed him how to use it. 'He was clicking it back and showing me how to use it. The safety and that,' he said. Cahill claimed that Kelly talked to him as he was leaving. 'He said he didn't want to know what we were doing but not to mess it up. He just said don't mess around.' On the day of the murder, Cahill said he was in a car with Dessie Dundon when Dundon asked Gary Campion if he would drive the motorbike. Cahill told prosecuting counsel that Dessie Dundon pointed Brian Fitzgerald out to him, outside Doc's night-club in Limerick. 'I walked past him. I didn't take much notice of him. It was just he was a big lad,' he said.

Cahill said that Dessie and John Dundon drove him out to Fitzgerald's home one day to see where the CCTV cameras were located. On the night of the shooting, he and Campion hid in some bushes near the house, as they lay in wait for their victim. Dessie Dundon phoned to tell them when Fitzgerald left work. When Brian Fitzgerald's jeep pulled up, Cahill described killing him. 'I shot him in the heart, then after a while I walked round and shot him in the head.' He said he didn't know how many times he fired: 'I just clicked it.'

After the shooting Cahill gave his helmet to Campion and left him to dispose of the motorcycle and the helmets. He said he left the gun in a hedge where Philip Dean later found it. He went back to Chaser O'Brien's house, had a shower and got changed out of the clothes he had worn for the murder. Then he was driven to Heuston Station in Dublin where he was met by Dougie Moran and driven to Connolly Station to catch the Belfast train. He said he booked into a hotel with McCarthy Junior, where they met John Dundon. 'He was asking me did the shit run down his legs and everything and I said yes but it never.' They stayed in Belfast for a couple of days before travelling to England.

Under cross-examination Cahill told defence counsel that he thought he was going to be killed in prison. He said he had been afraid of being killed by the prison officers or by 'politicals'. 'I was in the cell in Portlaoise and they were talking above me. They were saying the murder victim didn't get a chance.' Cahill said he was hearing screaming and voices in his head. He began seeing a psychologist in 2005: 'I was afraid of seeing the psychologist because I was still getting the screaming. Stuff I had done when I was younger, abuse and stuff. I was getting flashbacks. I could see the murder in pictures.' He agreed with counsel for one of the accused that he had told the psychologist he often talked to himself. The hit man said he was very concerned to get the evidence right but got mixed up with another murder that had been planned: 'I was getting everything jumbled up with the screaming and everything.'

During this period he wrote a ninety-day 'diary', covering the years 1997 to 2003. He detailed a wide range of criminal activity carried out by both him and others. He agreed with counsel that in the diary he had named around 100 other people involved in crimes, including drug trafficking, murder and arms offences, and detailed a trip to Germany to buy radio-controlled car bombs. However, Cahill then said that some of this was what the voices had told him to write.

Under further interrogation Cahill then changed his

testimony and said he could not be 'one hundred per cent certain' who asked him to carry out the shooting or who was to pay him €10,000. He said that no one had told him to shoot the night-club security man in the head. He could hear a voice saying 'give him one in the head'. Cahill said he had never fired a handgun before, although he had fired a shot-gun and a blank pistol in robberies.

In an extraordinary series of additional admissions, Cahill claimed that he had abused at least six children in Ireland and the UK, including one nine-month-old baby. He also said he had abused a dog and had fantasies about abusing a horse and having sex with his mother. When defence counsel asked what kind of horse was in his fantasies he replied: 'An ordinary little horse.'

The killer said he heard screaming in his head that sounded like his victims and it only stopped when he told the truth. He maintained that claims that he had previously made about being threatened by John Gilligan and Patrick 'Dutchie' Holland were untrue. The voices in his head had told him to say it. He also revealed that he had refused to leave his cell to meet a consultant psychiatrist from the Central Mental Hospital. The interview was conducted while the psychiatrist was standing in the door of the cell. Cahill was naked, wrapped in a blanket and sitting on a blue mattress on the floor.

As Cahill continued with his bizarre testimony, he changed his story once again. He said that John Dundon was not present when Brian Fitzgerald was pointed out to him or when they visited Brian Fitzgerald's house on a reconnais-sance mission. The crazed hit man could no longer be sure that John Dundon was present, although he could remember his brother Dessie being there. Cahill told Anthony Kelly's defence counsel, Michael O'Higgins SC, that he had been hearing screaming in his head during the three days that he had been on the witness stand: 'I got them when I was in my cell yesterday and when I was coming in the van.' He also said he had heard voices while he was giving evidence: 'Not when I'm speaking. I was getting them the other day. Just speaking and you will be OK.'

As the rigorous cross-examination by counsel for the four accused continued, Cahill said he had been involved in six murder plots, both before and after the shooting. He denied that he had ever fired a handgun before the murder and insisted that Anthony Kelly had shown him how to use it. He denied he had committed two murders in England, as he had told his psychologist in prison.

Michael O'Higgins SC then quoted from a statement made by the hit man's sister, in which she said he had lied about every member of the family. She maintained that he had stolen from them and betrayed them all in various ways. Cahill denied he had exaggerated abuse they had received as children and that he had been known as 'Billy bull-shitter' in his home neighbourhood in Birmingham. He had been expelled from secondary school after throwing a teacher down the stairs. Cahill was sent to a special school after that, but according to his sister he had stolen from there as well.

O'Higgins told Cahill that he was not the changed man he claimed to be. The senior counsel told the court that in December 2005, after coming forward to admit to the murder, Cahill threw boiling water in the face of a prison guard who, Cahill said, had 'looked out for me'. The killer denied that he had added sugar and soap to the water which would make the burning worse because the mixture would stick to the guard's face. Cahill said he never used sugar for this purpose, but 'sometimes I use it on my cornflakes'. The voices in his head had been telling him to attack the guard and he had not mentioned this to the prison governor because he thought he too was trying to kill him.

On 7 November, Mr Justice Peter Charleton directed the jury to acquit John Dundon of murder. He explained that he had come to this decision after Cahill's comment during cross-examination: 'I'm getting like voices and I don't want to convict someone in the wrong.' The judge explained that Cahill had gone on to say that he did not remember Dundon being present when the murdered man was pointed out at his place of work, or on a visit to the victim's house before the murder. Cahill had also said that while Dundon was present at a house where the murder was discussed, he was not present for the conversation.

On 15 November, the jury returned unanimous verdicts finding Anthony Kelly and Dessie Dundon not guilty of the murder. But they found Gary Campion guilty. There had been other evidence which independently corroborated Cahill's account of the actual murder. Alice Fitzgerald was able to identify Campion from his distinctive thick black unibrow. The former Murder Inc. linchpin, who was also awaiting trial for the murder of 'Fat' Frankie Ryan, was jailed for life. John and Dessie Dundon were delighted with the result. They laughed at their former pal before they were returned to their cells: Dessie was already serving a life sentence for the murder of Kieran Keane.

Anthony Kelly walked away from court a free man, arm-in-arm with his partner, Marie Cronin. Alice Fitzgerald was visibly upset as the verdicts were returned. She left the court opting not to give a victim impact statement. The Gardaí and Brian Fitzgerald's family were disappointed with the result of the trial. After such high hopes it had turned out to be a complete anticlimax. The testimony of the hit man, in which he depicted himself as a perverted lunatic, was incapable of convicting anyone. But almost five years to the day of the murder, at least Brian Fitzgerald's two killers, Cahill and Campion, were behind bars serving life.

The detectives involved were philosophical: one of the most dangerous hit men in the city was locked up for life, but they knew their war with Murder Inc. was far from over.

13. The Boy Who Cried

Wayne Dundon was uncharacteristically ebullient. For the first time in his criminal career the gang boss could not contain his sense of glee as he sat in the back of a prison van. The happy hoodlum was laughing and cheering out loud as he was taken from the Court of Criminal Appeal. The court had just reduced his sentence for threatening to kill Ryan Lee from ten years to seven. Dundon would be released from custody over two years earlier than he – or the fearful people of Limerick – had anticipated. The decision could not have come at a better time for the gangland brute. It cast a ray of sunshine over what should otherwise have been a grey day for Murder Inc.

In a bitter twist of irony, the appeal court in Dublin delivered its decision on 13 February 2008. This was the same morning that the trial of Dundon's two lieutenants who were involved in the arms conspiracy opened in Cork Circuit Criminal Court. As one court ruled that Dundon's original sentence was 'unduly severe', another court 255 kilometres away was being told that he wanted a large arsenal of assault rifles and rocket launchers for a 'war in Limerick'. The disparity could not have been more absurd.

The news that the hoodlum would be released in 2010, two years and two months earlier than expected, was a development that was greeted with astonishment by Steve Collins and his family. He told this writer: 'When I read that Dundon's sentence had been reduced I just couldn't believe it. I couldn't understand how I was reading on one page that he was getting three years off his sentence in one court and on the opposite page he's linked to buying rocket launchers in another court. It just didn't make any sense to me.'

Back in Wheatfield Prison Dundon celebrated his victory with his clan members. Five of them had not been so lucky with the appeal court and had no idea when they would see freedom again. When the party was over he began plotting an escalation in the war at home. John Dundon, who was as volatile and psychotic as his brother, would be released in a matter of months and was all set to take the reins. The Dundons had emerged as the undisputed strongmen of the crime family, with their cousins relegated to the level of foot soldiers. Even though the McCarthys were nasty thugs in their own right, the other half of the most infamous gang in Ireland weren't in the same league when it came to extreme violence. Wayne Dundon and his siblings had plenty of 'family business' to sort on the streets of Limerick. Over the next twelve months Murder Inc. would plumb the depths of depravity by claiming four more innocent lives. The world had not yet witnessed their true capacity for horror.

In Limerick the plans for regeneration were given a boost when President Mary McAleese visited the people of Moyross and Southill in January. The horrific gang warfare of recent years had forced the State to realize that the majority of decent people in the estates needed all the moral and physical support they could get. A visit from the Head of State was a symbolic gesture of solidarity. For one day at least there were no shooting incidents. But it did nothing to ameliorate the sense of dread and terror as the urban conflict rumbled on.

On 7 January 2008, the home of Kieran Keane's widow

Sophie was blasted in yet another drive-by shooting. Four days later, Murder Inc. brought their battle on to the streets of the city centre. At 5.40 p.m. on 11 January the city was thronged with Friday evening rush-hour traffic and shoppers. Jonathan Fitzgerald, who was about to be charged with the murder of Noel Crawford in December 2006, was walking on Parnell Street with his uncle Mark Moloney.

A hooded gunman jumped out of a getaway car in the middle of the street and opened fire on the eighteen-year-old, hitting him in the neck and leg. Mark Moloney had a lucky escape – a bullet meant for his nephew cut through his jacket. In full view of pedestrians and motorists the hit man ran after his seriously injured victim, who collapsed in Wickham Street. The would-be killer, believed to be Stephen O'Sullivan from Southill, then fled into the car, which drove off at speed towards Ballinacurra Weston. Fitzgerald was critically injured in the attack and was placed on a life support machine in hospital. He was lucky to survive and recovered well enough to be subsequently charged with Noel Crawford's murder. Three years later he was convicted and sentenced to life.

From their powerbase in Wheatfield Prison, the Dundons issued orders that ensured there would be no relaxation in hostilities. They wanted to stage a spectacular attack in the heart of the Keane/Collopy stronghold. The Murder Inc. men reckoned an attack on their enemy's home turf would have the desired effect of rattling their sense of security. Around 8.45 p.m. on 25 March a taxi drove into the heart of the Keane/Collopy territory of St Mary's Park in the Island Field. The gang's sentries who constantly monitored the only entrance to the estate paid no attention to the taxi as it drove slowly past the unofficial checkpoint. When the car turned into St Ita's Street it picked up speed. A man leaned out of the window with a machine-gun and unleashed a hail of at least fifteen bullets. Six houses were hit in the indiscriminate fusillade.

Gardaí said it was pure luck that no one had been killed or injured. The mobsters had shown no regard for the safety of innocent people, especially the dozens of children who were playing in the street and had to dive for cover. The attack happened in the middle of the Easter Holidays. It was later discovered that the car had been stolen in Rathfarnham, Dublin on St Patrick's Day by Murder Inc.'s associates. It was then stored and fitted with a false taxi plate to get past their enemy's watchmen. The subterfuge was typical of the treacherous Dundons. The taxi ruse was an unconscious nod to the legend of the Trojan horse, used by the Greeks to break the siege of ancient Troy, the same war that had inspired Limerick's motto. Although Wayne Dundon had never been in school long enough to hear the story of Troy.

The terror attack showed that no matter how many armed Garda patrols were operating on the streets, the Piranhas would not stop plotting new attacks. A few weeks earlier another hit man had got more than he bargained for when he walked into a city pub brandishing a sawn-off shotgun, intent on murdering a member of the Keane mob. A group of women jumped on the would-be assassin, whose target was sitting at the bar in a bullet-proof vest. They grabbed his sawn-off shotgun and gave him a severe beating. When Gardaí arrested the man he had to be hospitalized for his injuries before he could be questioned and charged.

Following the latest drive-by shooting, Fine Gael councillor and chairman of the city's joint policing committee, Kevin Kiely, demanded that tougher action be taken against the mobs. Kiely called on the Justice Minister of the day, Brian Lenihan, to consider internment for gang members to finally rid the city of the scourge. He said: 'It has got to the stage where emergency legislation is needed to deal with the matter and I think he has to look at internment so that these people can be locked away.' Local politicians were also demanding that the Government put troops into the estates to patrol the streets. In any other situation such calls would be laughed off as hysterical over-reaction. But after six years of an unrelenting conflict that showed no sign of abating, such demands were no longer so ludicrous. On 27 March, two days after the shooting in St Mary's Park, the Justice Minister and the Garda Commissioner Fachtna Murphy visited the city to be briefed on the ongoing crisis by Chief Superintendent Willie Keane and his senior officers.

Keane's senior detectives gave a detailed history of the feud and described the make-up and mentality of the mobs involved. They profiled the worrying number of young teenagers being recruited and catalogued the attacks, arms seizures and arrests. Limerick Gardaí had become particularly proficient at giving situation reports to Government ministers and their higher authorities. They clarified that one gang in particular was keeping the warfare alive – Murder Inc. Chief Superintendent Keane also revealed details of a major operation, codenamed Platinum, which was to be set up to trace the assets and wealth of the crime gangs.

The minister followed in the President's footsteps to visit Moyross and Southill to see for himself the physical evidence of the despair and desolation the violence was causing. Brian Lenihan later described the city as a 'tinderbox' and vowed to give the Gardaí whatever resources they required. The Commissioner ordered the return of the ERU to back up their hard-pressed colleagues on the ground. But despite the elite squad's presence on the streets, the blood-letting continued.

With time on their hands in prison, the Dundons focused on plotting the next moves in the war. Their dictates normally involved setting people up to be killed or maimed. There was nothing pragmatic or businesslike about their strategy. It was simply to keep fighting until they had wiped out all opposition. It hadn't dawned on the Piranhas, as it had on the Collopys in particular, that the feuding had descended into a monotonous war of attrition that no one was winning. The prisons were filling up with gang members who had been caught with drugs and guns in the implacable counter-offensive from the Gardaí. The 'Dumdum' Dundons were upset about losing the guns and drugs, which were expensive to buy, but they were untroubled by any concerns for the boy soldiers. There was a plentiful supply of expendable young fighters to lay down their freedom and lives for the ignoble cause. John Dundon dismissed them simply as 'fools'. One of the 'fools' was Stephen O'Sullivan, whom the Dundons called 'Stoner' because of his fondness for cocaine. O'Sullivan had visited his rapist father in prison a few weeks earlier to share the good news that he was a made guy in Murder Inc. Stoner had bragged that he was a key member of the gang.

The Dundon/McCarthys were still hell-bent on balancing the books for the murder of their henchman's brother, Noel Crawford. O'Sullivan had already shot and seriously injured the killer, Jonathan Fitzgerald, but that was not enough for the Dundons. They hated Fitzgerald and they wanted to get someone close to him. They deemed his uncle Mark Moloney a legitimate target in their terror campaign. Ger Dundon's partner, April Collins, would later say that she heard Ger and his closest lieutenant, seventeen-year-old Nathan Killeen, discussing a shooting. But such conversations were a recurring theme in the Dundon households and she didn't listen to the details. Nathan Killeen, who was from Southill, was the younger brother of twenty-three-year-old Ciara Killeen, the wife of John Dundon. He was a first cousin of O'Sullivan and despite his youth had amassed over ninety convictions for serious crime. Killeen came from a hopelessly dysfunctional family. His mother and father were alcoholics and drug addicts. When his father died from a drug overdose, his mother was incapable of minding Nathan or his twin brother Gavin. From around the age of eleven he and his brother had been living with John Dundon and Ciara.

Dundon moulded the rudderless young Nathan into a loyal enforcer for the mob. By his seventeenth birthday he was classified in Garda intelligence reports as being 'highly dangerous', with involvement in 'murder, drugs and firearms'. Unfortunately life with the Dundons proved to be too much for his sibling Gavin. Around this time the troubled teenager, who was also a drug addict, hanged himself because he could no longer take the relentless bullying and abuse. It was his only way of escaping from a life of misery shackled to the mob. Neither his sister nor his twin brother Nathan seemed too concerned. One Garda described Nathan Killeen: 'He was a vicious little thug despite his baby-faced appearance and there was nothing he wouldn't do for the Dundons.' Killeen was given the job of organizing the gang's next hit.

On Saturday, 5 April 2008, Limerick was looking forward to the Munster rugby team playing Gloucester at home in the quarter-final of the Heineken Cup. Thousands of fans from the rugby-mad city had travelled to the UK for the big match.

While the team were togging out for the game, O'Sullivan and his accomplice were putting on wigs and women's clothes for a match of their own.

Stoner was always eager to please his bosses. Earlier that morning, at 5.50 a.m. O'Sullivan had gone to the home of Paul Curtin, a convicted criminal who was feuding with the Dundons. He lived in O'Malley Park with his wife, Sylvia, and their three children. O'Sullivan, armed with a 9mm pistol, shouted through the letterbox ordering Curtin to come to the door. When he didn't comply, O'Sullivan smashed the window with a concrete block and went inside. It was later stated in court that Curtin came downstairs and was confronted by O'Sullivan who held a gun to his head and demanded the house key. Curtin managed to run back upstairs and O'Sullivan fired a shot after him, but missed. The enforcer fled and Gardaí were called. An alert was sent to all units to pick Stephen O'Sullivan up on sight. But his apprehension would come too late for one man.

Forty-year-old Mark Moloney lived with his partner of eight years not far from his mother's home at Claughaun Road, Garryowen. The unemployed petty criminal had no reason to look over his shoulder – he had no involvement in any feud. Moloney left his house around 2.45 p.m. to visit his mother and on the way planned to back a horse in the second major sporting event of the day, the Aintree Grand National. At the Garryowen House pub Moloney stopped to talk to a friend who was on a ladder painting the building.

Just then a stolen black two-door Toyota Celica came around the corner at speed. Stoner sat in the passenger seat nursing his 9mm automatic. He was wearing a blonde wig and a pink tracksuit top. Behind the wheel was twenty-year-old James Cronin, who was also wearing a woman's wig and clothing. Cronin's mother Marie was the partner of Anthony Kelly, Murder Inc.'s principal partner-in-crime. The young man had a full driving licence and the Dundons used him to drive them around in their bullet-proof BMW X5s. He was also employed as a car thief and getaway driver.

As the car was driving past Moloney, O'Sullivan sat out on the car window and leaned across the roof with the pistol in his hands. He opened fire on his target, hitting him several times in a hail of fifteen bullets. As Moloney turned to take cover behind a van the fatal shot hit him in the back and he collapsed to the ground dead. In less than two seconds the hit was over. The killers drove off at high speed. They had been instructed to burn the getaway car outside the city at Drombanna, the spot where Kieran Keane had been executed five long, bloody years earlier. It was a deliberate gesture to remind the Dundon/McCarthys' enemies that the war was not over.

After the car was dumped, Stoner was brought back to John Dundon's house on Hyde Road. The young killer was living in a caravan at the back of the house. Cronin had gone to another house to 'clean up'. After the murder James Cronin was overcome with remorse and broke down crying when he realized what he had just done. He realized suddenly that he wasn't a stone-cold killer. And that was a fatal weakness in the eyes of his malevolent bosses.

James Cronin's fate was sealed despite his apparent impeccable gangland credentials. Underworld sources, including former members of Murder Inc., who were interviewed in the research for this book expressed their shock and revulsion at the cold-blooded brutality that was perpetrated against the young man. Their chilling accounts of what happened revealed the extremes that gangland's most dangerous psychopaths were prepared to go to to protect themselves.

The same underworld sources, some of whom were close to April Collins, revealed how she recalled that Ciara Killeen had a bath ready for Stoner when he returned. John Dundon's wife was a central player in the gang and just as ruthless as any of the men. She supervised the drug trade and the collection of money. She also drove gang members, most of whom were disqualified from driving. During a search of her house Gardaí found a dealers' list that showed she was owed almost €100,000. Killeen had also been arrested for carrying a large consignment of heroin in 2001, but got off when she claimed the drugs belonged to her father who had died from a heroin overdose. Despite the fact that, like April Collins, she regularly suffered severe beatings from her husband, Ciara Killeen was staunchly loyal to him and the mob.

As O'Sullivan took a bath to clean off any forensic evidence, Ciara Killeen burned his clothes. Then she gave the killer clothes belonging to her brother and runners which were too small for him. Killeen was laughing admiringly at the thug and told him he was 'stone mad'. Around 5 p.m. April Collins and Killeen got into her car to drive O'Sullivan out of the city. After a short distance they were surrounded by armed Gardaí and O'Sullivan was arrested in connection with the gun incident earlier that morning in Southill.

Afterwards Killeen phoned John Dundon in prison and told him what happened. He was worried that Stoner might talk, but his partner reassured him that he wouldn't. Around the same time, Ger Dundon got a call from Wayne which was witnessed by April Collins. She would later reveal: 'I would hear both sides of the conversation as they are so loud. The Dundons all talk like travellers and talk loud. I can understand them after being around them so long. The call was about James Cronin.'

Ger told his brother that James was crying over the murder. He asked Wayne if he could trust him. 'Wayne said, "I'll ask someone and ring you back." Wayne rang back in ten minutes and said, "Don't trust him . . . do what you have to."' Ger Dundon curtly responded 'all right' and threw away the phone. James Cronin's fate had been decided. Murder Inc. had adopted a zero-tolerance approach – it was part of their new survival strategy. They had become paranoid about leaving 'loose ends'. Six of their most important members were serving life because they had been 'sloppy'. Gang members who had shown weakness and talked in the past had caused too much unnecessary aggravation. It didn't matter either that Cronin was close to Anthony Kelly. He would understand it was just business.

April Collins described how the atmosphere was tense the next day. She knew something was happening but didn't know what. The evening after the Moloney murder, April Collins heard Ger Dundon giving instructions to Nathan Killeen. Killeen was then driven away by his sister to meet James Cronin. The Murder Inc. lieutenant went with Cronin to Caledonian Park to bury firearms. A few hours later Nathan Killeen returned to Dundon's house with a shovel. He was laughing and announced to his boss, 'that's done'.

Ciara Killeen, for the second time in two days, took a killer's clothes and burned them. His runners were covered in blood and Ciara said, 'Oh my God, look at all the blood on your shoes; we'll have to burn them.' But Nathan didn't want to; they were new runners. His sister insisted. Ger asked his associate again: 'Is that done?' Killeen replied: 'Ya that job is done.' April Collins told how Nathan, Ciara and Ger were laughing and joking together. She wasn't told what happened because she wasn't trusted. Over the following days she wondered why she hadn't seen James Cronin who was always around the house. She didn't have long to wait to find out.

Gardaí had been questioning Stephen O'Sullivan about the incident at the house in Southill and the murder of Mark Moloney. Stoner wasn't as hard as he liked to portray and admitted his role in the two incidents. He also gave the Gardaí the location where the murder weapon might be hidden in Caledonian Park. Less than forty-eight hours after the murder, on 7 April, Gardaí began searching the waste ground and discovered the body of James Cronin in a shallow grave. He had been clinically executed with a single shot in the back of the head and dumped into the hole he had dug himself on the pretence of burying guns. He was partially covered in dirt. Two firearms and some ammunition were also found. The heartless killing showed that no one was exempt from the mob's malevolence.

When news broke that Cronin's body had been found, Ger Dundon and Nathan Killeen began to panic. It was obvious that Stoner had talked and it was likely that he might implicate them in the Moloney murder. The Piranhas were also concerned that the rapid recovery of Cronin's body would point the finger at them. The discovery of the body had also alerted Anthony Kelly to the murder, and he was said to be furious. The gangsters were worried it might cause further difficulties for them. Ger Dundon told his partner that he was going abroad for a while but would not say where. Ciara gave them a bag of cash to keep them going as the thugs went into hiding.

The two hoodlums travelled to England where Ciara Killeen and April Collins met them some days later in a safe house in London. Collins later told her associates and friends how Nathan Killeen described Cronin's murder in chilling and callous detail. Laughing, he said Cronin was crying before he shot him. According to Collins, Killeen said that he 'had to get rid of him' because 'he couldn't be trusted'. Dundon and Killeen discussed how they were 'afraid he'd talk'.

Killeen began imitating his victim, showing how Cronin begged for mercy and pleaded 'please don't'. The young killer went down on his knees to show the position of Cronin just before he killed him. Cronin was on his knees and crying when Nathan Killeen shot him in the head. Killeen's sister and Ger Dundon were laughing: 'He said he killed him down the field. He [Cronin] started to run; he hit James with the shovel and then shot him.' They knew by Collins's reaction that she was upset and they were wary of her, she later explained. For good measure Dundon gave her a beating and there was no more discussion about the matter.

Gardaí were fearful that Anthony Kelly might go to war with his former partners over the murder of his girlfriend's son. Instead he cut his ties with the mob and left Ireland. He split up with Marie Cronin, who never recovered from the loss of her only child. In 2012 she took her own life. The day after her son's body was discovered, Stephen O'Sullivan was formally charged with the murder of Mark Moloney. Ten detectives, accompanied by Chief Superintendent Willie Keane, were in the courthouse. Detective Garda David Bourke of Roxboro Road Garda Station gave evidence of charging the hit man with the murder. The teenage killer replied: 'Not guilty, I didn't intend to kill anyone.' He was remanded in custody. O'Sullivan had to be segregated in solitary confinement for his own safety. He had given cops information about where the guns were hidden and there was a risk that he might turn State witness against the mobsters. Murder Inc. sent the word out that they wanted him dead. Stoner, who had wanted to impress his bosses, spent over three years in solitary before pleading guilty to manslaughter in 2010. He never talked and was jailed for fifteen years.

The two murders again shone the national spotlight on Limerick for all the wrong reasons. John Devane, a local solicitor who defended gangland figures in the courts, offered to mediate between the gangs. Justice Minister Lenihan rejected his offer, commenting: 'We're dealing with a group of people whose range of depravity is very deep indeed.' Lenihan said the authorities would continue to directly confront those responsible. 'One of the great difficulties with mediation is that you recognize the legitimacy of these people and I don't believe they should have any legitimacy,' he declared. 'I think we have to engage in a relentless fight against them.' The Defence Minister Willie O'Dea, who had supervised an earlier 'truce' between Brian Collopy and Wayne Dundon, revealed that he refused a request to mediate because he said it was pointless. He believed it was time that the gangs were 'taken on'.

At the funeral for James Cronin, Fr John Dunworth compared the current travails of the ancient city with the threats of the past. 'Limerick is one of Ireland's oldest cities, dating back over a thousand years,' he said. 'It used to be a walled-in city to protect its citizens. Parts of the city are called after the gates through the old walls: Watergate, Thomondgate; the ruins of those walls are still seen today. In ancient times, the walls were manned by watchmen and if an enemy approached, they shouted "enemy approaching" to alert its citizens. Sadly today, the trouble lies within the city, but the citizens still need to be on the alert, danger is around us.' Murder Inc. member Jimmy Collins couldn't have agreed more.

On the afternoon of 23 April 2008, Jimmy Collins, April Collins's father, was standing outside his home on Hyde Avenue when Liam Keane and another associate drove by in a stolen car. The hate-filled thug had been released from prison five days earlier after serving a ten-month stretch for stealing and crashing Philip Collopy's A4 Audi car. Christy Keane's son had become a heroin addict and was spiralling out of control. He opened fire on Collins with an automatic pistol, firing a total of fourteen shots at Collins, who was luckily wearing his body armour, hitting him twice in the legs. Some months later the Murder Inc. enforcer laughed at his would-be assassins.

'It was three in the afternoon and I was standing at my door when I got sprayed by a Scorpion machine-gun. What saved my life was the fuckin' idiot didn't know how to use it,' the wife beater scoffed. 'He was only a young fella, couldn't have been more than fifteen. They pumped him full of heroin and sent him down here to do a man's job. They phoned me an hour after they shot me, when I was in the hospital, to say I'd been lucky, "We'll get you sooner or later." It's a war now and the streets are going to see blood pour,' Collins warned.

The gangster had been wrong when he described the weapon as a machine-gun. The Glock automatic used in the attempt on his life was found two weeks later when the ERU arrested Liam Keane and his accomplice Greg Crawford. The thugs were forced off the road by the elite cops at 1.45 a.m. on 4 May in Corbally, on the edge of the city. Gardaí had received intelligence that they were on their way to carry out another shooting. The car they were driving, a silver Mazda RX 80, had been stolen on 19 April from a house in Portmarnock, County Dublin. A Porsche was also taken from the same house. Detectives found the weapon in the footwell of the car. It was cocked and ready to fire. Keane was wearing latex gloves and Crawford had woollen gloves on. Ballistics tests confirmed it was the same weapon used to shoot Jimmy Collins. When he was questioned, Keane claimed he bought the Mazda for €500 in Limerick to 'pull birds' with and found the gun in a field. When asked why the mobs hated each other so much he shrugged: 'That's life; that's the way it goes.'

Four days later, after months of secret planning, Operation Platinum was launched, targeting the criminal assets of the city's mobs. The Limerick Garda division was the first to set up an Assets Profiling Office outside the Criminal Assets Bureau in Dublin. It was staffed by two local experienced officers and the profilers worked closely with their CAB colleagues. Gardaí began kicking in doors at dawn on 8 May 2008 in the biggest search operation ever seen in Limerick. It was the first time criminals across the city realized that the police had been focusing on their ill-gotten gains.

CAB officers, backed up by more than 250 Gardaí drawn from Limerick, Cork and Kerry, raided 120 homes across the city. The offices of solicitors and accountants were searched in Dublin and Limerick. Gardaí seized over €250,000 in cash, €200,000 worth of cocaine and heroin and a number of firearms. Three vehicles, two jeeps and a high-powered car, valued at €200,000, were seized from the Keane/Collopy mob. Twenty homes were also sequestered by the CAB.

On the other side of town the CAB seized the two armoured four-litre BMW X5 jeeps registered in the names of John and Wayne Dundon. The jeeps, valued at over €150,000, had been imported from Germany. The vehicles had been modified with bullet-proof glass an inch thick and armour plating that could withstand rounds from high-powered assault rifles. They were also built to absorb an under-car explosion. The vehicles came equipped with a public address system, which the mob used to taunt rival criminals inside the walls of Limerick Prison. Ironically the Dundons' treasured battle-buses were soon redeployed for a much more useful role when the ERU confiscated them to use in their operations against the gun gangs.

Operation Platinum froze bank and credit union accounts belonging to members of Murder Inc. They even confiscated prize bonds bought with one gang member's drug money. The search operation continued for a number of days and turned Limerick's gangland upside down. The Dundons and their henchmen believed that it was a response to the double murders in April. The sheer scale of the offensive left both sides stunned and running for cover. The authorities had dramatically escalated their efforts to smash the underworld's grip on the city. As a result the two sides began talking peace again – in a forlorn bid to get the cops off their backs.

Shortly after Operation Platinum exploded onto the streets, the gangsters announced to the local media that a truce had been agreed that this time apparently included the Keanes. It was claimed that through intermediaries Christy Keane and Wayne Dundon had been involved in 'negotiations' from their prison cells. While the ordinary citizens greeted the sudden declaration of peace with guarded optimism, the Gardaí were not so impressed. 'The Keanes and Collopys realized that the feuding was bad for business and would stick to an agreement. But the Dundons were the most devious creatures you could encounter and as sure as night follows day they would try and kill the people they claimed to be at peace with ... they just couldn't help themselves,' a local detective said, explaining his well-founded cynicism. He was soon proved right.

Garda management in Limerick knew that talk of peace among the criminal gangs in the city was nothing more than another attempt to pervert the course of justice. The senior officers had witnessed first-hand the immeasurable damage caused by Mikey Kelly's peace process in 2001. The chaos of the past seven years was due in no small part to the dead gangster's ploys to undermine the rule of law. There was a determination on all sides of the forces of law and order that that would never happen again in Limerick. In the end the only way to deal with organized crime was through the enforcement of the criminal law and the incarceration of the bad guys. No amount of fluffy libertarian 'love the criminal, not the crime' philosophy would ameliorate the Limerick mafia.

On 4 July, the youngest Dundon brother was arrested by Gardaí as he was about to board a flight to Amsterdam at Cork Airport. Ger Dundon was using a false passport in the name of Terence Ruth. He had returned from Spain, where he had spent three months with members of 'Fat' Freddie Thompson's gang. He claimed that he needed the forgery because his life was still in danger. Dundon was charged with three counts relating to the possession of a false passport and released pending a court hearing.

On 9 July Ger was back before Limerick District Court, where he was jailed for ten months for over thirty motoring offences. His solicitor John Devane told the court that his client was living under threat. 'He is aware there is a €1 million contract on his head because of who his family are. He cannot walk the streets of Limerick city or any other city in the country. He has been given motor vehicles by his family for his own protection and has a bullet-proof BMW,' said Devane.

On 31 July 2008 John Dundon was released from Wheatfield Prison after serving just over three-and-a-half years for making death threats against Owen Treacy. Just before his release a bullet-proof vest was delivered to the prison so that he could wear it from the moment he stepped outside. There was a wild homecoming party for the thug as Gardaí kept him under close observation. A few days later he caught a flight and went on a holiday with his wife.

On 27 August, Ger Dundon was jailed for nine months after pleading guilty to possessing a false passport. His defence barrister told Cork District Court that his client's use of the forgery was 'motivated by fear for his life'. There were some wry smiles in the courtroom as the barrister declared: 'While growing up in Limerick, his family became embroiled in a dispute with another family. As a result he has received very little education and is unable to read or write . . . he has received numerous threats against his life and I understand that's why he got the false passport and wanted to get out of the country for a few days.'

In pleading for leniency for the vicious thug the barrister said Ger Dundon's main concerns were his family and, without a hint of irony, said he wanted to go back to school. 'He is currently unemployed and I believe that the reason for this is the constant threats to his life,' the counsel added. In the meantime he was granted bail when he appealed the severity of both sentences to the Circuit Criminal Court.

That same month the Garda National Drug Unit scored another victory when the gang's mentor, Sean 'Cowboy' Hanley, was jailed for ten years for possession of a large consignment of amphetamines.

RIGHT: Dessie and John Dundon pose with a fellow prisoner whom they had tortured and beaten for fun

BELOW: Aerial photograph of dereliction in the Moyross estate

LEFT: Ger Dundon and his partner April Collins

BELOW: Family – April Collins with Ger and Wayne Dundon at home

The Molls – April Collins and Ciara Killeen

Nathan Killeen with his sister Ciara

Christopher McCarthy and Wayne Dundon

LEFT: Wayne Dundon arrives home from holidays

BELOW: Wayne Dundon and his wife at Dublin Airport in March 2010

Wayne Dundon dresses to go out

Looking after family pets

Strolling thugs – Wayne and Ger Dundon on the street, 2010

LEFT: Proud dad Wayne Dundon on his daughter's First Holy Communion Day

BELOW: Dundon escorts his daughter's Cinderella Carriage

Pictures show Wayne Dundon with his family, including his father Kenneth and wife Anne, on the day of his daughter's First Holy Communion

ABOVE: Murder Inc. member Christopher McCarthy stopped by a member of the 'Dublin Squad'

RIGHT: Masked member of the special team from the Garda National Support Services

The so-called 'Dublin Squad', which was sent to Limerick to take on Murder Inc.

Wayne Dundon is stopped and searched for first time by the 'Dublin Squad'

LEFT: Nathan Killeen being stopped and searched by the special Garda unit

BELOW LEFT: Cops stop and search Annabel Dundon on a city street

BELOW RIGHT: Ger Dundon searched by Gardaí while his partner April Collins looks on

ABOVE: Chief Supt Dave Sheehan with the new Regional Support Unit (RSU)

The other pictures show members of the RSU taking part in various raids and arrest operations against Murder Inc. members in Limerick

Ger Dundon is arrested for threats to businessman Mark Heffernan

Hit man Barry Doyle is arrested for the murder of rugby player Shane Geoghegan

The RSU breaking in the front door of Ger Dundon's home before his arrest

LEFT: Detectives searching waste ground in Ballinacurra Weston

RIGHT: Home of Wayne Dundon with an RSU patrol parked outside

Members of the 'Dublin Squad' searching for firearms in a derelict housing estate

Dublin officers stop Annabel Dundon in her car

LEFT: Former home of Ger Dundon and April Collins, which was trashed after she gave evidence against the mob

BELOW LEFT: NSS officers arresting a suspected gunman

BELOW RIGHT: Armed Gardaí on the streets of Limerick

ABOVE: March for Peace – Steve Collins and his wife Carmel lead over 5,000 through the streets of Limerick to protest against the gun gangs. Also in the picture are Steve Collins Junior, Cllr Kevin Kiely (left) and Mayor John Gilligan (right)

LEFT: Steve addresses the crowd

RIGHT: Steve at the grave of his murdered son, Roy

ABOVE: Steve Collins and members of his family saying goodbye when they were forced to leave Ireland under a witness relocation programme

RIGHT: Steve and Carmel Collins with the author before their departure

BELOW: Steve behind the counter of the Steering Wheel Bar

LEFT: Det. Supt Jim Browne and Chief Supt Dave Sheehan and their investigation team following the conviction of Wayne Dundon and Nathan Killeen for Roy Collins's murder in July 2014

RIGHT: Justice – Steve Collins with his wife and family leaving the Special Criminal Court after the verdict in July 2014

BELOW: The Collins family on the steps of the Special Criminal Court in Dublin after the Murder Inc. godfathers were jailed for life

The relentless police operations forced the gangs to observe a fragile peace. As a direct consequence Limerick experienced the first real lull in hostilities after seven long years of conflagration. Statistics demonstrated how the city's force of over 600 Gardaí had also made their mark on the law enforcement world. They enjoyed the top success rate for the investigation of serious crime in Ireland – and the highest clean-up rate of any police force in Western Europe. This was clearly evident in the number of shootings, which dropped dramatically from 103 in 2007 to 43 in 2008. In the same year Gardaí also seized 56 firearms. Between 2000 and 2009 there were 556 shootings recorded in the city compared to just 51 in Cork, a city at least three times the size of Limerick.

In the four-year period between 2005 and 2009 Limerick accounted for a quarter of all convictions for firearms offences in Ireland's three largest cities. In the ancient city's Circuit Criminal Court there were 162 convictions for fire-arms offences, compared to 447 in Dublin and 43 in Cork. When these convictions were analysed on a per capita basis per 10,000 of population, firearms convictions in Limerick amounted to 9.24 per capita, compared to 3.98 in Dublin. In the same timeframe there were twenty-eight homicides recorded, including gangland murders, of which twenty-three had been solved and convictions secured.

During 2008 the local drug units in the city seized €4 million worth of drugs, representing a 23 per cent increase on 2007. In 2001 there were fifty-six criminal proceedings involving drug dealers in Limerick. By 2007 the figure had climbed to 194 cases and in 2008 it reached a record 276. The daunting workload meant that resources were permanently stretched to the limit. But in September 2008 a new squad arrived on the streets which dramatically bolstered the powers of the local force in their war on the gangs. The Regional Support Unit (RSU) was about to give the mobs a major shock.

The idea of regionalized Specialist Weapons and Tactics (SWAT) teams had first been mooted by the Garda Síochána Inspectorate in response to the increasing use of firearms by organized crime gangs across the country. The ERU, which had been deployed to Limerick on a semi-permanent basis over the years, was the only specialist SWAT unit in the country. But it was Dublin-based and could not remain in Limerick indefinitely as there were huge demands on the unit to tackle crime gangs and terrorists throughout Ireland.

The Inspectorate's chief, Kathleen O'Toole, recommended that the Gardaí urgently required locally based specialist units to respond to emergencies. She wrote in a report to Government in 2007: 'The Inspectorate recommends that a second-tier local response be established. A cadre of police officers, trained to a greater level of proficiency in lethal, less lethal and tactical team operations, could be highly effective during this crucial period, particularly in more remote areas.'

On 3 September 2008 the RSU officially began operating in Limerick. A similar unit was also established in Cork. It was decided to deploy the SWAT teams on a trial basis, with a view to establishing similar units in all the other Garda regions outside Dublin. Each RSU consisted of two sergeants and ten Gardaí who were handpicked from the local divisions. They underwent a rigorous training programme in firearms and tactics, supervised by ERU and military instructors. The units wore combat-style uniforms with ballistic vests and helmets. They were armed with the same sophisticated lethal and non-lethal weapons used by the ERU. The arsenal included Heckler and Koch MP7 machineguns, Sig automatic pistols and non-lethal Taser guns to stun armed and dangerous suspects.

Each RSU was equipped with two custom-built highpowered, armour-plated Volvo XC 70 station-wagons to carry their weapons and equipment. The squad cars were deliberately decked out in bright insignias with banks of flashing lights to ensure maximum visibility. When they first appeared on the streets of Limerick the criminals didn't know what to make of them. But they would soon find out.

The new SWAT teams would quickly prove to be an invaluable physical and psychological weapon in the war against the gangs. The criminals had more respect for heavily armed blunt force. The first thugs targeted by the RSU were the Dundon/McCarthys, especially John and Ger Dundon. As one local Garda told this author, the squad was sent out with one mission: 'to break their balls, make them look small and show the public that these people were no longer untouchable'. A lot of local Gardaí who had tried to take on the Dundons and their henchmen had been followed to their homes and subjected to intimidation – all that was about to change.

The specialist officers took on the role of getting in the faces of the most dangerous gangsters on the streets. The cops wore balaclavas and baseball hats to protect their identities. One Garda close to the unit recalled their first confrontation with the Dundons. 'When the RSU arrived John and Ger were running riot around the place and the first encounter with them came very soon after that. John Dundon was trying to be a hard man one day so he was pulled over on a busy street and ordered at gun point to lie spread-eagled on the ground while he was searched in full view of the public. Then Ger got the same treatment just so as everyone understood that the game had changed,' the officer said, smiling at the memory.

'The unit patrolled the areas where they lived and did checkpoints at all hours of the day and night. The gangsters and their friends were stopped on the streets and searched at gunpoint. It made these feared hard men look small in the eyes of the younger kids who looked up to them. For the first time the public in the worst-affected areas of this city could see that there was a new force in play that would put manners on these boys and not stand back. The boys in the unit got a lot of people coming up and wishing them well and thanking them for being there. I think the introduction of the RSU was a very important psychological victory for the Gardaí and the decent people,' the officer continued.

'From the time the RSU was established they were the first through the doors of the gang members' houses during search and arrest operations. All searches were dynamic breach entry in full ballistic protective gear, which normally meant taking the jambs off the door and going in hard. We took no chances and all operations were done on the assumption that they would be met by armed and dangerous criminals. The gangs didn't know what to make of the unit and it was freaking them out.

'They thought the guys were from Dublin and they would complain bitterly to other Gardaí that they weren't getting fair play. The funny thing was that the likes of the Dundons never made any official complaints. After a while they all got the message and whenever we arrived through the door or pulled them over, they would put their hands up and lie down on the ground without a quibble,' the officer added.

The arrival of the RSU also uncovered some secrets which were rather embarrassing for some of Murder Inc.'s most macho men. In one raid they found Ger Dundon and Nathan Killeen in a rather compromising position. In an upstairs bedroom of a safe house they found the two hard men semi-naked and in bed with an eighteen-year-old foot soldier. The ardour of Dundon and his friends, who were all wanted for questioning, was suddenly stifled when they were tasered by the cops who feared they might be going for weapons. Ger Dundon was afraid that news might leak out about his ambiguous sexual appetites.

But just as it seemed like the tide was turning on Murder Inc., the gang hatched another murder conspiracy which would have lasting repercussions. It began with a short, handwritten note Wayne Dundon sent from prison.

14. The Contract

The obscure note was crudely encrypted to render it meaningless to all – except its intended recipient. The combination of squiggly letters and figures was scrawled in pen on a small, crumpled piece of paper. To the uninformed eye it was no more than an absent-minded doodle, scribbled in a moment of boredom. It read:

75 Pitchfork 75 SC blk jp pref morn.

This deceptively innocuous permutation of twenty-eight characters carried a dark message. It was the catalyst for an unprecedented chain of tragic events that resulted in the murders of two innocent men. But it would also have unexpected, drastic consequences for its brutal author. The murders created a reluctant hero, who in turn galvanized the State into a final showdown with Ireland's most pernicious gang. Ultimately, this coded prison message heralded the beginning of the end for Murder Inc.

The note was sent from prison by Wayne Dundon in October 2008. The gang boss wasn't prepared to chance using his mobile phone in case it was bugged by the police. They had already scuppered some of his more ambitious plans, including arming his mob for an all-out war. And this was too important to screw-up. The reference to '75 Pitchfork' was code for a contract worth €75,000. Dundon was offering the fee for the murder of the Dundon/McCarthy's most hated foe, Johnny McNamara, nicknamed 'Pitchfork' after Larry McCarthy Junior had stabbed him with one nine years earlier. McNamara had testified in court against the Murder Inc. boss and that would never be forgiven or forgotten. The drug dealer, a close associate of the Keane/Collopy mob, was top of the Piranhas' list for eradication. But the rest of the note contained a much more sinister message.

The reference to '75 SC blk jp pref morn' detailed another €75,000 contract. It was on offer for whoever murdered businessman Steve Collins. Dundon's message informed his lackeys that Steve drove a black jeep and the best time to hit him was in the morning, when he would most likely be without police protection. It was a measure of Wayne Dundon's resolve that the notorious miser was prepared to invest €150,000 to kill the two men. The coded message came to light when an associate of the gang tipped off Steve that his life was in danger. The anonymous gangster wanted no part in such an atrocity.

'I couldn't believe it and it was like a bolt out of the blue when I was handed that note,' Steve told this writer. 'We had been trying to get our lives back on some sort of track and we had put Dundon out of our minds. I had already lost two businesses over him and we were facing bankruptcy. I knew that we would have to look over our shoulders for standing up to this animal but realizing that he was now trying to have me murdered was terrifying.' When Steve was given the note he contacted the Gardaí who took the coded message seriously.

Local detectives were not surprised that the mob wanted to whack McNamara. He had previously been stabbed with a pitchfork, seriously assaulted and lost an eye in a shooting incident. In 2006 he had narrowly escaped when Murder Inc.

opened fire on him with a machine-gun as he walked into his house in Clonmore, Kilteragh. But the violent gangster wasn't exactly innocent. He had been responsible for several retaliatory gun and arson attacks on his enemies. And he was involved in the ambush that had led to the murder of Aidan Kelly a few years earlier. Targeting Steve Collins was a different proposition. Detectives were divided as to whether Dundon had the capacity to have an innocent businessman murdered. However, those most familiar with the Dundon mindset had no doubts.

Behind-the-scenes feverish efforts were made by the police, using their network of informants and the Crime and Security Branch in Dublin, to get to the bottom of the plot and stop it. Armed Gardaí were assigned to escort Steve to and from his work in his last remaining pub, the Steering Wheel in Roxboro. McNamara was also informed by the Gardaí that his life was in danger – again. Pitchfork, who since the last gun attack had been spending most of his time in his Spanish villa, laughed at the officers when they offered him personal security advice. After so many attempts on his life, he joked that he was an expert on such matters.

The plot to murder both men bore testimony to the long, unforgiving memories and the blind, irrational hatred at the core of the Dundon psyche. Despite the continuing talk of peace, the Piranhas were hell-bent on revenge and murder. There was no place in the world for their enemies; no matter how long it took to eviscerate them. Peace merely meant delaying the inevitable. In 2005 Wayne Dundon had vowed to kill Steve Collins when he was in a cell with his henchman Gareth Collins (no relation). And promises to kill were the only ones he ever kept. What happened next would put the gang on a par with a terrorist organization. It gave a chilling insight into the chaotic and pernicious world of Murder Inc.

The police and the ordinary citizens weren't the only people who had been dismayed to see the return of the unpredictable and volatile John Dundon in the summer of 2008. When Dundon came out of prison he took control of the gang and began throwing his weight around. And the first people to incur his wrath were his own gang members, including the McCarthys, who lived in constant fear of him and his brothers. They were regularly threatened, beaten and bullied by the evil monsters. April Collins, Ger's partner, described them to Gardaí: 'The Dundons are unbelievable people, they're monsters. They're very violent people. They terrorize everyone into doing things for them; people are frightened to say no in case they'd be killed.'

Her sister Lisa Collins, the partner of gang member Christopher McCarthy, Dundon's first cousin, also revealed what life was like in the mob: 'Ye have no idea what the Dundons are like – they are vicious and evil. We were just always afraid of them like, they were savages. Ye really have no idea what it was like being around them.' It was against this backdrop of fear and intimidation that John Dundon organized the murder of Pitchfork McNamara.

'John Dundon was always mouthing off, roaring and screaming at people and making threats,' recalled Lisa Collins. 'He was always saying that Pitchfork had to get it and "We have to do him . . . we're goin' to kill the cunt."' Dundon ordered her boyfriend Christopher McCarthy to steal a getaway car for the job. He threatened to kill his cousin if he didn't do it. At that stage robbing a car was not as easy as it sounded. By October the gang was under intense pressure from the Gardaí, especially the newly formed RSU. But that was no excuse for the deranged Dundon. Lisa Collins gave an extraordinary insight into John Dundon's unique style of persuasion.

'I remember one evening he came in and said to us, "Ye better get me a fuckin' car or I'll slap you around the place." He was coming over a few times a day telling us to get a car,' she told Gardaí in 2011. 'We were terrified of him. I know Christopher was his cousin but he was afraid of him too. He said [to Christopher] in front of me one night, "If you don't get me a fuckin' car I'll kill her." When he left me and Christopher were sitting down and I said, "What the fuck are we goin' to do?" Christopher was saying, "We'll just have to do it or he'll kill one of us."'

On 18 October 2008, McCarthy, Lisa Collins and another local car thief went looking for a getaway car. As they were driving through the countryside they spotted a Renault Espace seven-seat people-carrier parked along the road. The owner had just popped into a neighbour's house and left the keys in the ignition. The car thief jumped in and drove it off back towards Limerick.

The thieves parked the car at the Ballycummin Village apartments in Raheen, situated a half mile from McNamara's home, and reported back to Dundon. 'John just said, "Grand." A few days later he ordered us to drive him out to inspect the car. He didn't say much; he was just happy to have the car,' said Collins. Two days later Dundon instructed his cousin to show the getaway car to the hit man assigned to kill McNamara, twenty-three-year-old Dublin man Barry Doyle.

Doyle had become close to the Dundons through his brother Paddy, a killer for the 'Fat' Freddie Thompson gang in Dublin. Ger Dundon and April Collins had lived next door to the Doyle brothers on Spain's Costa del Sol for three months earlier in the year. Dundon was regularly beating his girlfriend there and wouldn't allow her to return to Ireland. April later told detectives that despite his fearsome reputation as a contract killer, Paddy Doyle was 'a real gent' who was had stood up for her and tried to stop Ger Dundon's violence. Her mother eventually sent her the fare and she escaped back to Ireland. However, the couple got back together when Ger returned. April lived in the midst of the Dundon/McCarthy clan and there was no way of getting away from him. She had also discovered she was pregnant with their second child.

Marbella was the European playground of international organized crime gangs including the Irish mobs. The British underworld dubbed it the 'Costa del Crime' – the little bit of Spain that fell off the back of a truck. While Dundon was staying there in February 2008, Paddy Doyle was executed in the Spanish resort. A hit team believed to be from an Eastern European gang ambushed Doyle while he was a passenger in an X5 jeep driven by his close pal, convicted armed robber Gary Hutch, aged twenty-seven – a nephew of veteran crime boss Gerry 'the Monk' Hutch.

The attackers used a machine pistol and hit Doyle several times. When he tried to make a run for it he was finished off with two bullets in the back of the head. Post-mortem results showed he had been hit fifteen times. The murder was well planned and carried out with military precision. The hit men had even moved CCTV cameras in the area before the ambush so that they wouldn't capture the action. The killing was believed to be in retaliation for Doyle's assassination of an English gangster in a contract hit in Amsterdam a year earlier. Doyle had murdered the wrong man. His ex-pat Irish bosses were suspected of also being involved in the plot because the killer was unpredictable and dangerous. After the murder Barry Doyle moved back to live with the Dundons in Limerick.

Doyle and his brother came from a respected family of street traders in Dublin's north inner-city. While Paddy was a dangerous criminal from his early teens, his younger sibling completed his Leaving Certificate. Barry worked for four years as a bricklayer and also played Gaelic football. But his brother pulled him into the dark world of organized crime, and when Paddy was murdered it completed his brother's transition to a fully-fledged gangster and killer for hire. Lisa and April Collins claimed that Barry Doyle, a heavy drinker, was impressionable and easily manipulated by the Dundons. They somehow convinced 'Doyler' that Johnny McNamara had helped organize his brother's demise. The Collins sisters also said Barry was frightened of Murder Inc.

On 29 October John Dundon contacted Philip Collopy to arrange a meet. Even though the Dundon/McCarthys and the Collopys had agreed another peace deal, the two gangland killers met in a public place – Cruises Street. Collopy and his brother Kieran met Dundon and Barry Doyle, and the four walked down the pedestrianized street in the city's shopping district. As they strolled among the shoppers they discussed peace and death. Dundon told the Collopys that before both sides could consider a lasting truce, he wanted to murder Johnny McNamara, who had just returned to the city from Spain with his partner. He said 'Doyler' was his hit man from Dublin. The maniac was effectively asking for the Collopys' blessing. Dundon said Doyle needed a description of the intended victim as he hadn't seen Pitchfork for a number of years. He particularly wanted to know if McNamara still had a 'smig', a goatee beard. Philip Collopy told him what he knew and the meeting ended. Immediately afterwards Collopy rang his associate, warning him that Dundon was plotting to kill him. He gave McNamara an ex-RUC-issue bullet-proof vest.

As the Dundons were busy plotting another murder there was a sense of renewed optimism in the city. The magnificent new Thomond Park rugby stadium dominated the skyline and had become the symbol of that new hope. On 18 November it would be officially opened with an historic match between Munster and the New Zealand All Blacks. There was much anticipation as Munster hoped to repeat its legendary victory over the formidable Kiwis of thirty years before. It would be a day for celebration. But unfortunately the mob would cast their long, dark shadow over the event.

On 7 November, there was a meeting in the sitting-room of John Dundon's home on Hyde Road. His partner Ciara Killeen and her brother Nathan were there. Barry Doyle, Ger Dundon, April Collins and another gang member, Liam 'Lika' Casey, were also present. John issued orders to Doyle that he was to kill McNamara the following day. He gave the hit man a description of his target, emphasizing that he had a beard. Dundon said he had 'everything sorted'. Nathan Killeen challenged him saying, 'You've nothing sorted.' Dundon shouted: 'I've everything sorted; the gun and the car are there. Everything is there; it just needs to be done.' That night, Ger Dundon told April Collins to book them into the Strand Hotel in the city centre with their three-year-old child. Two weeks earlier she had given birth to a second son, who was being minded by her mother, Alice. Ger Dundon wanted an alibi for what was to come.

On Saturday, 8 November, cold winds and heavy rain from

the Atlantic lashed Limerick. That afternoon twenty-eight-year-old Shane Geoghegan captained the Garryowen Thirds in a rugby match against Shannon. The burly rugby player, who worked for an aeronautical engineering firm, lived for his sport and his family. He was a popular young man, described as a 'gentle giant'. He lived with his partner, Jenna Barry, in a terraced house in Clonmore in Kilteragh. It was across the road from his beloved Garryowen club grounds where he had been tipped to one day be president. His home was four doors away from Pitchfork McNamara's. The rugby player didn't know the drug dealer. The only thing common to both men was that they had similar beards.

That evening Shane went to a friend's house around the corner to watch the Ireland v. Canada rugby match. Around 11 p.m. the stolen Renault Espace drove slowly into the cul-de-sac. Barry Doyle and his accomplice had picked it up a few minutes earlier at the apartment block in Raheen. They parked, switched off the lights and waited. Just before 1 a.m. Shane texted Jenna to let her know he was on his way home. Then she heard two loud gunshots.

It was still cold and wet as Shane Geoghegan walked the short distance home. He pulled a beanie over his head as he braced himself against the cold. At that moment he came into Barry Doyle's view. In the dim, yellow glow of the street light the killer saw his beard and thought that the stocky physique matched the description he had been given. Doyle would later admit: 'I saw someone walking across the estate. I got out of the car. I shot at him. He ran. I chased him around the back of the houses. I shot him again.'

When Doyle first opened fire Shane Geoghegan turned and ran for his life. The terrified rugby player ran in a zigzag line to avoid the bullets being fired at him. He was shot in the left shoulder, once in the right side of his back, once in the right upper arm and once in his abdomen. The injured man ran to a nearby garden where he tried to vault a six-foot wall, but wasn't able to get across.

As Doyle ran after his victim the gun jammed. He calmly slid the chamber of his Glock automatic to dislodge two unused rounds and re-loaded. He searched around some cars, until he heard Shane Geoghegan's heavy breathing. He found his victim cowering against the wall that had blocked his escape. Shane was clutching his side and trying to hide. Doyle stood over his victim who pleaded: 'Please don't.' He held the gun in his outstretched right hand, less than a foot from the back of Shane's head. He fired once more, killing the innocent man.

At that moment Jenna Barry looked out her front door. 'I saw a person running down the middle of the road to a navy people carrier. The wheels were turning and screeching and someone was shouting: "Drive, drive!"' she later told the Central Criminal Court. She sent her partner a text message telling him: 'I think there's been a shooting.' She tried to ring him but there was no answer. She also rang the police.

The Renault Espace was found on fire nearby in Rosbrien at 1.12 a.m., close to the Dundon/McCarthy stronghold of Ballinacurra Weston. Around the same time Gardaí found the body of Murder Inc.'s latest victim. He became the twelfth person to die at the hands of the mob in six years. Half of them were completely innocent people. The combined death toll attributed to the gangs on both sides of the feuding since November 2000 had reached nineteen.

Meanwhile, Doyle burned his clothes and a gang member hid the gun. At 1.30 a.m. he switched his phone back on. His girlfriend, Vicky Gunnery, with whom he had a one-year-old daughter, had sent him a text asking why he'd had his mobile turned off since about 8 p.m. the previous night. She lived in Dublin with their seriously ill child who had been born with a hole in the heart. The couple had a tempestuous relationship and she often accused him of having affairs. He told her to read the teletext the following morning and she would know where he had been. The next morning she read that a man had been shot in Limerick. 'I called him a scumbag,' she later told Gardaí. 'So you read the teletext?' he replied.

John Dundon and Barry Doyle arrived at the home of Lisa Collins and Christopher McCarthy around 2 a.m. Dundon was banging on the door and demanding to be let in. Doyle was wearing a new tracksuit and runners. He was quiet and tense while the boisterous Dundon was in high spirits. Lisa Collins later recalled: 'John Dundon was really happy in himself. I remember him saying to Christopher that Johnny Mc was dead. He was laughing the way he laughs – pure evil laugh. He said it a few times over and over, laughing.'

Around 6.45 a.m. John Dundon phoned Ger in the Strand Hotel to tell him the good news that Pitchfork McNamara was finally dead. April Collins drove with him and their child to the car park of Finnegan's pub on the Dublin road. They pulled alongside John Dundon and Barry Doyle who were waiting in another car. John was still jubilantly declaring that 'Johnny Mc' was dead. Then he phoned Philip Collopy to gloat. But Collopy rang Johnny McNamara and confirmed he was alive. He called Dundon back to inform him he got 'a pizza man' – his slang for an innocent civilian. Now Collopy was laughing at Dundon.

In the car John Dundon flew into a violent rage, screaming at Doyle that he'd got the wrong man. The motivation for his rage was not that he was upset over the death of an innocent man: Shane Geoghegan's life was of little consequence to the psychopath. He was in a fury because it meant that he and his clan looked stupid and were now going to be the laughing stock of the underworld. 'Are you sure it was him?' Dundon demanded from Doyle. 'It is him – I know it's him,' the bungling killer replied. The hoods were in a panic and drove off towards Dublin while Ger Dundon and his partner returned to the hotel. Doyle later went abroad to Turkey where the Dundons had a number of villas.

While he was away Doyle kept in touch with Vicky Gunnery to find out what was being written about the Geoghegan murder. She would later tell the Central Criminal Court: 'He asked me what were the newspapers saying about the murder in Limerick. I said, "They know it's you because they say it's a very close associate of Patrick Doyle." He said, "They have no proof."' But Doyle was wrong. Within hours of the atrocity, Gardaí had a major breakthrough in the case from the most unlikely source.

Detective Garda Sean Lynch and his colleagues at Roxboro Road Station were at the scene of the murder the following morning. News had quickly filtered out that an innocent rugby player had been murdered in a case of mistaken identity. The wind and rain had cleared for a sunny but cold morning. Lynch heard someone calling his name. He turned around to see two of the city's top gangsters, Philip and Kieran Collopy, standing on the other side of the police cordon. Sean Lynch was a veteran detective who knew them both well.

As Philip Collopy stood at the fluttering cordon tape he breathlessly told the stunned detective everything he knew. He was angry and upset that an innocent man was dead. One of the city's toughest criminals – a hardened killer – was unburdening himself at a murder scene, with his equally delinquent brother standing beside him. To describe the dramatic development as surprising was putting it mildly. Collopy spoke so fast that the detective urged him to slow down. He told the Garda about the meeting in Cruises Street with John Dundon, when Dundon asked if 'it was OK' to whack Johnny McNamara. He revealed that Dundon had phoned him earlier, laughing that they had got Pitchfork. The Murder Inc. gangster had even told Collopy how the gun had jammed when Doyle pursued his prey.

It was clear that Collopy and his brother wanted the people responsible to face justice. 'The cheek of Dundon wanting to kill my friend. They already killed a close friend of mine, Kieran Keane. Now they want my permission to kill another close friend,' Collopy stammered excitedly. He further astonished the detective when he handed him the mobile phone Dundon had called to use as evidence. He volunteered to make a full statement and said he was willing to testify in court. The following day Detective Garda Lynch and his colleagues interviewed the gangster at his home in the Island Field. The evidence he provided could all be corroborated. The Gardaí had been handed an opportunity to put John Dundon and his accomplice away for life.

The murder of Shane Geoghegan came as a depressing bombshell to the people of Limerick. 'Scum killing scum' was tolerable, but killing innocent people was crossing the Rubicon. Whenever the city had something positive to celebrate, a group of vile criminals cast a cloud over it. As Noddy McCarthy had warned at the end of the Kieran Keane trial – for every action there is a reaction. One local city councillor compared the shock and outrage to the aftermath of 9/11.

The sense of revulsion reverberated throughout Ireland and the wider rugby confraternity across the world. For the second time in six years, the Munster rugby family were united in grief to mourn an innocent brother who had fallen to merciless thugs. It brought back haunting memories of when they had gathered to bury Brian Fitzgerald on another cold winter day in 2002. City Mayor John Gilligan, who had been outspoken in condemning the gangs, summed up the feeling of the demoralized people. 'We were so looking forward to the visit of the All Blacks next week and the opening of Thomond Park, but all that seems so inconsequential now,' he told the *Irish Independent*.

Shane Geoghegan's funeral took place in St Joseph's Church on O'Connell Street on Wednesday, 12 November. It was a harrowing scene of raw emotion and grief. His distraught mother, Mary, his only brother, Anthony, and his girlfriend Jenna Barry were joined by the thousands who turned out to pay their last respects. A special press room was set up, complete with an audio/video link to the church, to facilitate the large media presence. The huge crowd applauded and cried as Shane's coffin – draped in the sky-blue and white of Garryowen rugby club – was placed in the back of a hearse to be taken for burial.

Very quickly the feelings of shock and despair turned to intense anger. The murder prompted a special debate in the Dáil, during which then Justice Minister, Dermot Ahern, described the perpetrators as 'scum'. He promised new laws to crack down on organized crime. The Garda Commissioner and his senior staff travelled to Limerick where he appealed for the public's help in finally ridding the city of the cancer of the gun gangs. The mood was changing from fear to anger among the law-abiding citizenry. A group of people planned to stage a silent, candle-lit procession through the Dundon/McCarthy enclaves, in a public act of moral defiance. However, it was cancelled at the request of the Geoghegan family, who didn't want to see any more innocent people suffer.

The murder had come as a profound shock to Steve Collins. Shane Geoghegan had been killed in mistake for Johnny McNamara. Wayne Dundon's scribbled note had suddenly become a terrifying reality. 'I was stunned when I realized that Shane had been murdered in mistake for McNamara – I could not believe that they had killed an innocent man in such a way,' he recalled. 'I went to the funeral and paid my respects to his family, decent people who never did anything wrong in their lives. I couldn't even begin to think what they were going through. I also knew that I was the second name on that list and it was likely they would come after me now. It had a dreadful effect on the family.' Following the murder the Gardaí increased their protection around the businessman.

As Shane Geoghegan was being laid to rest, bench warrants were issued for the arrests of Ger and John Dundon at Limerick District Court. Ger had been wanted since 24 October when the Circuit Criminal Court refused his appeal against the ten-month sentence for motoring offences. He was also due to appear on public order offences for urinating on a Garda patrol car and being drunk and disorderly on 13 October. John was due to appear on a charge of using threatening and abusive behaviour in Pineview Gardens in Moyross.

There was a surprise later that day when Ger Dundon walked into the court and gave himself up. He was immediately put in custody and sent to Limerick Prison to begin his sentence. The young thug had decided that a few months inside would help him to avoid the heat from the Shane Geoghegan investigation.

A week later he was brought back before the District Court under heavy armed guard. He pleaded guilty to the public order charges and was fined €400. The twenty-one-year-old had amassed seventy-four convictions in his short, chaotic life. The same day, beside the court building, the All Blacks and the Munster players gathered for a civic reception in City Hall. Later that evening, All Black legend Jonah Lomu remembered Shane Geoghegan when he officially switched on the city's Christmas lights. Lomu told the people of Limerick: 'We have lost somebody who is quite dear to the rugby community itself and I think you can be pretty sure that everybody that runs out on the paddock will be running out in memory of him, and hopefully they can piece something together in terms of respect to him.'

The following day there was a minute's silence for Shane Geoghegan before the big match started. He should have been one of the fans sitting in the gleaming new stands for the historic game. The silent tribute was replicated among the thousands of Munster fans packed into the pubs across the city to watch the encounter, which the All Blacks eventually won by a narrow margin.

The murder of a rugby player inevitably attracted considerable attention from the international media contingent in the city for the All Blacks match. The journalists sought out the protagonists who had turned Limerick into one of the most dangerous cities in Europe. Jimmy Collins had become the de facto spokesman for Murder Inc. He had appeared in a German TV documentary lamenting the curse of internecine feuding, which he blamed on social deprivation. In a blatant display of contempt Collins had also posed, bare-chested, along with his son Gareth and Christopher McCarthy, for an English magazine. The three thugs proudly showed off their tattoo-covered torsos, most of which featured handguns and the names of their dead pals. Collins had had the face of his friend 'Fat' Frankie Ryan inked into his shoulder. When Jimmy was approached by *The Times* of London, he was more than willing to talk.

The tactless gangster had no sympathy for the murdered man and instead whined about the universal outrage at his gang's crime. 'He was in the wrong place at the wrong time,' said Collins, who wasn't in a mood to divulge his own intimate knowledge of the crime. 'But I didn't kill him and I'm getting my house battered in [by the police] and my family harassed for it. Just because a rugby player gets killed there's holy war. There was never any of this fuss when my friends were getting killed and some were just as innocent.'

Collins denied that the mayhem had anything to do with organized crime. 'It's not about the drugs why this is happening. It's just that we hate each other's guts. They don't respect us so we're not going to respect them. This started with fists more than twenty years ago. It moved on to stabbings and went from there to executions; people getting killed not because they'd done anything but just to get at the families. I can't see it ever ending. I took part in peace talks only weeks ago. I shook hands with the men who tried to kill me. But that's over. Only the funeral parlours will do well out of this for years to come.'

Christopher McCarthy, also interviewed, agreed that he and his pals didn't see much of a future. 'The graveyard or jail' was their only option, he said. He was probably thinking of his lethal cousins.

Jimmy's long-suffering wife, Alice, was equally defiant,

and joked that in Ballinacurra Weston you are never more than twenty feet from a gun. The previous day their home had been raided by police at 5 a.m. 'The Guard's hands were trembling as he pointed his gun at me but I told him to fuck off when he told me to put my hands on my head,' laughed the woman who was repeatedly beaten by her peacemaker husband.

But Alice Collins and her clan would not be so glib in the future. She would soon be glad of the presence of the Gardaí in her family's life.

15. A Murder Too Far

On a cold, gloomy January morning in 2009, as a leaden sky hung over Limerick, the denizens of the Dundon/McCarthy enclave awoke from their drug and alcohol-induced slumbers to find a strange sight outside their doors. Lisa Collins urgently shook her partner awake – there was something he needed to see. Although bleary-eyed and groggy from too much weed, Christopher McCarthy's primeval instincts kicked in when he squinted through the bedroom curtains. Outside two jeeps and a car – all high-powered, top-of-the-range models – were parked in positions with different lines of sight to his house on Crecora Avenue. Between the dope and the wintry grey half-light of the morning, he could only make out ghostly shadows sitting motionless inside. The mobster grabbed his phone and started making calls – Murder Inc.'s stronghold had been invaded by an unidentified force.

Throughout the rat-infested wasteland the mob called home, wary eyes were peeping through windows in houses scarred and blackened from bullets and petrol bombs. The residents of the gangland equivalent of 'Sleepy Hollow' considered taking the Glock automatics from their hiding places. The hoodlums chattered excitedly on their phones as they tried to work out what was happening. They had never seen anything like this before. It couldn't be their enemies just sitting there, behind blacked-out windows, waiting for them to come out and play a game of 'bang bang'. As Jimmy Collins knew from first-hand experience, they normally drove past at high speed, with a drug-addled muppet hanging out the window firing a machine-gun. Anyway, there was a type of truce in place; and it was too cold and too early for mayhem.

The gangsters knew it wasn't the media because that circus had long since moved on from the Shane Geoghegan murder story. All the gangs had deprived them of fresh gangland stories by abstaining from killing or shooting anyone in the two months since then. In any event, the hacks weren't so brave, or organized, as to line up so provocatively outside the doors of the country's most feared crime gang. That left only one option, the thugs argued excitedly – the police.

The Piranhas had been expecting a visit from the 'shades' every day since the gang's tragic 'mistake', and everyone in the organization was prepared for it. But when the cops did make their move they would descend on the place in huge force. Inevitably the 'pigs' would come before dawn, kicking in doors for maximum surprise and confusion. The local Gardaí never sat outside like that – as if they were waiting to be invited in for tea. Nobody made a move as the rat-like instincts of the residents of 'Dundonville' told them there was an unidentified predator on their turf. The slouching drug dealers decided it was safer to stay indoors.

The men sitting outside could feel dozens of curious, nervous eyes watching them from the dishevelled houses. After an hour or so, as the day grew a little brighter, there was no sign of the mysterious cavalcade fucking off. The brave hoodlums sent their children out to investigate.

The youngsters found that the men in the jeeps and the car were friendly and chatty. They all wore dark-blue baseball caps with 'NSS' and 'Garda' emblazoned on them in gold letters. They wore vests, similar to their daddy's, only theirs had 'Garda' written on them. 'Tell your daddy we're the guards from Dublin and we're going to be around for a long time . . . this is going to be a really safe place now,' a friendly face told the curious children who ran excitedly to tell Daddy the news he was so anxiously awaiting.

The mobile phone network lit up again. In prison Wayne Dundon was briefed. The boss told his people to watch and wait, to see what 'the cunts are up to'.

The arrival of the mysterious squad that morning would be another game changer in the longest-running confrontation between cops and robbers in the history of the State. The local Garda force of just over 600 officers had been engaged in a Herculean battle and had managed to prevent all-out anarchy. But despite the efforts of the most successful local police force on the island, there was just no end in sight to the war as it entered a seventh year. There was an endless supply of expendable foot soldiers to fill the shoes of the 150-plus gangsters languishing in prison since the murder of Kieran Keane in 2003. The introduction of the RSU six months earlier had already contributed to a dramatic reduction in the use of firearms in 2008 – down to 43 incidents from a peak of 103 in 2007. But the murder of Shane Geoghegan had upped the stakes even further.

The death of another innocent man turned public opinion in the city firmly against the mobs, especially in the areas where their support came from. People were sick of the carnage and chaos being perpetuated by a small group of craven, sadistic morons. Pressure mounted on the politicians who responded by calling for action. That resulted in even more pressure piling on the police to end the chaos. Such was the workload in Limerick that Garda resources were permanently stretched to the limit. But following the rugby player's murder they were at breaking point. Every available detective was engaged in investigating the backlog of murders and other serious crimes that the gangs had already committed. They needed to build the cases that would put the likes of John Dundon out of circulation. Officers were showing the signs of stress and fatigue.

The caseload meant that they didn't have the resources to physically keep watch on the thugs and prevent further crimes from occurring. Garda management realized that they needed to take the fight to the gang to stop them even contemplating going out to wreak more havoc. The RSU had been deployed for that purpose and the team were getting good results. However, it was important to mount overt surveillance against the Dundon/McCarthys to show the public that these guys weren't glamorous or untouchable. The Gardaí needed to deploy more psychological pressure, or what the US Army term 'PSYOP' – psychological operations – to gain the upper hand. In their search for another line of attack, the Garda top brass resurrected tactics that had not been used for twenty years.

The new squad that suddenly appeared outside Christopher McCarthy's house in January 2009 was an extra weapon to complement the RSU. But this specialist unit had just one priority target – Murder Inc. – in a manoeuvre codenamed Operation Weston. This new tactical approach was the brainchild of Assistant Commissioner Derek Byrne, Commander of the Force's National Support Services (NSS), which encompassed most of the national specialist units. Assistant Commissioner Byrne was one of a dying breed among the senior ranks of Garda management – he was an experienced thief-taker who cut his teeth on the frontline. The Assistant Commissioner had been a young cop back in the late 1980s when the Central Detective Unit (CDU) established the famous Tango Squad to target Martin Cahill, the notorious crime boss known as 'the General'. The ad-hoc unit, made up of seventy enthusiastic young cops, was ordered to carry out round-the-clock overt surveillance on Cahill and his top lieutenants. The operation was a spectacular success and it forced the gang to make mistakes. Within eight months most of the General's closest associates were facing serious charges for armed robbery and drugs offences.

The murder of Shane Geoghegan clearly illustrated the need for such a radical approach in taking on the Dundon/McCarthys. Using the Tango Squad template, Assistant Commissioner Byrne had personally hand-picked six suitable officers from the various units within the NSS. In Limerick they were joined by four local Gardaí selected by the city's head of detectives, Detective Superintendent Jim Browne. A particular type of police officer was needed if the operation was to be a success. The officers selected had to be level-headed, patient, tough and resilient under pressure. They also required plenty of experience when it came to getting up close and personal with hardened, dangerous criminals. Operation Weston would not be an easy job.

The new version of the Tango Squad was told: 'Wherever they go you follow. Stop them, search them, and question them. Do the same to anyone they meet. There are no rules for this game – just don't break the law.' The plan in such operations is to put the targets on edge and force them to make mistakes. The ad-hoc unit, which became known as the 'Dublin Squad', were equipped with three high-powered vehicles, fitted with surveillance cameras. They were armed with Sig automatics and Uzi submachine-guns fitted with laser sights. Then they headed to Limerick.

One officer gave an insight into how the operation unfolded: 'We parked outside Christopher McCarthy's house the first morning to let them know that we were there. McCarthy's house was the focal point for the gang and they met there every day whenever they got up. Intelligence revealed at the time that it was from here that everything was organized. The first day we sat looking at them and they sat looking back at us. Then they sent the children over to talk to us to find out who we were. From then on it was just a full-on game of cat and mouse.'

The Dublin Squad wore baseball hats and deliberately ensured that Murder Inc.'s members could not identify them. 'It was important that we were not seen to be from Limerick because they had no way of trying to follow us or intimidate us. We adopted a robust approach with them from the very beginning,' the officer recalled. Later that morning McCarthy left the house in a car with Nathan Killeen and Jimmy and Gareth Collins.

Two of the jeeps followed while the car remained in situ. On a busy city street the jeeps hemmed in McCarthy's car and the hoods were ordered to lie on the ground to be searched. The car was also searched as a fourth officer stood covering his colleagues with an Uzi submachine-gun. And it was all done in the full public eye. When the thugs drove on up the road the RSU were on a checkpoint and they were put through the same humiliating routine again. The gang's new tormentors made the procedure an annoying daily ritual for the Piranhas.

If the gang members decided to walk, the Dublin officers walked behind them as the jeeps drove alongside on the road and up on the footpath. No words were exchanged during these bizarre strolls. When a target walked into a shop the cops stood inside with him and then left with him. Some of the thugs tried to make light of it by laughing that they were being protected from their enemies. But the strain began to show. Anyone who met the Murder Inc. men on the street or visited their homes was pulled aside, questioned and searched. 'The idea was to get the word out that getting involved with these guys would bring you under the spotlight,' one of the officers explained at the time.

'On one of the first nights a low-level drug dealer drove up to McCarthy's house. He shone his full headlights on us and the gang began trying to take our pictures but we were covered up. When the drug dealer left he was followed and pulled over. He was taken out of the car and searched. The guy was all apologetic and said he was only a low-level drug dealer for them and he had been ordered to light us up. He told us that you couldn't say no to these people. A week later he moved away and we didn't see him again.'

The sight of Limerick's most feared gangsters being spread-eagled on the side of the road became a welcome – and regular – spectacle for the people of Limerick. It demonstrated to the public that these feared men were not as powerful as they wanted everyone to think. They could no longer swagger as if they owned the city.

After a few weeks the Dublin Squad realized that their quarry were not very bright. 'The Dundon/McCarthy crew and their entourage were actually quite stupid and that was why they were so dangerous. They were the kind of lackeys who would do what they were told to without any consideration of the consequences,' an officer close to the squad revealed. 'The Dublin gougers would have bought and sold these guys and they wouldn't have had the same status that they enjoyed in Limerick. Some of them were no more than murdering zombies and that is not an exaggeration.' For a while at least it seemed like the tables had turned.

Despite the increased police presence, the extra units could not be everywhere and Murder Inc. still managed to do some shooting. In February 2009 brothers Darren and Joe Hehir, foot soldiers in Murder Inc., were injured in two separate punishment shootings in a disagreement over drug money. In one of the incidents the suspected gunman was a fifteen-year-old boy. It didn't matter that Joe Hehir was the boyfriend of Annabel Dundon. Limerick was also braced for trouble when crime boss Christy Keane was released from prison on 17 February. He came back to a gangland that had undergone dramatic change during the seven-and-a-half years he had been away. A month earlier his wayward son Liam had been jailed for ten years for possession of the loaded gun used to shoot Jimmy Collins. His father took a holiday in the sun to acclimatize to the free world before considering his next move. A week after the godfather's release there were more dramatic developments.

In the three months that had elapsed since the Geoghegan murder, the investigation had been gathering momentum. Armed with the information from Philip Collopy, Gardaí had built up a clear picture of who was involved. The investigation team had painstakingly built their case under the command of the city's recently promoted Chief Superintendent, Gerry Mahon. Officers compiled a list of suspects as they patiently waited for the optimum time to move in and make arrests. In the countdown to the planned swoop, interrogation teams made up of detectives from Limerick and the National Bureau of Criminal Investigation were briefed and assigned suspects to question. Surveillance teams had been deployed to locate and secretly monitor the targets to ensure that everyone was lifted simultaneously.

On the morning of 24 February 2009 the Gardaí made their move. Before dawn a large force of officers, spear-headed by the RSU, swooped on Murder Inc.'s stronghold of Ballinacurra Weston. In all fifteen gang members were arrested, eight women and seven men. At an earlier briefing that morning officers had been told their prime target was Barry Doyle. The decision to move in on the mob was prompted by his return to Limerick a few days earlier. John Dundon had left the country and was keeping his head down in the UK.

When the RSU smashed their way into the safe house at 106 Hyde Road where Doyle was staying, he barricaded him-self into an upstairs bedroom. But the cops quickly burst in on top of him and the hard man began crying like a baby. Sleeping on the couch downstairs was another young Mur-der Inc. recruit, twenty-four-year-old James Dillon. He was questioned and searched but wasn't on the list to be arrested. Dillon, who was a cousin of the Dundon/McCarthys, had been described as just another soldier in the mob and was of little interest. A few months later the police would become much more aware of the 'nobody'.

The fifteen suspects were taken to several stations across the city and county. Barry Doyle was taken to Bruff Garda Station outside Limerick for questioning because the inter-view rooms in the city's three stations were full. At the same time Doyle's girlfriend, Vicky Gunnery, was also arrested in Dublin. In the two days prior to the murder of Shane Geoghegan, mobile records had revealed that the couple exchanged over 220 texts. Detectives reckoned she had a story to tell, and she did.

Gunnery was not prepared to protect her boyfriend. She had been sickened by the murder and also by Doyle's neglect of their seriously ill baby daughter, whom he ignored. When the baby had been admitted to intensive care with breathing difficulties the killer went to Spain on a six-week holiday with his cronies. Gunnery quickly told detectives everything she knew, including his admission to her that he carried out the murder.

Meanwhile Barry Doyle had been questioned by four detectives – operating in pairs – for twenty of the sixty hours he was in custody. He had insisted throughout that he knew nothing about the murder and claimed he could not remember where he was on the night of 8 November. He offered no explanation as to why his mobile phone had been switched off that night. Detectives had put to him the allegations made by his girlfriend in Dublin and arising from his meeting with Philip Collopy. They presented him with the various text messages the couple had exchanged, which clearly implicated him in the crime. He was told to think of his girlfriend who was in custody and his sick child, who had been due to undergo scans on the day of the arrests.

During his fourteenth interview, on the evening of the third day in custody, 26 February, Doyle suddenly requested a consultation with his solicitor, Michael O'Donnell. After the meeting the lawyer asked to speak off the record with Mark Philips and Gerry Hanley, the detectives who had been interviewing his client. He said Doyle was willing to admit to the murder on condition that Vicky Gunnery was released from custody in Dublin. The officers flatly refused any such deal because it would amount to an inducement to confession, and such admissions would not hold up in a court of law. The solicitor consulted Doyle again. When the interview resumed at 7.52 p.m. the detectives started by asking the suspect, 'Did you shoot Shane Geoghegan?' He replied coldly: 'Yeah, I shot him.' Then he began talking.

Claiming to have had a change of heart after thinking about his sick daughter, Doyle admitted his part in the killing. The six-foot-tall gangster described in graphic detail how he murdered the rugby player. He even leaned against the wall of the interview room to demonstrate the hunched position he found his injured victim in. The detectives asked him how far he was from Shane when he shot him in the back of the head. Doyle held his hands apart, and agreed it was about a foot.

The assassin demonstrated how he cleared the weapon when it jammed and how he aimed and fired the final shot into his victim. Asked if his victim spoke, Doyle replied: 'Please stop.' He drew a sketch of the estate, pointing out where the getaway vehicle was parked. He marked where he was standing when he first began shooting, the direction Shane was walking in when he was shot and the spot where he found his victim hiding.

But despite his fulsome confession Doyle refused to implicate anyone else in his crime, which he freely admitted was 'vicious' and 'tragic'. He would not reveal his motivation for taking on the hit. Even though he was facing a mandatory life sentence Doyle was too afraid to name John Dundon as the man responsible for organizing the murder. Another young killer was prepared to take the rap rather than face the wrath of Murder Inc. In a last act of contrition, Doyle took off his rosary beads and asked the Gardaí to give them to Shane Geoghegan's family.

On Saturday, 28 February, Doyle was taken under heavy police guard to a special sitting of Limerick District Court where he was formally charged with the murder of Shane Geoghegan. Detective Garda Sean Lynch gave evidence of charging the hit man. When it was put to him, Doyle replied 'I have nothing to say.' He was remanded in custody.

Back at the investigation's incident room in Mayorstone Garda Station, Chief Superintendent Gerry Mahon and his team reviewed their options. They had a strong case against Doyle based on his own admissions and those of both Vicky Gunnery and Philip Collopy. But he wouldn't name his accomplice or John Dundon.

There was, however, enough to charge the psychopathic Dundon with murder based on Philip Collopy's statements and corroborative evidence. Collopy, despite his criminal background, would make for a compelling witness. Gardaí decided they would nab Dundon when he returned to the city so that he could be questioned. If they went ahead and laid charges, Dundon could be extradited but Gardaí would be unable to interrogate him.

When the rest of the mob was released from custody it became clear that Philip Collopy had become a State witness. Gardaí were concerned the gang would try to get him before he stepped onto the stand, and armed patrols were stepped up in Island Field. But just when it seemed that the net was finally closing on Dundon, cruel fate intervened.

In the early hours of 21 March Philip Collopy was drunk at a house party in St Mary's Park. Everyone was drinking, smoking joints and laughing when Collopy returned from the toilet around 2 a.m. He was wearing a shoulder holster and brandishing his favourite 9mm Glock automatic pistol. The gang's most feared enforcer had a fascination for guns. A few months earlier he'd got a pal to film him on a mobile phone firing automatic weapons on a gun range in Eastern

Europe. He liked to brag about his expert knowledge of firearms. A teenage girl later described how he was 'messing' with the pistol and unloaded the magazine. She was worried that it might be still loaded and asked him was it safe.

Collopy laughed as he put the gun to his temple and said, 'There's nothing in it . . . watch.' But in his drunken desire to impress, the gun expert and would-be State witness forgot the basics of handling firearms: to check and ensure there wasn't a round up the breech. As he squeezed the trigger the gun exploded. The bullet went through his skull and lodged in the ceiling above where three young children were asleep. Later forensic officers found a fragment of bone tissue in the ceiling. Panic ensued as Collopy collapsed in a pool of blood.

A patrol from the RSU was passing the front door as people ran out shouting for help. Collopy was rushed to hospital where he was placed on a life support machine. He died less than twenty-four hours later. The gangster, who had survived several attempts on his life, had done his enemies' job for them in a moment of bravado. Collopy's recklessness had inadvertently saved John Dundon from a life sentence and Murder Inc. had two reasons to celebrate. For the Gardaí it was the cruellest of ironies – and a huge setback. One officer commented to this writer at the time: 'The devil was minding his own – the fucking Dundons.'

Less than two weeks later another criminal who had crossed swords with John Dundon also died by his own hand. John Creamer had survived several attempts on his life, including being literally riddled with bullets at the hands of his Dundon cousin. He had miraculously recovered from his injuries and joined forces with the Collopy gang. He'd fled to the UK after attempting to murder Anthony Kelly in

Kilrush and was found dead in a London flat after taking a heroin overdose. His cousins didn't send flowers to his funeral.

In the meantime the pressure was beginning to tell on Murder Inc. Jimmy Collins and his cohorts had taken to filming the Dublin Squad as they sat outside their homes. In one telling episode the officers stopped and searched a thirteen-year-old who had been seen talking to the Murder Inc. men. As they talked to the kid they were examining his mobile phone just as he received a text from Collins. It read: 'Where in fuck are ya' . . . mov yer arse if you wanna b a drug dealer.' The kid was a courier for the mob. The cops tried to advise the boy that this kind of life would only end in disaster. But the youngster shrugged his shoulders and laughed. He was already beyond saving.

Inevitably the mob fell back on its favourite 'peace' tactic in a bid to get the cops off their backs. A week before the arrests in the Geoghegan murder, Jimmy Collins had decided to use the media in his fight for the right to roam the streets unfettered. In an interview in a national newspaper he claimed the 'Dublin guards' were trying to ensure that the latest peace pact didn't succeed. He complained bitterly that the squad was the source of all the trouble in the city and demanded that they be 'reined in' by Commissioner Murphy and brought back to Dublin. He even praised the local Gardaí who had been on his case for most of his life. 'The Limerick guards are great,' he said without a hint of irony.

But while the gang was talking peace in public, behind the scenes it was plotting another murder. The proposed victim would also be an innocent man; only this time his death would not be an accident. Wayne Dundon wanted the second man on his list executed and he didn't care how many cops were breathing down the necks of his henchmen. He needed Steve Collins dead.

The plot to murder the businessman illustrated how far removed from reality Dundon and his siblings had become. They were devoid of any sense of humanity or reason. They were completely impervious to the tragic consequences of their botched efforts to kill their long-time rival Johnny 'Pitchfork' McNamara. It didn't seem in any way important to them that their hit man, Barry Doyle, had confessed and was now charged with murder. The unprecedented level of police attention didn't put them off either, and they were indifferent to their media portrayal as Public Enemy Number One. It was as if they lived on another planet and in another dimension. Dundon wanted his revenge and nothing else mattered. He wasn't even prepared to allow the dust to settle before the gang's next senseless act of terrorism. The sadistic monster knew he had the 'fools' on the outside to do his evil work.

Contrary to popular perceptions about contract killings, there was nothing sophisticated or well organized in the planning of Steve Collins's assassination. This became clear from the combined testimonies of five people associated with Murder Inc. – Lisa, April and Gareth Collins and brothers Anthony 'Noddy' and Christopher McCarthy. In evidence they gave in the Special Criminal Court, the supergrasses revealed that the plot was first mooted in mid-March 2009. Nathan Killeen called around to Gareth Collins, who was staying with his sister Lisa and her boyfriend Christopher McCarthy. Collins had been released from prison in January 2008 after serving three years and nine months of a five-year sentence for possession of a firearm.

Killeen had a proposition for his pal. 'He asked me would I be interested in driving a car for him and that there would be a few quid in it for me. I asked him what was involved. He told me he'd explain more if I'd say I'd do it,' Collins later told Gardaí when he broke his code of silence. Killeen told him it was connected to 'the pub up the road', which he understood to be the Steering Wheel. Collins claimed he knew it meant that they were going to kill the publican and he refused.

Killeen made a phone call to someone in prison and told the person on the other end to tell 'the other fella I want him'. Wayne Dundon phoned back a few seconds later and Killeen gave the handset to the reluctant gang member. Collins said Dundon offered him €20,000 to 'drive a car'. He also offered him a kilo of 'dirty stuff' – heroin. Collins told Gardaí, 'I got a bad feeling then and I knew it was something serious because they were offering me €20,000. Wayne tried to sweet talk me first and then got aggressive.'

Dundon reminded the recalcitrant thug that he owed the family. Shortly after his release from prison Collins robbed a car in Limerick to get back to Portlaoise where he was living with a girlfriend and his daughter at the time. But the car belonged to Murder Inc. and the next day his sister April called to tell him Ger Dundon was out for his blood. Dundon claimed there was a kilo of cannabis weed hidden in the car and he wanted it back. When Collins said he couldn't find it, Dundon demanded that he pay €4,000 for the drugs with another €1,000 on top to compensate for the car – which had already been stolen. If Collins didn't pay up he was a dead man and it didn't matter who he was related to. Jimmy Collins, however, smoothed the waters and it appeared to be forgotten – until he refused to drive the getaway car for

Wayne. 'He started getting aggressive, saying I had stolen weed belonging to Ger and that I was driving the car.'

When the call ended Killeen seemed convinced that Collins would do the job and explained what they were planning. The gangster later told Gardaí: 'They were going to whack Steve Collins the father above in the pub over what happened with Wayne getting ten years over it. He [Killeen] said he was going doing the whacking and I was going doing the driving. He told me they had it all planned out and they had a fella who was watching the Casino which opened about 11 a.m. every morning and it was Steve Collins that opened then. It was definitely Steve Collins, the father, they were going for. He said he had the thing [gun] and was just waiting for a car to be sorted. He said they couldn't rob a car in Limerick as it would cause too much heat around.'

In early April 2009, Killeen was in Lisa Collins's house and spoke to Gareth. The Murder Inc. enforcer called Collins over to the side of a burned-out house to talk. Killeen always held his hand over his mouth whenever the 'Dublin guards' were around. If they had a line of sight on him, the killer wouldn't speak at all because he wrongly believed that the NSS crew were using directional microphones to listen in on their conversations. Unfortunately they had no such technology. 'Nathan explained to me that they had a car, a high-powered Mercedes and that they got it from "smokes town", which was slang for Dublin. He told me they were getting ready to go now soon and that he had his sister Ciara buy hats, scarves and gloves and stuff,' Collins later claimed.

In the meantime Operation Weston was being wound down by Garda HQ. It had been going on for just over three months and had seriously disrupted the gang's operations. But such high-intensity operations were expensive and could not be sustained indefinitely. When the cops disappeared the mob came back on the streets. On the morning of Holy Thursday, 9 April, Nathan Killeen called to Lisa Collins's house looking for her brother. He was accompanied by James Dillon, who had been staying with Barry Doyle in a safe house. Dillon was a cousin of the Dundons and, like everyone else in the gang, was terrified of them.

'Nathan said to me, "Come on so, we're going doing that in a few minutes." I said no I told ye before I'm not doing it. He snapped at me. He was cursing me and said, "What's going on?"' Collins said that Killeen then made a call and hung up. A few seconds later Wayne Dundon was on the phone again. 'This fuckin' fella won't drive the car,' Killeen told his boss before handing the phone to Collins. The gangster claimed that Dundon said, '"You just drop them up and drop them back down again." He wanted me to drive Nathan up to the Steering Wheel pub. Nathan would go in the pub, whack Steve Collins and would come back out,' Collins would later tell the Special Criminal Court. But Gareth Collins still refused to take part in the killing.

In his statements to Gardaí Gareth Collins claimed Dundon then warned him: 'I'll be out of here in a few months and you're fuckin' dead you little prick ya.' Both Christopher McCarthy and Lisa Collins would also testify that they had witnessed some of the exchange between Killeen and Gareth Collins. As he walked away, Collins said Killeen was still on the phone to Dundon. He was staring at Collins who claimed he heard him say: 'What will I do? Will I give it to him?' The last time Killeen had that type of conversation with the Dundons, James Cronin had ended up in a shallow grave with a bullet in his head.

Killeen then told his boss, 'James Dillon is here,' and

handed the phone to the young man. According to Gareth Collins, Dillon was 'stuttering on the phone as if he couldn't get a word in'. In Wheatfield Prison meanwhile, Anthony 'Noddy' McCarthy was sharing landing G with the rest of Murder Inc. including his cousins Wayne and Dessie Dundon. He would tell the Special Criminal Court in 2014 that sometime after 9.30 a.m. on the morning of 9 April he heard Wayne Dundon roaring from inside Lebanese criminal Hassan Hassan's cell. Noddy McCarthy walked into the cell and saw Wayne Dundon on a mobile phone shouting and screaming: 'You'd better do this; you never do nothing for our family; you'd better do this or you'll be sorry. If you don't do it then you and your mother are going to be sorry.' McCarthy said his cousin was 'hyper'. He said that after Dundon got off the phone, when Noddy asked his cousin what was up, he replied that he had 'ordered James Dillon to go kill Roy Collins'. This apparent confusion over the target for the murder was because McCarthy had mixed up their names. Noddy McCarthy had already been in prison almost two years when Wayne Dundon arrived outside the Collins family's pub in December 2004.

McCarthy claimed he told Wayne that he should not talk to James Dillon like that as he was 'only a young fella'. He was their cousin and was not involved in violence. The convicted murderer maintained he was disgusted because at the time there were ongoing peace talks taking place to end the feuding as part of the Limerick regeneration project. He said he then heard Wayne Dundon say to his brother Dessie, 'that fucking muppet Gareth Collins wouldn't drive the car neither'. McCarthy said he then returned to his own cell, where he was 'very stressed out' and 'very angry' about what had occurred. He said in court: 'I didn't want it to happen. I was trying to figure out ways to stop it.'

Noddy McCarthy said he considered talking to Dessie Dundon and reminding him that there had been a big outcry over the murder of Shane Geoghegan; for 'something like this' there was going to be an even bigger uproar. The gangster claimed that he wanted to contact a member of his family to tip off Steve Collins, but in the end he did neither.

Around the same time Nathan Killeen and James Dillon went to the Steering Wheel pub in a taxi to check if their victim was there. They were both described as being 'out of it' on heroin and one of them got sick along the way. Killeen walked into the Steering Wheel pub while Dillon went into the Coin Castle Amusements arcade next door, which was owned by Steve's eldest son, thirty-five-year-old Roy. They jumped in a taxi and went back to Lisa Collins's house where they changed their clothes. They made a petrol bomb and left to pick up the stolen car.

That morning was no different to most mornings for Steve Collins. Two armed Gardaí from Roxboro Road Station escorted him from his home to the pub and they got there at 7.50 a.m. Roy arrived to open up the arcade for the day around 11 a.m. He had taken on the business after returning to Ireland from the UK nine years earlier. Life was good for the businessman. Roy was in the final stages of completing his dream home that he had built in picturesque Killaloe along the Shannon on the border with County Clare. He was planning to get married and he lived for his two daughters, twelve-year-old Shannon and eight-year-old Charlie. His father was very proud of his eldest boy. 'Roy and I were more friends and buddies than father and son. He came to see me as he always did before opening. The next day was Good Friday and he was going to go to IKEA in Belfast where he had spotted a bargain kitchen. He left me in good form and went in next door,' Steve recalled.

Around noon the stolen Mercedes, driven by Nathan Killeen, pulled up outside the arcade and James Dillon went inside. When the Murder Inc. foot soldier spotted Roy he pulled an automatic pistol and fired one shot, which hit the father-of-two in the chest at close range. Dillon turned and ran to the getaway car. As it sped down the road Killeen collided with other cars four times before he abandoned the vehicle and set it alight about a mile away.

Steve Collins didn't hear the single shot. The first he knew that something was wrong was when a member of staff ran in to say someone was bleeding next door. When the publican rushed into the arcade he found his son in the corner. He was bent down on his hunkers and gasping for breath. 'I went over to comfort him and he said: "Dad I've been shot." I could see the bullet on the ground and he kept saying that he couldn't breathe. I tried to move him to his side and he couldn't move and every time I moved him it was making it worse so I jumped up and I called the ambulance. I held Roy and he just held on to me. He told me he loved me and he loved his mother and then Steven Junior came and we were both comforting him. When the paramedics came they gave him a shot of adrenaline and he bucked up a bit. Roy gave me a thumbs-up when we got him onto the gurney and into the ambulance.

'Steven went with him and I went back in to get the CCTV for the Gardaí to see exactly what was after happening. Steven rang me and said it wasn't looking good and that Roy had taken a bad turn. As they got to the hospital, he had a heart attack. I dropped everything and I rushed out to the hospital. I could see the doctors working on Roy inside and we were told to wait in a family room and that they would tell us when he was OK. I thought he was going to be OK. I couldn't believe when the doctor came and told me that Roy had had another heart attack and they couldn't bring him back . . . so we lost him . . . we lost our beautiful boy.'

Within minutes of the shooting being reported, local Gardaí and the RSU converged on the Dundon/McCarthy stronghold. Before the cordite had even cleared in Roy's arcade everyone knew who the culprits were. A detective unit from Henry Street Station spotted Dillon and Killeen walking with hoodies pulled tight over their heads. The killers bolted in two different directions back towards Crecora Avenue. Several squad cars descended on the area and a house belonging to one of the McCarthys was surrounded. Dillon was found hiding under bunk beds in an upstairs room, while Killeen was located concealed under insulation in the attic.

Meanwhile, in Wheatfield Prison, Noddy McCarthy read on the teletext service that a man had been shot in a pub in Limerick. Sometime after 2 p.m. that afternoon he met Wayne Dundon on the top of the prison landing and told him about the shooting. Wayne tapped on the wrist of his watch hand and told him: 'Steve Collins didn't believe me when I did that in court.' Dundon was referring to a gesture he had made to Steve during his trial for shooting Ryan Lee. McCarthy said he asked his cousin if the man was shot in the leg, to which Dundon replied, 'As for him being shot in the leg, he's dead . . . I warned James Dillon to kill him.' Wayne Dundon always kept his malevolent promises.

The rapid response of the local Gardaí quickly paid

dividends. James Dillon, the Dundon's latest 'fool', didn't have a chance to clean up after the horrific crime. Forensic examination found firearms residue on his hoodie and a glove he was wearing. Then, after twenty-six interviews over the following days, and a visit from his grandfather Bart, who had reared him, Dillon finally admitted: 'I shot Roy Collins.' But just like Barry Doyle and the other young men who did Murder Inc.'s bidding, he would not implicate Killeen or Dundon. He was prepared to sacrifice his life for the sadistic thugs.

Steve Collins also knew the killer's family. 'Dillon was just another example of the disposable muppets the Dundons used. He had been well reared and did his Leaving Cert. His grandfather, Bart Dillon, was a great community man and his uncle was an international weight-lifter. But when he got in with those evil animals they dragged the kid down with them and he murdered my son and destroyed our family,' Steve said. The young heroin addict was charged with murder and remanded in custody. Nathan Killeen was released because there was insufficient evidence with which to charge him.

The murder of Roy Collins was a murder too far – and his father decided to stand up and demand an end to Murder Inc. His bravery would create a domino effect that ultimately brought down Ireland's most dangerous criminal gang.

16. A Hero Stands Alone

The murder of Roy Collins, coming so soon after the destruction of Shane Geoghegan, was a seminal moment in the story of Murder Inc. The gang wars that had blighted Limerick for too long could no longer be tolerated. A band of anarchic nihilists had declared war on civil society. Like Mafia godfather Toto Riina's gang in Sicily, the Dundon/McCarthy mob was shown to be one of the most bloodthirsty organized crime consortiums in Western Europe. In many ways they posed a far greater threat to society than the gang who murdered journalist Veronica Guerin twelve years earlier. These barbarians had infested and corroded every level of civilized society, but now the time had come to eradicate them. The Piranhas held the record for deliberately murdering more innocent people than any other criminal gang in the history of the State. Not even the fluffiest liberal could find anything in the character of these predatory creatures worth defending. This was the tipping point; this was the beginning of the end of the mob.

The murder attracted unprecedented publicity and anger. Thousands of people in Limerick signed books of condolences. The public were demanding action. The NSS Dublin Squad and the ERU were redeployed to Limerick once again. Working together with the RSU they turned over gangland. A large number of officers from the National Bureau of Criminal Investigation were deployed to work with the local detective branch on the murder investigation. Gardaí and

Steve Collins already knew who was responsible for this out-rage. The gunman Dillon was just another dispensable fool. There may not have been hard, irrefutable, 'beyond reason-able doubt' evidence for a criminal court, but anyone involved in the business of crime in Limerick knew the obvious sus-pects. It didn't take the legendary deductive powers of Sherlock Holmes to work it out. Wayne Dundon was the only person in the world with a clear motive. In the *Sunday World* three days later, this writer named Dundon as the prime suspect for the outrage. The public had a right to know who had been responsible for murdering Roy Collins.

'I knew straight away who was involved. I knew I had no enemies. I knew that the Dundons were behind this,' Steve Collins commented with conviction after the crime. 'I didn't need to be told who was involved, so the main thing was to go out and do something about this, to stand up and say that no one would suffer again the way my family had suffered.'

On 13 April, an overcast day, Steve and Carmel Collins and their children were joined by thousands of mourners for the funeral Mass of their beloved Roy. For the second time in just five months a family was bidding farewell to a loved one who had been so cruelly taken from them by the Dundon/McCarthys. There were impassioned pleas from the altar for an end to the madness. The Bishop of Limerick, Dr Donal Murray, told the congregation, 'We all appeal and pray that this madness, this utter madness will stop.'

The Church of Ireland Bishop of Limerick and Killaloe, Bishop Trevor R. Williams, joined the chorus of condemna-tion when he said the community's response showed that people would not 'put up with the callous desecration of human life'. 'The sudden death of a young man is a huge blow and when it's the result of senseless violence, it seems even more meaningless and it strikes at all of us and we see the darkness and the pain that's inflicted by such acts,' he said.

Local curate Fr Sean Harmon, a friend of the family, issued a powerful, heartfelt appeal to Roy's killers: 'Today, I appeal on my own behalf and on behalf of the people of Limerick that you men of violence will look deep into your hearts and see the great evil that you are committing and the untold heartbreak and pain you are bringing to the families of the victims. Spare a thought too for the fact that by your evil deeds, you have besmirched the precious name of your ancient and beautiful and cherished city of Limerick.'

Business in Steve Collins's Steering Wheel dropped after the murder of his son. Many of his customers, who came from the working-class ghettoes of Southill and Ballinacurra Weston, were afraid of being intimidated by the gangsters for supporting Steve. He never re-opened Roy's arcade. He commented at the time: 'They have shot and injured Ryan; they have murdered our son and they have practically destroyed our livelihood. I will never open the arcade again. I just couldn't bring myself to. All we have now is intense fear that the Dundons will come back again and take another member of our family. My children cannot go out anywhere any more because it is just too dangerous. I just wish that they got me instead.'

Predictably, the 'pond life' that inhabited Murder Inc. did not show any hint of remorse or regret, and they continued to openly intimidate Steve Collins. A week after he buried his son, the grieving father was parked along Childers Road in Weston talking to his son Steve Junior, who was in another car. They were spotted by members of the Dundon/McCarthys. The thugs pulled alongside the Collinses' cars and began making threats and gesturing with their hands, shaping them into guns. April and Lisa Collins were also in the car jeering at the grieving father and brother.

'They were shouting abuse at my son, saying that he was next to get it . . . It was crazy,' said Steve, who followed the car intent on confronting them, but a red van blocked his way. 'This was intimidation and it was all well planned. As I did that . . . they came over the walls from an estate in Weston, twenty-five of them with sticks, chains, bottles, and attacked the car like a herd of wild animals. I had to get away in a hurry and barely made it through the gates of the level-crossing. I don't know what would have happened if I had been stopped there . . . they probably would have killed me.'

Later Steve Junior went back to the Weston area with Gardaí to see if he could identify the men. He told this writer: 'There were thirty of them just standing around there, the way they do, intimidating and laughing and joking. They thought it was very funny.'

The mindless, tribal hatred of the Dundon/McCarthys stiffened Steve Collins's resolve to stand up and become a voice for the downtrodden silent majority whose lives had been blighted by the scourge of organized crime in Limerick. He decided to shine a light on their dark, vile world. Steve went to the media and campaigned for tough new anti-gang legislation which was being drafted at that time by Justice Minister Dermot Ahern. His warm, likeable personality and his articulate honesty when he spoke of what had happened to him and his family turned him into a popular hero. He became the embodiment of Irish political philosopher Edmund Burke's dictum: 'When bad men combine, the good must associate; else they will fall, one by one, in unpitied sacrifice in a contemptible struggle.' Although cast into a desperate, bewildering world not of his making, he decided to make a grand gesture against the mobs.

'Carmel came up with the idea of a march through the streets of Limerick to send a message to these people that enough was enough. We watched the red protests in Thailand and were impressed. So we decided, OK if we can get the people on the streets everyone would have a Munster jersey, a Man United jersey or Liverpool jersey. We wanted to let the innocent people demand justice for the innocent victims and make the politicians listen to what we were saying, that enough was enough,' he explained.

Within the space of ten days Steve and Carmel Collins organized the biggest public march against organized crime ever seen in Ireland. On Sunday, 10 May, the family marked the Month's Mind of Roy's death with at least 5,000 people, who all turned up wearing red in solidarity with the family. I took part in that solemn and dignified protest; it looked like the estimate of 5,000 was conservative – it seemed more like 7,000 people were there. Many of those who turned up on that warm, sunny afternoon made no secret of the fact that a lot more people would have attended only they were afraid of the rabid Dundon/McCarthys. The Piranhas had sent their lackeys to observe and try to intimidate, but when they saw the sheer size of the crowd, the thugs slithered back to Weston.

The walk from Pery Square to City Hall on Merchant's Quay took place in solemn silence, without slogans, chants or placards. Among those who took part was Brian Fitzgerald's father, Martin, and Tony Geoghegan, the uncle of Shane Geoghegan. John Hennessy, the solicitor under twenty-four-hour Garda protection since the assassination of his client Baiba Saulite, had travelled from Dublin with his bodyguards to be there. These people were all victims of Murder Inc. Even criminals turned up to show their solidarity and send a message that the mindless butchery was not done in their name. It was an emotional and heart-warming day on the streets of Limerick – the day the decent people demanded the return of their lives from the terrorists who had destroyed everything in their wake.

Mayor John Gilligan, who had been outspoken in his criticism of organized crime in the city, prepared his speaking notes carefully beforehand. He included the words 'irrespective of the size of the crowd' because of his fears that the people would not turn up. Happily, he didn't need to use them when it came to delivering his fiercely passionate speech on the steps of City Hall. He said the people of Limerick were not prepared to allow those who 'introduced the death penalty to our streets' to continue their terror.

'This will have ended when Steve Collins and his family no longer have to look over their shoulders in fear, and the people who have inflicted these dreadful wrongs on them are no longer in a position to do so any more,' declared the Mayor to loud cheers and prolonged applause. When he described the mobs as 'cruel, heartless monsters', the applause and cheers of agreement grew so loud that they could be heard kilometres away in the heart of the mob's territory on the other side of the city.

When his turn came to speak, a determinedly composed and genuinely heartened Steve Collins took to the podium. He had to wait some time for the longest, loudest applause of the day to peter out. Steve had a simple message: the time for talking was over; now it was time for the authorities to take up the baton.

'This has been a traumatic time for our family, which we

felt should not have gone without some kind of message to the thugs who have destroyed our lives and have let us down and have let the good name of Limerick down,' Steve told the crowds. 'By your actions here today you have spoken and said we have had enough of the low-life mutants that have eaten into the fabric of our society like a cancer that must be cut out. Let's hope that this action yields some kind of reward going forward because, believe me, nobody wants to go through what my family has had to endure. From the bottom of my broken heart, thank you all,' he said before being hugged by his wife and surviving children. In that memorable moment it appeared that all of Limerick wanted to put their arms around the Collins family.

The huge sea of red filled the square in front of the courts complex and City Hall in Merchant's Quay. As everyone observed a minute's silence, the Tricolour fluttered and the afternoon sun struck the shimmering water of the Shannon behind the speakers. Then a lone uillean piper played the 'Lament for Limerick'.

The following week Justice Minister Ahern introduced hard-hitting new anti-gang legislation. The measures included making membership of an organized crime gang an offence and allowing the use of the non-jury Special Criminal Court to hear gangland trials. A new surveillance bill also gave Gardaí powers to use covertly gathered evidence in the courts against the criminals. The innovative laws appeared draconian in some ways, but in light of the need for a proportionate response it was necessary. The Irish Council for Civil Liberties sent representatives to Limerick in a bid to dissuade Steve Collins from supporting the legislation. 'These people didn't come to see me when my son's civil rights were taken away with his life,' Steve told this writer.

'I have always seen the introduction of these laws as my son's legacy . . . it helps me to think that he didn't die in vain.'

The indifferent Dundons were not bothered by the backlash following Roy Collins's murder. Wayne's only regret was that he hadn't got the real target, Steve Collins. But Dundon was nothing if not assiduous when it came to threats – the courageous businessman was still firmly in his sights.

The Dundon/McCarthys were determined to parade their contempt for their victims at every opportunity. On 9 June, a month after the Limerick march and the introduction of tough new laws, John Dundon posted an astonishing video on YouTube entitled 'Boys in da Hood'. Dundon, who had been joined by his brother Ger and Nathan Killeen, had been staying in London since the murder of Shane Geoghegan. He had just purchased a new C63 AMG Mercedes car worth €100,000.

As the clip started they revved the engine of the high-powered car. The loudmouth brothers sneered and taunted their old adversary, Christy Keane. 'Christy if yer lookin' for me I'm somewhere in eh . . . 'Europe,' John Dundon guffawed. 'I know where you are. Here Christy, as you can see I didn't lose my hair.' Ger Dundon then appeared and shouted: 'See you soon, motherfucker.' Dundon pointed to a grinning Killeen, who had joined him after being questioned about Roy Collins's murder, boasting that he might be with his 'favourite getaway driver'. Later in the five-minute clip the psychopath emerged from the sunroof of the expensive car to illustrate how he could shoot Keane. Posing as if he was carrying a rifle, he laughed: 'I might come out of the roof that way.'

Three days later the grinning thugs had the smiles wiped

from their faces. John Dundon and Nathan Killeen were injured when Dundon crashed the car on a road in Essex. He was being chased by police after failing to stop at a checkpoint. The American-registered car was travelling at speeds of over 180 kph when Dundon lost control at a roundabout. The car rolled over a number of times before landing on its roof. John checked himself out of hospital after four days even though he was still in need of treatment. He was afraid that Christy Keane's men might turn up for a bedside chat. Killeen, who was more seriously injured, remained in hospital for a number of weeks.

Dundon, now facing a potential charge in the UK, returned to Limerick to cause havoc. His behaviour had become increasingly erratic and unpredictable. Elaine Walsh, the partner of Murder Inc. thug Gareth Collins, later commented to Gardaí: 'I remember that it was a quiet summer until John Dundon came home. It was the end of the summer when John Dundon came back.'

In June Gary Campion was jailed for life for the murder of Murder Inc. member 'Fat' Frankie Ryan. The hit man smiled and said nothing as he was led away to start a second life sentence. In the same month this writer received a solicitor's letter at the *Sunday World* from Wayne Dundon. The sensitive gangster threatened to make a complaint to the Press Council of Ireland concerning coverage of his criminal activities. Specifically, he complained that my stories about him were lacking in truth and accuracy. His complaint became the front-page story and we didn't hear from the deranged killer again.

A few weeks later Nathan Killeen returned to Limerick. He joined forces with John Dundon and they went to see Gareth Collins. Dundon wanted to punish the lackey for refusing to drive the getaway car in Roy Collins's murder. However, Collins managed to get away and his partner fled the house with her two children. Killeen and Dundon went into the house and urinated everywhere.

On 5 August 2009 John Dundon presented himself to Gardaí who had a warrant for his arrest on a string of motoring offences, mainly for driving without insurance or without a licence while disqualified. Hours earlier several shots had been fired at his house in Hyde Road, but no one was injured. He was released on bail. Between 5–8 August, while on bail awaiting a court hearing, Dundon was stopped six times. He had also been arrested in Dublin while driving a stolen car. On eight separate occasions he also broke the curfew conditions that had been laid down as part of his bail.

On 2 September the RSU had to clear Limerick courthouse after Dundon attacked his solicitor, John Devane. In the corridor outside the courtroom the gangster, who was still on bail, grabbed the lawyer by the throat and flung him to the ground. He also threatened Devane in an angry tirade of abuse. Around twenty officers inside the court rushed to the lawyer's aid and Judge Tom O'Donnell cleared the courtroom. Dundon, who was not due before the court, was then involved in a stand-off when he and his entourage briefly refused to leave the building.

Devane, who was visibly shaken, returned to the courtroom and informed the judge that he had been physically attacked. 'I've just been assaulted in the hall and I'm too upset to go on,' he said. Devane was publicly criticized by Steve Collins and Councillor Kevin Kiely, Chairman of the Joint Policing Committee, for not having Dundon charged with assault. But it was believed at the time that the solicitor was simply too scared to make a complaint. Devane later revealed that he had been warned that he would be a 'dead man walking' if he had pressed charges against his client. John Dundon had made it clear that his family were not discerning about who their violence was aimed at.

Later that day John Dundon dished out more indiscriminate brutality. This time the victim was Gary Killeen, the sixteen-year-old cousin of Nathan Killeen. The teenager was just another glorified gofer who drove cars for the Dundons. That afternoon Killeen was sitting in a car waiting to drive Ger Dundon when John asked him for a lift to court. The teenager explained he couldn't oblige because he had already been asked by Ger to go somewhere else. Dundon was not happy and stormed off into his house. A few minutes later he returned with a handgun and shot Killeen once in the leg as he sat behind the driver's wheel.

As John stood laughing, Ger Dundon began shouting abuse at his brother for causing the inconvenience. 'Whadda fuck did ya do that for, ya cunt . . . he was driving me,' Ger ranted. He pushed Killeen into the passenger seat and drove him to hospital. John Dundon had no reason to worry about getting into trouble because no one, including his unfortunate victim, would say anything. The status of Killeen's cousins in the mob made no difference and there was no protest about the act of casual barbarism. Arbitrary violence was an accepted way of life in Murder Inc. The RSU were on the scene within ten minutes and later invited Killeen to make a statement. He refused. In the words of Ger's girlfriend, April Collins, 'There was no discussion of this shooting afterwards.' After the incident, Gary Killeen cut his ties with the gangsters and moved out of the city to get away from them. He never returned.

Steve Collins continued his crusade against the gangs, and

he was publicly acknowledged for his bravery in September 2009. The new Mayor of Limerick, Kevin Kiely, held a civic reception for Steve and his family in City Hall. On 12 September Steve Collins was again acknowledged for his outstanding bravery in standing up to the scourge of organized crime when he was honoured with a Person of the Year Award. The nation had taken him and his family to their hearts. Less than a week after Steve was fêted at the glittering ceremony in Dublin, John Dundon was remanded in custody. He was subsequently jailed for a year on a multitude of motoring offences. The people of Limerick, including his own increasingly nervous gang members, were relieved to see him locked up. More time was subsequently added to his sentence when he was convicted of being in possession of a stolen car. Dundon would be off the streets for a total of nineteen months.

The year 2009 did prove to be a turning point of sorts for Limerick as the number of firearms incidents dropped to twenty-nine from forty-three the previous year. It was the lowest number in seven years. But the war with Murder Inc. was far from over.

17. The 'Ditch Rat'

The adage goes that a picture can paint a thousand words. It refers to the notion that a single image can convey a complex story more effectively than the written word. The picture of the Dundons posing with a terrified fellow inmate in Wheatfield Prison achieved that goal. It told the public everything they needed to know about the brothers from hell. It was taken in February 2010 on a mobile phone on 9G, the landing that housed John, Dessie and Wayne Dundon, along with their fellow gang members. The image confirmed how the sadistic siblings ruled the prison landings through fear and intimidation.

The Piranhas had already orchestrated murders, shootings, drug-trafficking operations and an international arms smuggling conspiracy from the comfort of their cells. So terrorizing and bullying fellow inmates with impunity was merely a recreational hobby. The picture proved that non-Murder Inc. prisoners were as much victims of the gang's savagery as the people of Limerick.

The picture in question (plate section 2, page 1) featured a pathetic young Dublin criminal who was tortured and humiliated by the Dundons for fun. It was their unique way of relieving the boredom of being inside. The victim had been badly beaten, stripped and part of his head shaved. With a red marker-pen the brothers then wrote 'fuck me' on their victim's forehead and bare backside. The unfortunate addict was chained to a bed and the Dundons ordered other terrified inmates on their prison wing to take turns beating him.

In a final act of degradation, John and Dessie laughed and smiled as they posed for pictures with their victim as Wayne took them on his mobile phone. The disturbing image was smuggled out of prison to this writer by inmates who desperately wanted to be rescued. It was, quite literally, a cry for help. The long-suffering residents of the prison, most of them ordinary villains, wanted the world to know how the sadistic monsters had made their lives unbearable. They accused the prison authorities of leaving them to the mercy of the psychopaths in return for a hassle-free life. When the picture was published on the front page of the now defunct *Irish News of the World*, it was greeted with shock – and seriously embarrassed a prison system which was supposed to protect the civil rights of its inmates.

The prisoners revealed how Murder Inc. inflicted a regime of intimidation and horror. They controlled the landings and most of the prison. It was a real-life version of the brutal hell-hole jail portrayed in the 90s' US TV series *Oz*. Their story was corroborated by prison staff sickened by the way the mobsters could do what they wanted.

One of the prisoners told this writer: 'Everyone is scared of them, including the screws, and they seem to be able to do what they like. The Dundons control phones, drugs and weapons in here, which are the most important things in any prisoner's life. There is no such thing as the word "no" to them. When people come in Wayne Dundon takes their phone or any drugs they might have on them.'

The convict continued: 'They get a few junkies to bring in the gear [heroin and cocaine] for them and in return the junkies get a few €50 bags for themselves and they are not beaten up. They are like the brutes you see in one of those hell-hole prisons in the movies.'

The sources for the story described Wayne Dundon as being particularly deranged and dangerous. His menacing presence struck fear into the hearts of everyone around him. No one dared smoke on his landing because he did not approve of the habit. 'If any eejit lights up, they can expect a serious beating from him because he doesn't like it. He is always looking for someone to play pool with in the recreation room. If you beat him he will kill ya. One guy, who didn't know the rules of the game and beat Wayne, was hammered with a ball and a pool cue. It was the same in the gym, if you were using a machine Wayne didn't believe in queuing and if you didn't get off immediately then you were beaten.'

When John Dundon was sent to Wheatfield in October 2009 for a series of road traffic offences, he found it hard to acclimatize again to prison life. So he took some pills to relieve the monotony of being locked up. 'John was in a cell with a Dublin guy who gave him pills to take his mind off things. But Dundon went around the place off his head beating up people just for the hell of it,' the inmate revealed.

Wayne took his brother aside to chastise him. 'Wayne went wild at John and told him: "You are a Dundon and you do not take drugs. We have to show these cunts who is boss around here."' He then gave the drug dealer a severe beating for giving drugs to his depraved brother. 'These bastards really are a scourge. It is bad enough to be caught and locked up. Most lads just want to get on with it and do their time in peace. But these fuckers are making life so bad it is almost unbearable . . . there are guys who have attempted suicide to get away from them,' the source added.

The publication of the embarrassing picture coincided

with the much-dreaded release of Wayne Dundon in March 2010. He had served five years and four months for threatening to kill Ryan Lee. An inmate told this writer at the time: 'Just before he was released he told people he was like Santa. "I've written a list and checked it twice," he told everyone. It meant the scumbag had a list of people he intended dealing with when he got out.'

While the Gardaí and the people of Limerick braced themselves for the godfather's return, there was widespread relief on the landings in Wheatfield Prison. The other inmates had a party. For one young drug addict in Limerick, however, Dundon's return was too much. He owed the gang money and had been beaten up several times already. He was told that Wayne wanted to see him as soon as he got out. The twenty-year-old hanged himself a few weeks beforehand. He was one of at least four young men, including Nathan Killeen's brother Gavin, who took their own lives after being victimized by the Dundons.

The publication of the torture picture and the accompanying story had the desired effect. The day after the newspaper appeared, prison authorities ordered a shakedown on the landings where the Murder Inc. gang was being housed. John Dundon was put in solitary confinement and Dessie was moved out of his cell. Seven mobile phones and drugs were seized in the swoop. The young prisoner in the picture was quietly granted immediate temporary release to make up for his horrendous ordeal.

When Wayne was released on the morning of Friday, 19 March, he was picked up by his cousin Dougie Moran in a custom-built, bullet-proof BMW jeep. It was part of a batch of three Moran had ordered for himself and his family. Two of them had been seized from the Dundons in Limerick and were now being used by the ERU. Wayne Dundon's first priority was to find out who had leaked the picture to this writer. Three former inmates were 'interviewed' by his mob in Dublin and Limerick. The gangsters' phones were confiscated so Dundon could check if they had the picture and if they had forwarded it on to another party. Luckily for the three men they were not involved.

The following Tuesday morning Dundon returned to Wheatfield Prison with a group of his henchmen, demanding to speak with senior prison staff. The gang boss was furious that his brother had been placed in solitary and demanded John be returned to his prison landing. A source in the prison later told this writer: 'He was in a temper and he made a veiled threat that if John wasn't taken out of segregation then he would deal with it in his own way.' After that the prison authorities decided to begin moving the Murder Inc. members around the prison system, to prevent them building another powerbase. John was eventually released from segregation but was promptly transferred to another jail.

Gardaí in Limerick and Dublin mounted a major surveillance operation to keep tabs on Wayne Dundon. Ten minutes after Moran picked him up at the prison gates armed officers pulled them over and searched the vehicle. They wanted the godfather to know that he was a marked man. Over the following week he was spotted in Dublin meeting with members of the criminal gang led by Eamon 'The Don' Dunne, who had violently usurped his old boss Marlo Hyland three years earlier. Dundon also met with dissident Republicans and representatives of two notorious traveller crime clans. He was determined to reorganize the gang's drug business.

Dundon also informed several lower-level criminals in Limerick and around the country that they would be donating to his 'coming home' fund.

Steve Collins told a newspaper that his family were hoping that the criminal would move away from Limerick. 'I think it is time for him to move his wagons. I hope he will see that there is nothing here for him any more. I think he is finished in Limerick as far as I can see. There is no more damage they can do; the guards are on top of them.'

On 28 March, Wayne Dundon and his wife, Anne, flew to Cancún in Mexico for a luxury two-week holiday. Three days later Steve Collins was invited to a meeting in the office of the Justice Minister Dermot Ahern. Steve and his family were deeply distressed at Dundon's return to Limerick. He recalled: 'Willie O'Dea organized the meeting because he knew how terrified we were that this animal would come back to kill again. No one doubted that we were still top of Dundon's list of targets.' The meeting was attended by Willie O'Dea, who was then Minister for Defence, the Garda Commissioner Fachtna Murphy and senior department officials. The item on the agenda was Murder Inc.

The experience of the Collins family had motivated the minister to introduce the severe new anti-gang legislation the previous year. The minister later commented: 'I was deeply moved by the plight of this family. They were decent, ordinary people who had suffered unimaginable pain at the hands of the Dundon/McCarthys because they did their civic duty. I felt as the Minister for Justice I had a responsibility to do whatever I could to protect Steve and his family.' Ahern told Steve he was concerned that his regular appearance in the media denouncing mob violence was continuing to make him a target. 'I told Steve I didn't want to silence him but I was very worried that his commentary would provoke these thugs further because it was obvious that they were capable of anything,' Ahern recalled.

Commissioner Murphy said he was immediately providing full-time armed protection to Steve and his two surviving sons, Steve Junior and Ryan Lee, who were seen as Dundon's prime targets. Each one was assigned two armed officers on a 24/7 basis. A uniformed Garda was posted permanently outside the Steering Wheel pub and the family home was also closely monitored and a state-of-the-art security system installed.

Commissioner Murphy reassured the businessman that he was also sending the 'Dublin Squad' back to Limerick to coincide with Dundon's return and to step up operations against the mob. Then Steve broached the subject of what the State was prepared to do to compensate him and his family for the long-term horrors they had endured. Their lives had been destroyed because they had more than fulfilled their part of the 'social contract'. His wife Carmel and the children had been left shattered and traumatized. Their lives were non-existent. Carmel had become a prisoner in her own home, too afraid to face the world outside. The children could not go out for a night without being constantly vigilant against attack.

Following Roy's murder the family had been offered a place in the WPP but quickly found out that it was a complicated and not-so-user-friendly process. Steve explained: 'The programme they had was designed for criminals. Most of them are on the dole anyway, so you whisk them away and give them a few bob, a place to live and a job maybe. I asked what happens to us. They said, "We'll get you over maybe to Austria, and your parents and sisters and brothers can meet you once a year, maybe down in Marseilles." I was mystified and asked for somewhere I could speak English and they came back with Canada. But pub work or electrical contracting would be ruled out, they said, as these would make me traceable. They said I could train as a carpenter. I asked them were they having a laugh expecting a fifty-five-year-old man to train as a carpenter, but they were serious.'

When he asked the people in charge of the programme in Garda HQ how starting a business might work, they had no response for him. Steve commented: 'It was hard enough to get a loan from a bank manager here who knows your track record, so how in the hell could I walk into a bank in Canada, under a new name, and ask for money to start a new business? They couldn't answer. We would just be dumped there and left to get on with it. I could not believe that this was how the State treated innocent people who helped them put criminals behind bars. I brought all this up with Dermot Ahern.'

To add to the intense stress, the businessman explained to the meeting that he was on his knees financially. He had huge borrowings on businesses which had been burned down, closed or undermined because he had testified against Wayne Dundon. He needed help from the State or else he was going under. Ahern vowed to do what he could. A senior civil servant was assigned to investigate a suitable package for the family whereby the State would buy his properties and business. But the wheels of bureaucracy turned painfully slow, and it would take almost two years before a solution was found.

Two weeks before Dundon's prison release the deliberate murder of yet another innocent man had been a brutal reminder for Steve and the people of Limerick that the feuds had not gone away. The authorities were also well aware that the Limerick problem had not been resolved. Bread delivery man Daniel Treacy, Christy Keane's nephew and Owen Treacy's brother, was shot four times on 22 February 2010. The thirty-five-year-old, who had no involvement in crime, was delivering bread to a Topaz garage at 6 a.m. when thirty-one-year-old John Coughlan walked in after him. He produced a Glock automatic pistol from a plastic bag and shot Treacy three times in the head and once in the groin. Coughlan was not a hit man and had never been in trouble with the police before. But a desire for vengeance for the murder of his younger brother Darren had been smouldering in his soul for the past five years. That morning he decided to settle the score sheet.

Daniel Treacy's brother Richard, and his cousin, Joseph Keane, had been jailed for kicking eighteen-year-old Darren Coughlan to death. It was a case of mistaken identity – they thought he was a criminal aligned to the Dundon/McCarthys. Darren was another victim of the collateral damage caused by the mindless feuding. Now that futile act of violence had claimed a second life.

After shooting the bread man John Coughlan went to the home of another man who had been present when his brother was killed. Luckily for the accomplice the door wasn't answered. The electrician then travelled to the city centre where Patrick Keane, another of Treacy's uncles, normally operated a mini-sweeper for the council. The gunman approached the machine but realized that it wasn't Keane behind the wheel – fortuitously he had been redeployed that day. Coughlan was later arrested and charged with murder. At his trial in October 2013 his defence claimed that he was suffering from paranoid schizophrenia at the time of the shooting, which would have substantially diminished his responsibility. However, the jury found otherwise and he was jailed for life.

When Wayne Dundon returned from his holiday the Gardaí reactivated Operation Weston; the officers from the NSS were dispatched to make their acquaintance with Ireland's most hated crime boss. Garda management had decided to increase their efforts to turn the Piranhas into gangland pariahs. The hot-tempered thug was furious when the Dublin Squad jeeps parked right outside his door. He stood staring menacingly at them in the forlorn belief that they might get scared. Dundon then tried to videotape the officers, who pulled balaclavas over their faces. Everywhere he went the cops followed. He quickly discovered that other gang bosses were nervous about meeting him.

One of Dundon's visitors certainly got more than he planned for. The operation had been running for just twenty-four hours when a Cork-based Lithuanian gangster arrived at the thug's house. Dundon and his pal hugged like Mafia bosses before disappearing inside for a private chat. While he was there the officers ran a check on the visitor and discovered he was a member of Lebanese mobster Hassan Hassan's criminal organization. Hassan had been released from prison a week before Dundon. On the same day Gardaí escorted him to Dublin Airport to ensure he caught a flight out of the country. The man visiting Dundon had been photographed delivering a passport to Hassan at the airport that morning.

It also turned out the Lithuanian was a person of major interest to their colleagues in Cork. He was wanted on charges relating to false imprisonment and firearms offences.

He was also wanted by the Police Service of Northern Ireland on firearms charges. The squad called their colleagues in Cork. As soon as the criminal and Wayne Dundon reappeared outside the Lithuanian was arrested and taken into custody. The Murder Inc. boss was not happy.

In the meantime Dundon was extorting cash from criminals in the travelling community. The travellers were terrified of the gangster, whom they nicknamed the 'Ditch Rat', the lowest insult a traveller can bestow on his enemy. But Dundon's fellow travellers tended to call him this far behind his back. He paid several visits to one particular crime clan in Rathkeale, County Limerick – followed in convoy by his police tormentors. In the weeks following his release from prison it was estimated, through Garda informants in the traveller community, that Dundon had taken up to €100,000 from the clan. Whenever the police kicked in his front door for legal searches the Ditch Rat immediately went to visit travellers – under the watchful eye of the Gardaí – and demanded that they give him the cash to pay to repair the damage. But there was nothing the NSS could do as no one would make a complaint.

The Ditch Rat was also putting the squeeze on heroin and cocaine dealers in several counties. Like the travellers, few of them refused to pay up. One detective familiar with the extortion demands explained: 'Each drug dealer got a call and it was not a preamble to a negotiation. They were told that they were working for Dundon now and if they didn't like it then that was just tough. They were given a figure and it had to be delivered by a set date. It rarely led to anyone being shot – because the criminals targeted were too afraid not to comply.'

But the constant Garda pressure was beginning to take its

toll on the gang members. They were increasingly paranoid about the anonymous officers who were making their lives unbearable. In one incident an officer lost his expensive wristwatch while he was searching Christopher McCarthy's car. The cop had no idea where he'd mislaid the precious timepiece. The following day McCarthy, an incorrigible thief, walked up to the Dublin Squad and handed them back the watch. The Murder Inc. man sneered: 'Youse think yer real smart leaving that bug in me car ... ya must think I'm a fuckin' eejit.' McCarthy's suspicion had proved to be advantageous.

In another extraordinary incident the Dublin Squad were following Nathan Killeen, who was going to a traveller halting site to drink and take drugs with relatives. He had made several efforts to lose them but the persistent cops stayed with him. Earlier he'd visited a grotto near a local church and blessed himself as if in solemn prayer. One of his Garda tormentors shouted to the Murder Inc. hard man: 'Make sure to say a prayer for Roy Collins, Nathan.'

At the halting site the officers parked their two jeeps in full view to remind Killeen of their undivided attention. But the drunk and clearly stoned killer, who was sitting with another man drinking from a plastic jug, had taken enough harassment. Killeen rummaged around a horse trailer outside his relative's caravan and dragged something out. He walked over to one of the Garda jeeps and swirled the heavy-looking object over his head before tossing it onto the bonnet of the vehicle. It was the rotting, decomposing carcass of a dog that had been killed by Killeen a few weeks earlier. The animal had been barking too much so the gangster cut its head off, leaving it to rot in the open beside the caravans. No one had bothered to move the rancid dead dog, which clearly posed a serious health hazard to the children playing around it. The incident spoke volumes about the psyche of the people at the heart of organized crime in Limerick.

The cops manoeuvred the jeep, knocking the carcass off the bonnet. Killeen then came back and threw it onto the second vehicle. The detectives couldn't tolerate the pungent smell and were forced to withdraw to clean their jeeps. The body was left at the halting site.

At dawn on 23 April disaster struck for Murder Inc. as a large force of Gardaí descended on the Dundon/McCarthy stronghold. The RSU smashed in the doors of several houses, including those of Ger and Wayne Dundon. The cops had come with warrants for the arrest of seven members of the gang on charges of extortion and intimidation. For the previous two years the thugs had been terrorizing former night-club owner Mark Heffernan for payment of €80,000. They had been hired by a former business associate of Heffernan to collect money from him even though Heffernan did not owe it. The situation came to a head on 17 February 2010 when Ger Dundon, Gareth Collins and brothers David and Christy McCormack tried to abduct the businessman as he drove his father's jeep in Garryowen.

He later told this writer what happened: 'I was about to go into a shop when a car driven by Gareth Collins swung in beside me. Dundon was in the front seat and I saw the McCormack brothers getting out of the back with hammers. I wasn't sure if someone had a gun. I drove off at speed and down a dead-end street to get away from them. As I was turning the jeep around to go back out, the McCormacks came running around the corner – one had a bar and the other a hammer.'

Heffernan continued: 'Gareth Collins drove his car into the road and blocked it. Dundon got out and ran at my jeep with the McCormacks, yelling at me to stop and get out. At the same time I could see that someone else had opened the boot of the car. I knew that if I didn't get away I was going to be dead. I drove through red lights and up the middle of the road. I could see them all the time in the rear view mirror coming after me. I rang 999 and then I drove into Roxboro Road Garda Station.'

Mark Heffernan had once worked for Steve and Roy Collins and knew the family well. Through the entertainment business he also knew Brian Fitzgerald. Heffernan realized that once someone came into the sights of the Dundon/ McCarthys there would never be peace for that person again. Taking on Murder Inc. was like having an unstoppable juggernaut barrelling towards you at high speed, and being unable to get out of the way.

The murder of Roy Collins had convinced him of that. Even if they backed off and assured Heffernan that he was safe he knew their word was as sincere as a whore's kiss. 'I realized then that I had only one option open to me. I knew that you couldn't trust the word of these savages with a handshake,' Mark recalled. The businessman went to see Steve Collins to ask for advice. 'I told Mark there was only one way to deal with these people and that was through the law. Once they came into his life, I told him, there was no going back,' said Steve. On 6 March 2010, Mark Heffernan made an official complaint to Gardaí about the two years of harassment and terror he had endured. It would prove to be another significant turning point in the fortunes of Ireland's most dangerous crime organization. A major Garda investigation was launched, codenamed Operation Redwing.

On 23 April, the operation came to fruition when Ger Dundon, Jimmy Collins, Gareth Collins, Christopher McCarthy, Patrick Pickford and the two McCormack brothers were arrested. They were later charged with a variety of offences including making threats to kill, demanding money with menaces and violent disorder. In one fell swoop most of the gang's middle management tier had been taken out. The seven hoodlums were denied bail and remanded in custody. The odds were stacking up against the Dundon/McCarthys.

Like Shakespeare's Macbeth the bloody means of obtaining power was going to bring about the gang's downfall. The Dundon/McCarthy mob's unrivalled reputation for savagery and the murder of innocent men was their fatal flaw. Their propensity for making threats and their determination to follow them through would be their undoing. At the same time Steve Collins's powerful media campaign and the march through Limerick the previous year had galvanized the public and the State authorities into a realization that this situation could no longer be tolerated.

The grieving father had shown people like Mark Heffernan that once the mob came into your life there was no option when it came to the survival principle of fight or flight. The only option was to stand and fight. The arrest of the seven gang members was part of the domino effect now taking place. As a consequence of the new anti-gang legislation introduced after Roy Collins's murder, all the thugs were sent forward for trial at the Special Criminal Court. The full resources of the State were gradually being mobilized to encircle Murder Inc. For the first time the mobsters, who were well versed in the arts of war, were the ones under siege.

The gangsters were arrested fourteen days after the Collins

family marked the first anniversary of their son's murder. To commemorate the occasion Steve had a plaque erected at the arcade where his son had been gunned down. Family, friends and well-wishers gathered at the Steering Wheel pub to watch Steve unveil the memorial for his boy. It had a simple message on it for all who passed by:

In memory of Roy Collins, 1974–2009.
A wonderful son, father, brother and friend,
taken from us here on April 9 2009.
The world is a dangerous place not because
of those who do evil
but because of those who look on and do nothing.

On 3 May, Steve Collins attended an appointment with Gardaí at Henry Street Garda Station where he was quizzed under caution about allegedly making threats against Wayne Dundon. The brazen godfather had made an official complaint over comments Steve had made in an interview which featured in an English TV documentary focusing on crime in Limerick. In the show Steve watched the infamous You-Tube clip 'Boys in da Hood', featuring John Dundon. When the show's presenter, Donal MacIntyre, asked Steve what he would do if his family were attacked again, he said that he would do the same to them. Everyone, bar Wayne Dundon, saw it as a throwaway remark. But the disingenuous Ditch Rat told cops he was afraid that the businessman was going to have him killed. When it suited Dundon he would use the law.

The investigation was assigned to detectives from Cork because the local Gardaí could not guarantee their objectivity in what was clearly a vexatious claim. But the cops were only doing their jobs and had to be seen to be even-handed. Steve was questioned for three hours and a file was subsequently sent to the DPP. There were no grounds to make a charge. On another occasion Nathan Killeen also ran to Gardaí in Roxboro Road Station to make a complaint against Steve Collins Junior. His victim's brother couldn't help himself when he spotted the enforcer one day and he had assaulted him. The complaint went nowhere. In a separate incident, despite the ongoing campaign of intimidation, one overzealous senior Garda officer, who wanted to be seen as impartial, saw fit to have Steve Collins charged with serving alcohol after hours at his last remaining premises. In the end common sense prevailed and higher authorities had the charges dropped.

Two days after Steve was questioned, his son's killer, twenty-four-year-old James Dillon, was sentenced to life imprisonment. The trainee butcher who had fallen under the control of Murder Inc. pleaded guilty. Detective Sergeant Kevin Swann, one of the lead detectives in the murder investigation, told the Central Criminal Court that Dillon had come from a good family. He had developed a drug problem and had become embroiled with the Dundon/McCarthys six months before he was sent out to kill. He had left the family home and was moving between addresses in the gang's stronghold of Ballinacurra Weston. Steve Collins then read a victim impact statement on behalf of his family.

'Evil came into our lives on that fateful day and took the love of our lives in a callous act, a cowardly act, an unforgivable act, a total waste of a good life,' he said, as tears welled up in his eyes. 'Now, every day, we have to look at Roy's two beautiful daughters lost in confusion as to where their daddy has gone; their little hearts broken beyond repair, too young to understand, too afraid to contemplate what's gone on and why.' In what was a deeply poignant sight, Bart Dillon, the killer's white-haired elderly grandfather, wept as he listened to Steve's statement. He had lost his beloved grandchild to the malevolence of the mob and it had had devastating consequences for another family.

On Saturday, 8 May, Steve Collins was a guest on Marian Finucane's popular RTÉ Radio One show. He was interviewed about his son's murder and asked about his reaction to the conviction of his killer earlier in the week. He said of Wayne Dundon: 'He's a dangerous guy, a very, very serious criminal. You're dealing with crazy people; these are scum, these are pond life, unbelievably sick people.'

As the broken-hearted father was airing his opinion on Dundon, back in Limerick the Murder Inc. boss was displaying his complete lack of tact, sensitivity or style. The soulless killer hired a pink Cinderella carriage for his daughter's First Communion in a tacky demonstration of his tasteless vulgarity. The Ditch Rat spared no expense for the big day. He splashed out on designer dresses for his wife and daughters, hired a professional photographer and threw a party for family and friends in a city hotel. Two white horses with pink plumes, driven by a coachman in a top hat and tails, transported Dundon's daughter from Hyde Road to the local church. His wife drove in front as the gangster hung out the window proudly recording the gaudy spectacle.

When the convoy arrived at the church the ordinary people, who had scrimped and saved to pay for their children's big day, were forced to make way for the garish parade. Such was the reality of life in this hellish enclave of Limerick that it was inevitable that a number of the innocent children in the church that day would end up slaves to Wayne and his rabble of cut-throats. The rest of the parents there that day either didn't have the money to put on the same show – or they lacked Dundon's sense of 'taste'. There was no doubt that there was a motive behind the gangster's vulgar ostentation. It was another act of public contempt and defiance.

The pictures of the Communion pageant appeared on the front pages of a number of the Sunday tabloids the following morning. On Monday morning the city's *Limerick Leader* newspaper also ran pictures of the big day, aptly describing it as a 'vulgar display of wealth'. In the same story, Mayor Kevin Kiely said he would be demanding an investigation into how a man, who claimed to be unemployed, could afford to pay at least €8,000 for his daughter's Communion. 'It was an insult to the law-abiding public who had suffered the worst of the economic downturn,' he said.

As soon as the paper hit the streets that morning Dundon flew into a rage. The intense police attention was one thing, but now the media had opened up a new front on the war against him and his reviled clan. In a clear sign that the pressure was getting to him, Dundon stormed into the offices of the *Limerick Leader* to make a complaint. The menacing mobster complained bitterly to the newspaper's editor, Alan English, who later published an exclusive interview with the godfather. It was a most enlightening and illuminating piece of journalism. 'Ye've been writing about me for years and I have never once complained. I'm fair game. I've been a bad person; I've done wrong things,' Dundon ranted aggressively to English as he waved that morning's paper around. 'Say what ye like about me. In for a penny in for a pound. It's all hearsay anyway, what the papers write about me. But my daughter was very upset. This has hit a nerve,' he stuttered, as he grew more agitated.

'All travelling people do a big day for their children's Communion. I'm a traveller; my wife's a traveller. We didn't make out that our daughter was the best. We didn't spend €8,000. There were 500 people in that church in Southill and not one person complained about the carriage. They all waited for my daughter at the end; they all showed respect. Everybody at the church congratulated us on the carriage and said how beautiful our daughter was,' he continued, sounding remarkably like a Limerick version of Don Corleone. Inevitably you have to wonder what would have happened if someone had dared say anything negative to Wayne that day.

His tirade resumed: 'I can read and write myself. I'm educated; I was in school until I was sixteen. The papers in Dublin write whatever they want about me and my family. We don't care about the tabloid papers but I don't like seeing stuff like this in my local paper.'

English later described how Dundon apologized whenever he swore. The newspaper editor said he projected a menacing presence but for the most part had remained calm. Once he started talking he couldn't seem to shut up. He complained bitterly that he had been the victim of a miscarriage of justice, claiming that he never threatened Ryan Lee. English described how the gangster became particularly animated and agitated when asked about Steve Collins and the murder of his son. Dundon's animosity towards the businessman was obvious. His responses told their own story.

He claimed that he had been forced to become a virtual recluse since his release from prison – because he was afraid of Collins. Pointing at a picture of Steve Collins on the front page of the paper in his hand, he said: 'I can't leave my house in case Steve Collins sees me and says I threatened him again. All he has to do is say that and I get another ten years. Steve Collins doesn't like me. He's blaming me for killing his son. I've never been charged with anything. The trial is over. His son is dead twelve months, why is he still talking about me? I was in prison . . . it's nothing to do with me. Collins is interested in me; I have none in him.'

Then in an extraordinary outburst Dundon said he had no pity for what happened to Roy Collins: 'What's it to me? Why should I be sorry? It's nothing to do with me,' he said, asking and answering his own questions. 'He's [Steve] going through a hard time. Everybody who loses a family member does, but can he not leave me and my family alone? Do I have to pay for other people's sins? I'm very worried about the way the guards are carrying on with the Steve Collins affair, about what's being said. It's all innuendo; there's no facts. I'd like Mr Collins and his vendetta against me and my family to be left alone. Let justice take its course. Why can't every Joe Soap in this town get the coverage that he's getting?'

When he was asked why James Dillon, a nobody in the criminal fraternity, would take it on himself to shoot Roy Collins, he bluntly replied: 'I don't know . . . ask James Dillon.'

Dundon dismissed the city's crime problem that, of course, had nothing to do with him or his ilk. 'I hear [Ballinacurra Weston] is a no-go area and my experience is completely different. I'm not saying nothing happens but there is petty crime wherever you go. Drugs? What drugs? They say all the problems are caused by drugs in this town. It's all lies. It's caused by social deprivation, people with no jobs. Have I caused thousands to lose their jobs? Why aren't the bankers on the front page and singled out like me?' Then, in an oblique reference to the red march through Limerick a year earlier, he said: 'They're not lining up on the streets of Limerick, five thousand complaining about the bankers costing them their jobs. This town is one depressing little place.'

A week later, Wayne Dundon packed up his family and moved to the UK to live with his traveller cousins. He could no longer take the pressure of the relentless police harassment. Dundon and his clan spent their time moving between London and Kuşadasi in Turkey where he owned a villa. While there he was accompanied by two Kurdish minders, in recognition of his status as an international hoodlum. When he was approached by a reporter, Dundon threatened to kill him.

By the summer of 2010 most of the Dundon/McCarthy gang, including three of the Dundon brothers, were behind bars, either serving sentences or awaiting trial having been denied bail. The new laws meant that their cases would be heard in the non-jury Special Criminal Court to prevent the intimidation of juries in Limerick. The mob's reputation ensured that none of them could get bail. In July they were joined by Nathan Killeen, after he was arrested for breaking into a house and demanding money with menaces while out of his head on drugs. In the early hours of 24 July, Killeen and Niall Carey from Hyde Road broke into the home of a man and demanded payment of €10,000. But the victim called the Gardaí and later identified the two thugs. People were no longer afraid to go to the police.

As the Garda success rate mounted, gun crime continued to decline in Limerick. In 2010 the number of reported shootings dropped to twenty, the lowest figure in a decade. Drug seizures were also increasing. 'Fat' John McCarthy, one of Murder Inc.'s drug dealers, was nabbed with €150,000 of heroin. He was subsequently jailed for fourteen years, while two other members of the gang got four years each.

In September Wayne Dundon suddenly reappeared in the city for the funeral of his uncle, Patrick 'Pa' McCarthy. As soon as he arrived the trouble started again. On 29 September the mob tried to murder their hit man James Dillon in Limerick Prison when they purposely spiked his heroin with poison. Dundon was worried that the young man was weak and might become a State witness once the reality of a lifetime in prison sunk in. He was like James Cronin – a loose end that needed tidying up. And it didn't matter that he was a relation.

The heroin was smuggled in to Nathan Killeen, who was on remand there with several other members of Murder Inc. Even though he was a drug abuser himself Killeen refrained from using the contaminated 'gear'. Within hours Dillon collapsed and was later treated in intensive care. When he recovered the impressionable gang member considered making a statement about the Roy Collins murder to the police. But he was warned to keep his mouth shut.

The following day Dundon attended his uncle's funeral and helped to carry the coffin. The self-styled godfather wasn't greeted with a warm welcome by his McCarthy relatives. The constant police activity and the gang's horrific, mindless crimes had resulted in most of the clan being incarcerated. The State was bringing its full weight to bear on Murder Inc. and they were front-page news, confirming their position as Public Enemy Number One. The dim-witted gangsters were beginning to weary of the publicity and notoriety they had once thrived on. The fun was going out of their nasty game. The public were also sick of the mob and no longer prepared to take their intimidation and threats. Under the surface of the gang's seemingly solid infrastructure, cracks were beginning to show. The disintegration began with the gang members who had been locked up for the Heffernan extortion case.

Around 2 p.m. on the same day as the funeral, 30 September, the simmering tension boiled to the surface when Nathan Killeen attacked Gareth Collins in Limerick Prison – and got more than he bargained for. There had been bad blood between the pair since Collins refused to drive the car used in Roy Collins's murder. Killeen filled a sock with batteries as a makeshift weapon. Then he lunged at Gareth Collins on the landing. Collins had always been treated as an easily bullied weakling in the gang, but he was no longer prepared to take the abuse. He quickly over-powered Killeen, giving him a severe pounding in the process, and emerged as the victor against Murder Inc.'s favoured enforcer. Killeen was later set upon again and seriously beaten by other members of the gang, who had been infuriated by the attempt to poison James Dillon. It was a grievous loss of face for Killeen and the Dundons. He shared a cell with Ger Dundon and was seen as the brothers' most trusted lieutenant. The commotion between the former allies was so loud that Gareth Collins's mother, Alice, could hear the shouts in the visiting room where she was waiting to see her husband, Jimmy. News of the confrontation was quickly relayed to the women on the outside.

At 5.45 p.m. Nathan Killeen's sister Ciara – John Dundon's wife – went to the home of Alice Collins. Ciara Killeen was with her sister Linda, Ciara Lynch, the partner of Dessie Dundon, and a friend, Kathleen O'Reilly. The women wanted to exact revenge on Alice for her son's earlier victory over

Nathan Killeen. They were armed with a sledgehammer, a steering-wheel lock and a car jack. The women attacked Alice Collins who was forced to cower in the hallway as a range of metal objects flew through her open front door. Outside Ciara Killeen was shouting about putting a 'bullet through her head'. The other women beat the side panels of Alice's 1997 Suzuki jeep with the sledgehammer as she called the Gardaí.

When the police arrived Collins beckoned them inside her home. She didn't want to talk to the officers in front of Wayne Dundon. He had arrived before the cops and was standing close by, watching the commotion. She heard him ask: 'Why are the guards following her into her house?' Alice later made a statement of complaint about the incident at Roxboro Road Station and returned to her home. She washed the floors and left the front door open for them to dry.

Around 8 p.m. Wayne Dundon walked into her sitting-room unannounced and sat down. She later described how he was in a 'very agitated state' and was 'foaming at the mouth' as he shouted threats. He said his brother John was not happy and would 'hunt people down' if his wife Ciara went to jail over the earlier incident. Dundon then threatened her young-est son, Jimmy Junior, who had no involvement in crime. 'Our John will give some fool ten grand to kill Jimmy, how about that?' he snarled viciously. Alice Collins said she froze and asked why Dundon was picking on her quiet son. 'Cos it's always the quiet fellas who get it,' he replied.

Wayne Dundon promised to keep the pleasure of killing Gareth Collins for himself. He told her: 'I am going to kill Gareth myself personally. He's goin' to stand in front of me and look at my face, my face will be the last face he'll see.' As he got up to leave the house, Dundon reminded her: 'Alice, you're digging your own grave; we've a knack of making people disappear.' Then he left.

In the space of six hours Alice Collins had suddenly found herself in a blood-curdling situation. She had lived in the midst of the gang long enough to know that the Dundons never made idle threats. And when it came to receiving punishment of the most extreme kind it didn't matter who you were connected to in the mob's structure. Nevertheless, Alice Collins bravely pursued her complaint and the four women were subsequently arrested and charged with assault and causing criminal damage. But she didn't report the threats Dundon had made – she knew that would be a step too far. The cracks in the mob's relationships had suddenly become a large fissure.

Later on that same night, 30 September, Dundon attempted to lure Christy Keane and his nephew Kieran Keane Junior into a murder trap. It was chillingly similar to the plots which had resulted in the murders of Kieran Keane's father and Michael Campbell McNamara. Two armed and masked men burst into the home of Kieran's nineteen-year-old girlfriend and held her hostage. They tried to force the young woman to lure her boyfriend and his uncle to the house. When the gangsters arrived they were going to be shot dead. But the fractures within the Dundon/McCarthys' code of silence were also growing and an informant tipped off the Gardaí about the plot. The gunmen made their escape just before armed detectives arrived to rescue the woman.

Wayne Dundon ended his whirlwind visit home when he left Limerick and returned to the UK a day later. For a short time at least there would be an uneasy calm in Ballinacurra Weston.

Meanwhile the prison authorities had clamped down on

the Murder Inc. bully boys behind bars. Following the publication of the torture picture, the policy to keep the Dundons and their cousins separated and regularly moved between prisons was stepped up. Members of the once most feared gang in Ireland gradually began to realize that they were no longer men of 'respect'. Several of them, including Noddy McCarthy and Dessie Dundon, were beaten up by criminals from Dublin.

The gang was coming under attack from every conceivable angle. It was also unravelling from the inside. Murder Inc. was about to implode.

18. Breaking the Siege

The tension within the gang was close to breaking point – and April Collins was the first to snap. She decided that she had had enough of living a life of terror at the hands of her partner Ger Dundon and his family. The twenty-three-year-old mother of the thug's two children put on a brave, defiant face to the cops and to the media who came to annoy the mob, but in reality she had endured an eight-year relationship that was a nightmare of constant savage beatings and abuse. Dundon had kept her a prisoner in Spain a few years earlier while he pulverized her with his fists. The only respite periods she got from her ordeal were thanks to the police – who orchestrated Ger's frequent spells behind bars. When he wasn't there, his brothers beat her if she stepped out of line. April had the hospital records to prove what life was like living amid Ireland's most dangerous men.

April blamed Ger and John Dundon for the imprisonment of her father Jimmy and brother Gareth. They had terrorized businessman Mark Heffernan at the behest of the Dundons. She was also facing charges for threatening the victim's sister in a bid to force him to retract his evidence. Using intimidation against the gang's enemies and their families was expected from the Dundon women. April was also tired of living with the constant threat of drive-by shootings and arson attacks in the depths of the night. The unprecedented level of Garda attention that the mob's outrageous crimes had attracted was taking a heavy toll too. She had grown up the hard way and was beginning to realize that she had sacrificed enough of her life to a group of mindless, murderous morons.

Ciara Killeen's attack on April's mother Alice, and the death threats made by Wayne Dundon, were the last straw. In the aftermath April, Alice and April's sister Lisa ran the daily gauntlet of being bullied and intimidated by the other molls whom they had once called friends. Alice Collins advised her daughter that it was time to get away from the savages. In October 2010 April Collins made her decision and ended the dysfunctional relationship with Ger. Her brave move set the backdrop for an unlikely series of events which would end Murder Inc.'s ten-year siege of Limerick.

In the feuds between the crime families, the role played by women was unique to Limerick gangland. The women, like their gangster partners, were a breed apart from the rest of the underworld rabble. What they lacked in testosterone they more than compensated for with copious amounts of hatred and desire for vengeance. Their involvement in the chaos was another factor peculiar to the dynamic of serious crime in the city.

Mothers, wives, girlfriends and daughters from the neglected ghettoes were often the root cause of inter-family feuds, and they were blamed for fanning the flames of hatred and keeping the disputes alive. They rejected peace deals and goaded their menfolk into battle. Women and girls fought and stabbed each other in the street, the courts and the schoolyards. Mothers also instilled the poison in their children, raising a new generation that knew how to hate its enemies. It once prompted outspoken Limerick city councillor John

Gilligan to remark that as long as women continued to be so entrenched in the violence, there would be little chance of resolving the feuds.

Women have always played their part in the various Limerick sieges, both real and metaphorical. The gangland molls were following in the footsteps of their sisters in history. In the ancient city 'well versed in the arts of war', women had always been prepared to protect their territory – but with more honourable motives. During the sieges of Limerick in 1642 and 1691 women fought alongside their men to save their city. When the walls were breached they used stockings filled with rocks as weapons to throw at the invaders. Their role was equally significant in the siege that beset Limerick in the first decade of the twenty-first century. The women in Murder Inc. in particular were staunchly loyal to their men, despite the neglect and physical abuse they suffered. They moved drugs, guns and money and generally kept the war running when their brutal partners were in prison – or convalescing after being wounded in action. And they all produced heirs for their sadistic partners. The Dundon molls were also privy to details about the murders, shootings and drug deals. But they were strict observers of the code of *omertà*. In various Garda intelligence reports compiled through the years of warfare, women like April Collins and Ciara Killeen were described as hardened, fully integrated members of the gang. The female lovers and partners were the last ones anyone – particularly the Dundon brothers – expected to break the silence. It was ironic that it was the women who eventually brought Murder Inc.'s citadel of evil crumbling down.

With Ger Dundon locked up and facing a likely five-year prison sentence, it was the opportune time for April Collins to finally make the break. She was heavily pregnant with their third child when she ended the disastrous relationship. She also had two sons, aged five and two, to care for. Collins was happy to go it alone without the benefit of the mob's dirty money because Ger had never been of much support in the first place. The youngest Dundon brother refused to accept the split. She and the kids were his property and no one else's. 'You don't say no to these people,' was how she described Ger and his clan. He phoned her constantly in a bid to change her mind. Typically his technique involved threats of violence.

On 24 November 2010 a recording of an authorized prison phone call Ger Dundon made to April Collins highlighted the tensions between them. It was one of 116 such conversations that were recorded between the couple in the period before and after the separation. Dundon asked his eight-month pregnant girlfriend if she 'went off' with another man, which she denied. The conversation then turned to the attack by Ciara Killeen on Alice Collins. It quickly descended into an angry exchange. Collins told Ger Dundon that his family were 'lowlife scumbags'. She said: 'They [the Dundons] are the biggest shower of scumbags that I have ever met in my life.'

'You fucking scumbag; don't be ringing me no more. I don't want anything more to do with you. Do you understand that? I'll fix you when I have my child. Now don't fuckin' ring me again,' she was heard to say. April Collins stopped visiting him and didn't want him to see the children either. On 20 December she gave birth to their third child, another boy.

April had clearly shown that she had poor taste in men when she hooked-up with Ger Dundon at the tender age of fifteen. But she knew nothing else of life beyond the stultifying, enclosed world of the Dundon/McCarthys. She grew up in a home where her gangster father Jimmy was good for nothing, except committing crimes and violent assaults. He regularly beat her mother Alice and was the subject of several barring orders. In this primal world the male was dominant, and domestic abuse was seen as a necessary fact of life. So it was hardly surprising that when she found a new lover, he was just as violent and dangerous as the other men in her tragic life.

Shortly after she had her child, in early 2011 April Collins began a casual affair with a notorious rapist, Thomas O'Neill, who was a childhood friend of Ger's. In November 2010 O'Neill had been released from prison after serving six years for a horrific sex attack. In January 2004 the then sixteen-year-old and three other teenagers from Ballinacurra Weston gang-raped a thirty-five-year-old woman in Cratloe Woods, a remote area on the outskirts of the city popular among courting couples. O'Neill was the ringleader of the gang that attacked the woman and her boyfriend as they sat in their car.

Armed with a golf club, a screwdriver, a wheel brace and a shovel, they ordered the terrified pair out of the car. They then hit the woman on the shoulder with the golf club when she refused to give one of them a kiss. O'Neill and his accomplices pounced on the boyfriend, believing him to be a Garda, and shouted: 'Do him.' The man was beaten and bundled into the boot while his girlfriend was pushed onto the bonnet and savagely abused. She was dragged into the car and the four youths took turns raping her. They threatened to burn the car with her boyfriend still inside if she resisted. At one point they opened the boot and hit the man repeatedly with the golf club. In July 2004 O'Neill got ten years after pleading guilty to violent rape, false imprisonment and assault.

While inside O'Neill had become a sworn enemy of the Dundons, especially Wayne, for whom he had a deep hatred. The teen rapist, described in a subsequent trial as 'dangerous, volatile, unmanageable, unruly and depraved', was well able to take on the gangsters. When O'Neill came out he made no secret of his plans to take over Murder Inc.'s business. He also vowed to kill Wayne Dundon, who at that stage was still living in London. Ger Dundon wouldn't tolerate his former partner hooking up with anyone. But forming a relationship with a hated enemy was treason of the highest order. The relationship remained a secret and in the meantime Ger had other things on his mind.

On 4 February 2011, the Special Criminal Court jailed Ger Dundon and David 'Skull' McCormack for five years each for their involvement in the campaign of intimidation against businessman Mark Heffernan. They both pleaded guilty to violent disorder. Two weeks later, on 18 February, Jimmy Collins, Gareth Collins, Christopher McCarthy and Patrick Pickford all pleaded guilty to demanding money with menaces. On 16 March three of them were each jailed for seven-and-a-half years. Patrick Pickford got a four-year sentence, with two years suspended. On 7 April, Christopher McCormack received a five-year term for violent disorder, with the final two years suspended. The various hearings were told that Heffernan was forced to live under twenty-four-hour armed Garda protection because he had stood up against evil. The cases, all part of Operation Redwing, were heard in the non-jury court as part of the State's response to the murders of Shane Geoghegan and Roy Collins.

While his former 'colleagues' were waiting to hear their

fate, Barry Doyle's trial for the murder of Shane Geoghegan opened in the Central Criminal Court in Dublin on 22 February 2011. Looking dapper in an expensive grey suit and pink shirt, Doyle sat in the dock clutching a book entitled *The Damage Done: Twelve Years Of Hell In A Bangkok Prison*. When asked how he intended to plea, he replied 'not guilty'.

But before the trial could even get off the ground there was a sinister twist. A detective from the National Bureau of Criminal Investigation walked into courtroom No. 6 of the Central Criminal Court and recognized a face he knew sitting on the jury bench. The eagle-eyed detective knew the man to be an associate of a west Dublin crime gang, which was closely aligned to Murder Inc. The matter was brought to the attention of Mr Justice Paul Carney, who immediately discharged the jury. He told the jury panel: 'For reasons I'm not going to go into at this stage I have to discharge you from service. You're not to attend with the jury panel tomorrow.' The following morning a new jury was sworn in and the trial commenced.

From the outset the State appeared to have an open-and-shut case. The prosecution came to court armed with the extensive admissions made by Doyle, all of which were recorded on video. The killer had given a detailed description of how he carried out the heinous crime. Doyle had even helpfully mimicked the position Shane Geoghegan was in when the hit man fired the fatal shot into his head. There was also considerable corroboration to back up his admission. His former girlfriend, Vicky Gunnery, was prepared to testify that he had confessed his involvement in the murder to her. There was also extensive phone and text traffic to corroborate what she had to say. The evidence which crime boss

Philip Collopy had offered to give before he'd accidentally shot himself would have been the icing on the cake. But even without his input the prosecution was confident they could convict the Murder Inc. assassin.

Doyle's defence team argued that Gardaí had offered inducements and applied psychological pressure before he confessed. His counsel claimed the detectives were asking the killer to tell them what they wanted to hear on the condition that Gunnery, who was also in custody, could then return home to their sick child, who had been due to have a heart scan the day they were arrested.

The jury heard that Doyle's solicitor, Michael O'Donnell, had tried to do 'a deal' with investigating Gardaí – Doyle would confess if Vicky Gunnery was first released from custody. Detective Sergeant Mark Philips told the court he and his colleague had rejected this deal, knowing any admissions made this way would constitute inducement and consequently would not stand up in court.

Vicky Gunnery gave evidence that after Doyle switched his phone back on around 1.30 a.m., a half hour after the murder, she texted him to ask why he had turned it off. 'He told me to read the teletext in the morning,' she said. She said she did this and learned that a man had been shot in Limerick. She said Doyle rang her from Turkey some days later and asked what the newspapers were saying about the murder. 'They know it's you because they say it's a very close associate of Paddy Doyle,' she informed him. 'He said they had no proof,' she recalled in court.

However, despite the apparently strong evidence, the jury failed to reach a verdict after the month-long hearing. The panel of five men and five women had been instructed to return a unanimous verdict. This was because two jurors had been discharged from the panel of twelve before deliberations began. (With a full jury panel a court can accept a majority verdict, in the absence of a unanimous one.) The jury spent a total of fifteen and a half hours considering the evidence before telling Mr Justice Carney they could not agree. On 25 March the court ordered a retrial and Doyle was remanded in custody.

Back in Limerick the tension was continuing to fester between the once staunchly loyal gangster molls. On 10 March, despite the threats from Wayne Dundon, Alice Collins pursued her complaint against the women who had attacked her and her property. As a result Ciara Killeen, her sister Linda, Ciara Lynch and Kathleen O'Reilly were convicted of assault and criminal damage and each received ten-month sentences, suspended for a period of eighteen months.

In the same month, while in Portlaoise Prison, Ger Dundon asked a priest and a nun to contact April Collins. He had been moved to Portlaoise from Limerick Prison after smashing up his cell when his sister Annabel told him of his partner's affair. He wanted her to return his calls and bring the children in to visit. When the Good Samaritans called to Collins she told them to 'get lost'.

On 14 March 2011, Dundon finally spoke to his former partner and demanded to know what she planned to do with the children if she was jailed for threatening Mark Heffernan's sister. He wanted Wayne and his wife to rear them. And he was prepared to seek a court order to make it happen. April was having none of it. She told him: 'Do you think you would have a leg to stand on in court? You are the biggest fuckin' idiot going. Look who you are. Look at your family. Look at your background.' Ger contacted Wayne to see what he could do.

On 23 March Wayne Dundon's wife Anne gave birth to their third child, Wayne Junior. She had returned home from the UK to have the child in her native town. The following day Dundon arrived in Limerick to see his first son. He had slipped back on a ferry to avoid media and police attention. Murder Inc.'s malevolent influence on Ballinacurra Weston had begun to wane since his departure and the imprisonment of so many gang members. The row between the Collinses and Nathan Killeen had also resulted in a serious rift in the gang. Dundon's vacant house in Hyde Road had been set on fire in January, an attack that would have been considered unthinkable a few years earlier. When he returned the damage was still under repair at the taxpayer's expense. Dundon, like his entire clan, had never worked a day in his life.

At 11.15 a.m. the following morning, 25 March, April Collins had an unexpected visitor. She was hoovering the stairs at the home she had once shared with Ger when Wayne Dundon walked in and tapped her on the shoulder. His face was contorted with a terrifying anger that she recognized with dread. 'What's going on with you and Ger? You're not letting the kids up to see him; Annabel's been telling us,' he demanded. Dundon began shouting into her face, as froth and spittle gathered at the edge of his mouth: 'If anything happens to my brother over you, I'll kill you for it. I know your brother Gareth got my house burned. Tell him from me, he won't get away with it. He won't make it through the prison gates.' Collins was terrified and began to cry. She knew that Wayne Dundon never lied when he made such threats.

Then he threatened her mother. 'If your mother pulls up

outside the house one more time, she won't drive again. She will be going in a body bag and you know our threats are serious, so tell her that from me.' The mobster then told her to get out of Ger's house. He stared at her one more time before turning and storming out. April decided she wasn't going anywhere.

The following day, to make a point, Dundon temporarily 'kidnapped' her oldest boy, Dessie, by taking him to the shops. It was a reminder to April Collins that if she didn't do what she was told, the Dundons would take her children away – after all, they were Dundon property.

At 2 p.m. on Sunday, 3 April, John Dundon was released from Cloverhill Prison after completing his sentences for motoring offences and car theft. He was wearing one of his favourite red-and-white check shirts and looked trim, having shed almost five stone. April Collins and her family were on his mind. He was still raging that two weeks earlier his partner, Ciara Killeen, had received a suspended sentence for threatening Alice Collins. The recalcitrant women needed to be taught a lesson. When he arrived at his house at 80 Hyde Road – two doors away from where April Collins was still living – Wayne was standing outside waiting for him, and so were the police.

He later told Gardaí: 'I shook Wayne's hand and said it was nice to be out. I met my daughter, baby Annabel, then me and Wayne went for a walk.' The dangerous brothers walked down Wolfe Tone Street and Edward Street. The Dublin Squad officers followed close behind. The two killers were paranoid that their homes were being secretly bugged by the cops and reckoned the street was the safest place to discuss business. The new anti-gang laws enacted after the murders of Shane Geoghegan and Roy Collins had included powers for Gardaí to plant surveillance equipment in suspects' homes.

That evening Ciara Killeen threw a homecoming party for Dundon. Despite being out of prison for less than seven hours, he left the party at around 9 p.m. and walked to April's house. He began beating on her door but she didn't answer. She recalled later: 'He was shouting, "I want to see my nephews, you tramp; I know you're in there. When I catch you I'm going to fucking kill you."' Dundon then went back to his party. Later, between 1 a.m. and 2 a.m., Collins was in bed when she heard voices in her back garden. When she looked out she saw John Dundon and an associate on top of a shed. She asked him what he was doing. Dundon replied: 'I'm looking for a good place to bury your mother.'

Thomas O'Neill began spending more time with the frightened Collins to protect her from her estranged in-laws. To further annoy the Dundons, she was seen kissing and embracing the rapist outside her house on Hyde Road. By then she had made the biggest, most profoundly important decision of her life. April Collins was all too familiar with the Dundons' single-minded pursuit of their enemies. She knew that she was effectively a dead woman walking. April and her mother Alice went to visit Jimmy Collins in Limerick Prison to ask his advice. He knew that the Dundons were determined to spill Collins blood. The gangster, who had hated the police all his life, agreed that there was only one course of action available – contact the Gardaí and make an official complaint.

On 7 April 2011 Alice and April Collins stopped Detective Garda James Hourihan while he was patrolling Hyde Road. They told him their lives had been threatened by Wayne and John Dundon and they wanted to file a complaint. The following day the mother and daughter, both partners of career gangsters, sat down with Gardaí and made their statements. The women gave details of the various threats which had been made by John and Wayne Dundon, including the death threats made against Alice by Wayne the previous September.

For the Gardaí it was a welcome development. The Murder Inc. gang was beginning to disintegrate from the inside out. On Saturday, 9 April, April Collins left home with her children and went to stay for a week with Thomas O'Neill in Murroe, County Limerick. That evening Annabel Dundon went there to confront her brother's former partner. Dundon shouted at Collins: 'You might as well enjoy it while it lasts, 'cause it's not goin' to last very long. There's a bullet coming your way.'

April made a formal complaint and the DPP subsequently directed that Annabel Dundon also be charged with making threats. At the time of writing Annabel, who is living in the UK, is wanted by Gardaí.

At dawn on the morning of Monday, 11 April, the RSU moved in and arrested John and Wayne Dundon at their homes. Wayne was taken to Roxboro Garda Station and John to Henry Street Station. They were questioned by three teams of detectives over a period of twenty hours. As he paced around the interview room, Wayne punched his fist into his other hand and claimed his brother's partner was setting him up. 'Do you think it's coincidental she made a statement on the same day she ran away with a man we don't approve of?' he asked. But John Dundon was more talkative.

When the allegations were put to John he claimed she had fallen out with his family after they caught her taking drugs. 'April Collins is a Looney Tune, unstable person,' he scowled.

'She is a member of a notorious family and even the Gardaí objected to her bail [for threats against Mark Heffernan's sister] 'cause she would cause danger even though she was pregnant. I'm flabbergasted she is the type of person you believe. This is a witch-hunt against me by the Gardaí in Limerick.'

Dundon said the witnesses at his homecoming party would back up his alibi. He continued to rant: 'I have accounted for my movements through twenty hours of interviews and you have no other verification but some crackhead's allegation. She has no corroborating evidence and I have a full house of people. This is a witch-hunt. My liberty is at stake.'

Then, in a thinly veiled reference to the failure to convict his henchman Barry Doyle a few months earlier, he sneered at the officers interviewing him. 'Will you investigate it and run like a rugby player with it? Will you go for a scrum with that?'

On 12 April the DPP agreed to charge the Dundons with making threats to kill. The following morning the brothers were taken before Limerick District Court where they were formally charged with making threats to kill Alice Collins as well as her son Gareth and daughter April.

There was the by now customary heavily armed Garda presence for the appearance. The State objected to bail for both men. Wayne Dundon's solicitor said that his client was anxious to attend his son's christening, which was due to take place the following Sunday. Judge Tom O'Donnell refused bail after hearing evidence from Gardaí that Dundon was residing in the UK and had property in Turkey and Bulgaria. He said he didn't wish to sound 'disingenuous' but suggested that 'perhaps the christening could be rescheduled'.

The court then heard John Dundon's bail application. The loudmouth was sickened that he had only been out of prison for eight days. Judge O'Donnell was forced to halt the hearing after Dundon began shouting abuse at Detective Garda Denise Moriarty as she was objecting to his bail. 'Go fuck yourself,' he shouted at the Garda. Then he roared at the judge: 'Go fuck yourself. Fuck you. Fuck you, you clown.' Judge O'Donnell said he was 'not going to put up with that type of behaviour' and stopped the proceedings.

Judge O'Donnell described Dundon's performance as 'appalling'. As Gardaí took him from the courtroom, John Dundon struggled and shouted: 'Get your fuckin' hands off me.' When Wayne was being processed later on that day in Limerick Prison he spotted Gareth Collins. 'You're dead you little prick,' he warned his former lieutenant. Neither of the brothers succeeded in getting bail at subsequent hearings. Although they didn't know it then, they would never be free men again. April Collins was going to make sure of that.

On 20 April Alice Collins contacted Detective Garda James Hourihan, who had been appointed to act as a liaison officer with the family. She told him that she wanted to meet Detective Superintendent Jim Browne. She had something important to tell and would only talk to him. Ironically she wanted to talk to the mob's most hated foe. When Browne made contact, Alice informed him that April had decided to completely break her code of *omertà*. The mother and daughter had consulted Jimmy Collins, who agreed that she should come clean with everything she knew. That afternoon, April Collins and her mother sat down with Detective Superintendent Jim Browne and Detective Sergeant Brian Sugrue in a room in Henry Street Garda Station.

'I know things about some murders I want to make a statement about even though I'm terrified,' she told the two detectives. 'I couldn't say anything until they were all locked up because I was afraid I'd be killed.' Then over the next number of hours she proceeded to unleash the darkest secrets of Ireland's most dangerous mob. She told them everything she knew about the murders of Shane Geoghegan, Roy Collins and James Cronin.

The mother-of-three was determined to finally see justice done because she had nothing left to lose. The Dundons' predilection for extreme violence and terror had left her with no choice. The brutality and fear they used to control the world around them had ultimately proved to be their collective fatal flaw. In that moment of honesty, April Collins smashed a huge hole in Murder Inc.'s impenetrable wall of silence. This was the turning point the Gardaí had long been waiting for. It was the game changer in the longest-running criminal investigation in Irish history.

When the State's new witness finished dictating her statement at 6.23 p.m. a top secret investigation was immediately set up in an incident room at Roxboro Garda Station. It had to begin the mammoth task of compiling prosecution files around her evidence. Detective Sergeants Denis Treacy and Kevin Swann, two of the city's most experienced cops, were given the job of corroborating every word of Collins's devastating testimony.

Her new evidence copper-fastened the case against Barry Doyle, which had been scheduled for a second trial in February 2012. It also gave the investigators the break they needed to charge John Dundon with Shane Geoghegan's murder. She implicated Wayne Dundon in the murder of Roy Collins and Nathan Killeen in the execution of James Cronin, the would-be gangster who cried. In the meantime armed patrols were dispatched to watch the homes of the two women while decisions were made about their suitability to join the WPP.

On 19 May, April Collins received a three-year suspended sentence after pleading guilty to intimidating Mark Heffernan's sister. Even though she had once been one of their prime targets, the Gardaí described the twenty-three-year-old as being 'young and impressionable'.

In the meantime, April's brother Gareth Collins had contacted the Gardaí and said he also wanted to talk. On 1 May he met detectives in Limerick Prison and told them about being pressurized by Nathan Killeen and Wayne Dundon to drive the getaway car in the Roy Collins murder. He also revealed how the gang boss had vowed to kill Steve Collins after being convicted of threatening to kill Ryan Lee in 2005. Like his sister he was prepared to testify in court. A month later Gareth Collins's girlfriend, Elaine Walsh, also made a statement. Murder Inc. was unravelling and the breach in their wall of silence was growing so big that the cops would soon be able to charge through. The liberation of Limerick City from the clutches of organized crime had begun.

But despite the fact that the world was closing in on the mob they still wanted to remind Steve Collins that they had not forgotten him. On Monday, 4 July, a three-bedroom cottage he owned was extensively damaged in an arson attack. It happened just hours after a 'For Let' sign had been erected on the property. The building was situated a few doors down from Steve's former pub Brannigan's that had been gutted in 2005 and never re-opened.

The Dundons' henchmen showed no concern for the safety of others as they also lit a fire outside the house, beside a gas central-heating boiler. If the boiler had exploded, fire officers said, it could easily have killed an elderly couple, both aged eighty-two, who lived next door. At the time Steve told this writer: 'This is the most sickening part of this whole thing. These scum have no concern for the well-being of anyone. I'm more upset about the neighbours than I am about the damage they caused. The fire brigade saved us from having two deaths on our hands. They shot Ryan; they murdered Roy; they burned down our pub; now this. When will it ever stop?'

19. Downfall

The Dundons first realized the full extent of April Collins's disloyalty when Barry Doyle was served with additional evidence in the run-up to his second trial for the murder of Shane Geoghegan. The fact that she was prepared to become a supergrass was unconscionable. It underlined the gang's urgent need to eradicate Collins and her mother before John and Wayne's trial for threatening to kill them commenced in February. Orders were sent from prison, through the women who still remained loyal, to have April and her mother murdered at all costs. A bounty of €100,000 was placed on both their heads. But by then the women were under round-the-clock protection by armed Garda bodyguards. Even the most avaricious, brain-dead hit man knew better than to take on the contracts. Outside the prison walls Murder Inc. no longer commanded the same level of respect as before. The Piranhas had finally become pariahs.

April Collins's debut performance as a State witness against the mob was Barry Doyle's second trial that began on 16 January 2012. Doyle's defence team embarked on the same strategy of claiming that their client had confessed to Shane Geoghegan's murder under duress. However, this time April Collins provided crucial evidence that shed even more light on the crime. She described in detail witnessing John Dundon giving Doyle instructions on how to carry out the murder of the intended target, Johnny 'Pitchfork' McNamara. The star supergrass also told of the meeting the morning after the murder, when John Dundon and Barry Doyle realized that they had killed the wrong man. There was extensive corroboration to confirm her story.

Ger Dundon's ex-partner proved to be an articulate and honest witness as she endured robust cross-examination from Doyle's defence team. Her testimony stood up to intense scrutiny during the three-week trial. On 15 February the jury returned a unanimous guilty verdict after deliberating for six hours. Shane's mother Mary comforted his weeping girlfriend Jenna Barry as Mr Justice Garrett Sheehan handed Doyle the mandatory life sentence. The dapper gangster, who had tried to follow in his brother's footsteps, smirked as he was led away.

The Geoghegan family turned down the opportunity to make a victim impact statement. Counsel for the prosecution, Sean Guerin SC, told the court that they felt the crime and the conviction spoke for itself. Garda Superintendent John Scanlan later described the verdict as a time of great sadness for the Geoghegan family – not a moment for triumph. And in a clear reference to the use of April Collins's testimony in further trials, the officer warned that the investigation was not over. He said: 'It's a good result for the decent people of Limerick. But there are other persons who will have to be considered.'

A week later, on 21 February, the trial of Wayne and John Dundon opened before the Special Criminal Court in Dublin. Thirty-three-year-old Wayne was charged with five counts of making threats to kill and two counts of obstructing the course of justice at addresses in Limerick City over a seven-month period between 2010 and 2011.

The charges included making a threat to kill or cause serious harm to April Collins and making a threat to April

Collins to kill or cause serious harm to her brother Gareth and mother Alice. He was also accused of threatening to kill Alice Collins and her sons Gareth and Jimmy Junior on 30 September 2010. And he was charged with intimidating potential prosecution witnesses, Alice and April Collins, with the intention of obstructing the course of justice in the case which related to the attack by the four Murder Inc. girlfriends on Alice Collins. John Dundon was charged with threatening to kill April Collins and making a threat to kill her mother, Alice Collins, on the weekend of 3–4 April 2011. The brothers denied all the charges.

Alice Collins recounted for the court what had occurred when Wayne Dundon walked into her home on 30 September 2010. Under cross-examination she denied that she had made the allegations up to ensure Wayne Dundon was 'off the scene' for a substantial period. She told his defence counsel that even if Dundon was convicted she 'might only stay alive a bit longer'. She said that she had waited seven months after the initial threats before making a statement because she was in fear for her life. She told the court: 'You don't make a statement against him and survive it.'

When it was April Collins's turn to be called to testify she was flanked by four members of the ERU as she entered the courtroom. She was by then six months pregnant with Thomas O'Neill's baby. As she gave her evidence an armed Garda remained close by. She refused to make eye contact with the two brothers, apart from when she was asked to point them out for the court. The gangsters stared at her with hate-filled eyes. This wouldn't be the last time that they had to look at their brother's former partner in court.

The mother-of-three spoke quietly and looked down when she was being asked to relive the threats. Collins was repeatedly asked to speak up. When the presiding judge, Mr Justice Paul Butler, asked her to look up when talking, she replied: 'I don't want to take notice of Wayne and John Dundon.' Wayne averted his gaze to the ground or to the side, while John continued looking intently at the woman. It was clear he deeply regretted not killing her when he had the chance. Collins was repeatedly challenged about her relationship with a dangerous criminal and convicted rapist. John's counsel said Ger had been concerned about his children associating with O'Neill, a sex offender. But Collins responded: 'He wasn't a paedophile. He made a mistake when he was fourteen and received a prison sentence for it. He wasn't one bit violent towards me or my kids.'

When asked by Wayne's counsel as to why she never complained to Ger about him making threats against her mother, she replied: 'No, that's his brother at the end of the day. If I told him what Wayne said he would have told Wayne and Wayne would have come over to my house and beat me up.' In response to repeated suggestions that she was making the whole thing up because there was bad blood between the Dundons and the Collins family, she replied: 'I'm not telling lies. These men threatened me and I believe they are going to kill me and my family.'

Before the closing statements the defence teams for the brothers sought to have the case against the two Dundons thrown out on the grounds that the prosecution had failed to produce any evidence to corroborate the testimony of two unreliable witnesses. Brian McCartney SC for John Dundon urged the three presiding judges to ignore the Dundons' reputation as criminals: 'I'm not silly enough to ignore the elephant in the room in this case, but the name Dundon is nothing else – it's not a reputation; it's nothing other than a name.'

Padraig Dwyer SC, representing Wayne, told the non-jury court: 'Wayne Dundon comes before this court as a household name. Over the years there has been a complete tidal wave of adverse publicity about him. In this particular case the obligation is on the State to use such resources at its disposal to corroborate the evidence of the two witnesses. There was a complete failure on the part of the State to deploy these resources.' However, the court refused the application to have the cases thrown out.

On 16 March the court convicted Wayne Dundon of making threats to kill Gareth and Jimmy Collins Junior and also on two charges of intimidating April and Alice Collins on 30 September 2010. The court acquitted the mobster of making threats to kill April, Alice and Gareth Collins on 25 March 2011. John Dundon was found guilty of making threats against April Collins on 3 April 2011 but was acquitted of making threats against her mother in the early hours of the morning of 4 April. The court adjourned sentencing for a month. When it returned, the Special Criminal Court jailed the most feared brothers in gangland for a total of eleven years between them. Wayne Dundon was given six years; John got a sentence of five-and-a-half years.

It was a stunning victory for the Gardaí and society in general. Murder Inc. was imploding in full public view. But the war was still not won. To paraphrase Winston Churchill, it was the 'end of the beginning of the end'. Behind the scenes, Gardaí were working closely with the Chief State Solicitor's office in Limerick preparing a case to charge John Dundon with the murder of Shane Geoghegan. They were also preparing murder charges for Wayne Dundon and Nathan Killeen for the execution of Roy Collins. The tide of war had turned decisively in favour of the good guys. But just like in the dying days of World War II, there was plenty of fighting still to be done before they reached Berlin. And the war against the Dundons was still creating refugees.

On the morning of Sunday, 25 March 2012, Ireland was basking in unseasonably hot golden sunshine. That same morning Steve Collins left Ireland with his wife Carmel and their two children, Steve Junior and Leanne. (Ryan Lee had opted to stay in Ireland where he continued to receive police protection.) After months of secret negotiations the family, who had paid the ultimate price for standing up against the mob, had opted to leave Ireland as part of a witness relocation programme. Steve Collins gave this writer the job of breaking the news of his family's heavy-hearted departure. The State had finally, after two years, organized a financial deal to buy the family's remaining assets and attempt to compensate them for their mammoth ordeal. Special arrangements had been made between the Irish Departments of Justice and Foreign Affairs, in conjunction with Garda HQ, and the authorities in the host country where the family were going to live. As part of the arrangements Steve had insisted that he was not going to change his name – he had sacrificed enough and he was not going to give up that right.

In the three years since Roy's murder the family had found it impossible to impose any semblance of normality on their lives. They were under constant police protection and Steve's last remaining business, the Steering Wheel, was struggling to make ends meet. Despite having full-time armed guards Murder Inc. had continued to play mind games against the family. The ongoing stress, together with the grief and anguish, was taking its toll. 'We don't have a life worth talking about any more and it is having a serious effect on our mental and physical health,' he explained. 'We had decided never to leave Ireland, especially where our Roy is buried, but it has just become unbearable and we decided to try and start somewhere else afresh.' But it wasn't all gloom on that glorious morning. It was just nine days after the Special Criminal Court had found the Dundons guilty of threatening to kill and Steve said he was leaving on a high note.

'It is very satisfying to see them being convicted and having the prospect of yet another long stretch behind bars – and all because they think they can threaten and kill who they like,' Steve commented just before he boarded his flight at Shannon Airport. 'That is why I would like to ask them one question today: How do you feel now lads? And what have you achieved? Nothing. The truth is that they have been brought to their knees and their so-called empire is imploding around them. The State and the Gardaí have proved they have the power to pursue these savages who are nothing more than mutant pond life. When they are sitting looking at their cell wall I hope they reflect on why they lost their liberty.'

Then Steve Collins summed up what he thought were the reasons for Murder Inc.'s spectacular downfall: 'In return for the pleasure they got from terrorizing my family they will be spending years, maybe even the rest of their lives, behind bars. My family were never a threat to them but they were incapable of rational thought – they were too arrogant and stupid to realize what was coming to them. I am happy that I have done my bit to damage them. Now they have been reduced to killing each other like the animals they are.'

The hard work and professionalism of the Gardaí in Limerick, with the assistance of their colleagues in the national support units, had turned the tables on organized crime in the city that a few years earlier was the murder capital of Ireland and Europe. The offensive against Murder Inc. and its feuding rivals had taken on a momentum of its own – it had become an unstoppable rout. The Garda crime figures spoke for themselves. In 2007 at its peak, there were 103 shootings in the city, one-third of the total number recorded in the entire State. By 2012 that figure had dwindled to just seven. The following year there were just eleven such incidents. The murder rate had also dropped dramatically. There was just one murder in each of the years 2012 and 2013 – and neither of them was gang-related. The smashing of Murder Inc. had turned Limerick from one of Europe's most violent cities to one of its most peaceful.

While Murder Inc. was being pummelled from all sides, the tables had also been turned on their violent enemies. A veritable procession of the city's top gangsters were also either awaiting trials or serving long sentences. Among them were several members of the Collopy family mob, including its leader Kieran, who had been convicted for threatening to murder a member of their own gang following an internal row. When it came to turning on their own, Limerick villains just couldn't seem to help themselves. The notorious sons of murdered crime boss Eddie Ryan, Kieran and Eddie Junior, had also been captured in possession of firearms and jailed for up to ten years each. Over the space of five years at least 150 gang members were incarcerated for an assortment of serious offences including drug trafficking, possession of firearms, drive-by shootings, attempted murder and murder. It confirmed that Limerick's local police squads were the most successful in the country.

On the morning of 17 August 2012 John Dundon was taken from his cell in the Midlands Prison in Portlaoise by

Gardaí to be charged with the murder of Shane Geoghegan. He was then driven in convoy under army escort back to the Special Criminal Court where he was formally arraigned. It was exactly six months and two days after the conviction of his henchman Barry Doyle. The testimony that April Collins had to offer was combined with more than enough independent corroboration to sustain a charge against the psychopath. Dundon had benefited from an extraordinary stroke of serendipity when Philip Collopy got too drunk to remember if he had a bullet up the breech of his gun, but the happenstance was reversed when the 'Dumdum' brothers threatened to kill their own people.

The decision by Alice Collins and her two children to break the line and testify against the Dundons had convinced other members of Murder Inc. to break ranks too. Lisa Collins, Alice's other daughter, came forward in October 2012 and made statements about the murders of Shane Geoghegan and Roy Collins. She had witnessed John Dundon instructing Barry Doyle to kill Johnny 'Pitchfork' McNamara. She and her partner Christopher McCarthy, Dundon's first cousin, had stolen the car used in the Geoghegan murder. Dundon had threatened their lives if they didn't do it.

A month later there was confirmation that the once-powerful partnership of the Dundon and McCarthy clans was at an end when Christopher McCarthy officially came forward as a State witness. The hardened criminal had had enough of the Dundons' threats and bully-boy tactics. Lisa Collins and her partner were granted immunity from prosecution for the theft of the car in return for their testimony.

The dramatic development gave Gardaí enough of a case to have Nathan Killeen and Wayne Dundon charged with the murder of Roy Collins. On the morning of 22 February

2013 the two hoodlums were taken from their cells in Port-laoise Prison and transported under military escort to the Special Criminal Court in Dublin. The two killers sat impassively beside each other in the dock for the brief hearing. Counsel for the State told the court that the DPP had certified the case should be dealt with in the non-jury Special Criminal Court as the ordinary courts were inadequate to deal with the administration of justice in this instance. Dundon's counsel raised his concerns about media coverage of the case.

The development had sent the Dundon brothers and their trusted sidekick into a state of panic. They knew all too well that with such a range of witnesses queuing to testify against them they were stumped. Somehow the supergrasses would have to be silenced before John's case, the first of the murder trials, got up and running in June 2013. The psychopath's only way out was to convince the Collinses and his first cousin to withdraw their evidence. But he possessed few powers of persuasion other than having them murdered or making them too terrified to testify. For either approach to work he needed time. Given the weight of detailed evidence the prosecution had put together, Dundon knew that he was facing the likelihood of conviction. However, he tried to use this to his advantage in getting the delay he wanted.

On 15 May 2013, his legal team made an application for an adjournment in the interests of a 'fair trial' after they had received thousands of pages of what they described as 'thrown together' investigative material. They told the court that 26,082 pages of evidence, 1,226 disks of CCTV footage, two hard-drives and a memory stick had been disclosed to Dundon's solicitors at the beginning of the month. But the State objected on the grounds that there were 'serious concerns' for the security of the proposed witnesses. The prosecution also said 'very many' of the documents had been made available to the defence in a previous related case. When the court ruled that the trial would commence as scheduled on 4 June, John Dundon, who was appearing via a video link from Portlaoise Prison, asked to address the court president, Mr Justice Paul Butler.

As the killer's menacing face filled the screen, he leaned into the microphone and said: 'I know I'm a Dundon but I'm a human being and I know you want to fuck me up the ass, but do you want to find me guilty now or find me guilty on another date? To me, there is no fair trial there.' When Mr Justice Butler said the court would rise, Dundon could be heard saying 'OK, OK, run away', before then shouting 'ya big fat pig' as he stood up and turned away from the video-link camera.

Dundon subsequently appealed the decision to the High Court and it also refused to adjourn the trial. When the legal process didn't work, the increasingly desperate criminal went on hunger strike.

Two days before his trial was due to begin Dundon, who had been refusing food and water for a number of days, collapsed. He was rushed to hospital under heavy police and army guard. He was discharged that night and returned to prison. The following morning, 4 June as scheduled, Dundon refused to wear any clothes when he was brought before the court. The three judges were greeted with the bizarre sight of Dundon being pushed into the courtroom in a wheelchair wearing only cycling shorts.

Mr Justice Butler looked at the defendant and then at his lawyers and asked if anybody had anything to say about Dundon's 'state of dress or undress'. When it was explained that the gangster had refused to get dressed the judge replied: 'If he is not dressed appropriately in court he will be absent from the court.' The case was put back for hearing to July, while Dundon's lawyers went to the Supreme Court to appeal the decision not to adjourn the trial for a year. Throughout this process his mounting legal bills were being paid by the Irish taxpayer. Dundon, who never worked a day in his life, had claimed to be unemployed and was in receipt of free legal aid. When the Supreme Court appeal failed, Dundon pulled another delaying stunt when the trial opened again on 2 July.

Looking gaunt and appearing in a wheelchair for the second time, the ruthless criminal told the presiding judge, Mr Justice Nicholas Kearns, that he had sacked his legal team. Dundon's barrister told the court that he had withdrawn his instructions from them and that the accused wished to 'conduct proceedings' on his own behalf. When asked by Mr Justice Kearns if he could confirm the accuracy of what was said, Dundon replied: 'Yeah.' However, after the murder charge was read to him by the court registrar, Dundon said: 'I plead not guilty but it's a different legal team I am looking for.'

The judge told him he had agreed he wished to defend himself and had been asked only 'a few moments ago' to confirm this. Dundon replied: 'I thought you meant a new legal team.' The judge told him, 'You have elected to do the case yourself and you will do the case yourself.' When Mr Justice Kearns said the trial would begin at 2 p.m. that afternoon, Dundon said: 'I'm out of me depth here. I don't know nothing about the law; I haven't a clue, I thought I had a separate legal team. I left school at the age of nine.' The court ignored what was a rather crude attempt at derailing the trial process. The judges had made their point and there was nothing more to say.

But John Dundon hadn't yet run out of attempts to thwart the trial process. At lunchtime he was found collapsed in his cell and was rushed to hospital with a cut to his head. The following day a hospital consultant said he could find no reason why Dundon had fallen. The medic said that Dundon had two superficial cuts to the back of his head and that despite several tests – including an MRI scan – there was no obvious reason for his unconsciousness on arrival to the emergency department the previous afternoon.

Having finally run out of options Dundon hired a new legal team. This time he was represented by his former solicitor John Devane, whom he had once attacked in Limerick court. The gangster's new counsel, Brendan Nix SC, assured the court: 'There will be no messing around . . . I won't be party to any obfuscation,' he said.

The trial lasted a month, during which Dundon's former associates gave their damning testimony. The once-feared psychopath could only stare and make threatening gestures at Lisa and April Collins and his cousin Christopher McCarthy as they related how he had ordered them to steal a getaway car and instructed Barry Doyle to do the killing. Their testimony was supported by independent evidence, including the mobile phone handed over by Philip Collopy on the morning after the murder and the CCTV footage.

On 13 August John Dundon was convicted of the murder of Shane Geoghegan. As Mr Justice Kearns read the eighty-four-page judgment, Dundon chose to tune out and listened to loud rap music on his earphones. The court ruled that the evidence, including that of the State witnesses, pointed 'overwhelmingly' to John Dundon's guilt.

The judgment read:

This case is all about credibility. While that may be said of many criminal cases, it is particularly true in this case where all the principal suspects and those suspected of having information were closely associated and involved with each other at the time of Shane Geoghegan's murder in November 2008. Gangland rules of 'silence in all circumstances' usually prevail in the aftermath of a serious crime where such persons, or one or more of them, come under suspicion of involvement in it. Such attitudes create serious difficulties for the Gardaí in the investigation of crime and serious problems and risks for any member of such a group who afterwards leaves the group and decides to come forward as a witness against his or her former associates.

The court said it had treated the main prosecution witnesses as accomplices for the purpose of evaluating their evidence. It said that by not availing of an opportunity to warn Gardaí of the intended killing, the inaction of April Collins was reprehensible, but it acknowledged that she was in fear of being killed herself.

The court's ruling continued:

Plainly terrified of the accused, she was nonetheless steadfast in her account of what was said and what was done. She did not present herself as some sort of innocent and admitted to her own wrongdoings in the past and provided explanations when asked why she said and did certain things. She said she now lived in fear for her life and was under Garda protection 24/7.

That afternoon John Dundon returned to his cell to begin a life sentence for murder. He was due to celebrate his thirty-first birthday less than two weeks later. Prisoner number 1850 would mark many more birthdays locked up.

There was more trouble in store for the crumbling mob. On 3 September, Gardaí from Limerick visited Anthony 'Noddy' McCarthy in Cork Prison after he too said he wanted to join the growing line of supergrasses. Noddy, the older brother of Christopher McCarthy, was serving life for the murder of Kieran Keane back in 2003. In a detailed statement he outlined witnessing Wayne Dundon 'roaring on the phone' in Wheatfield Prison as he ordered James Dillon to take part in the murder of Roy Collins.

When Noddy McCarthy had finished dictating his statement to the two detectives he said: 'Like I said, what I've told ye is the truth, I'm going nowhere. I'm getting nothing out of this only a load of enemies. The reason I'm talking to ye is because a lot of innocent people have been killed.'

The eagerly awaited trial of Wayne Dundon and Nathan Killeen opened before the Special Criminal Court in Dublin on Thursday, 1 May 2014. Even before it commenced history was made – it was the first time that a trial in Ireland would be heard by three female judges. The presiding judge, Ms Justice Iseult O'Malley, was joined by Judge Margaret Heneghan and Judge Ann Ryan. The State hired one of the country's most formidable and capable barristers, Michael O'Higgins SC, to lead the prosecution. He was joined by Sean Guerin SC. Opening the case for the prosecution O'Higgins outlined how Roy Collins had been murdered on 9 April 2009, commenting that he had been shot with a single gunshot in the chest.

The barrister said it was the State's case that Wayne Dundon had directed the murder from prison, while Nathan

Killeen was the getaway driver and James Dillon the gunman. There was evidence that shortly beforehand, Nathan Killeen was in Roxboro Road Shopping Centre, where the deceased owned his arcade and his father, Stephen Collins, owned a pub.

Prosecuting counsel said the court would hear evidence that in the aftermath of the killing, detectives spotted Killeen and Dillon, who took flight and ran when Gardaí called out to them. They were both arrested a short time later hiding in a house. He said that the testimony of five witnesses, the three Collins siblings and two McCarthy brothers, was the 'meat of the case'.

The prosecutor outlined how the five witnesses were connected to the accused and described the associations of Gareth Collins and the McCarthy brothers as criminal in nature. O'Higgins said that if the court accepted the evidence of the witnesses, it would be satisfied that Wayne Dundon was part of a joint enterprise, was the organizer, designer and a legal participant. He said that, along with witness evidence, there was also strong circumstantial evidence in respect of Nathan Killeen, including CCTV footage, forensics and DNA. 'The seminal issue is whether the accused are involved,' he concluded.

One of the first people to give evidence was Steve Collins, who yet again had to relive the moment that he found his son gasping for breath seconds after he had been shot. Steve, Carmel and their children had returned from their enforced exile to face the monsters that had torn their lives apart. They attended every day of the emotionally draining twenty-nine-day trial, with court dates spread out over two months.

It was one of the biggest gangland trials ever heard in an Irish court and set a precedent as six close associates and members of the Murder Inc. mob – the three Collins siblings, the McCarthy brothers and Elaine Walsh, the girlfriend of Gareth Collins – testified against the accused men. For weeks defence counsel for the two gangsters put the witnesses through intensive cross-examination – scrutinizing and challenging every word of their testimony. They also questioned their motives and credibility as reliable witnesses.

On Tuesday, 15 July, the three judges returned to deliver their verdict after deliberating for two weeks. It took Ms Justice O'Malley two hours to read out the court's detailed forty-five-page judgment.

It was clear that the case against Nathan Killeen was the stronger of the two before the court. There was firearms residue on his clothing when he was arrested and there was CCTV footage and other evidence that showed that he was in the company of the actual hit man James Dillon on the morning of the murder. The court said that this corroborated the testimony of Lisa Collins, who had given evidence that Killeen told her that morning that he was going to shoot Steve Collins and to listen out for 'the sirens' to start.

In the case of Wayne Dundon the court had to rely on the evidence of Noddy McCarthy. He testified that he and Dundon were inmates in Wheatfield Prison on the day of the murder and that Dundon told him he had ordered the killing. Although it was suggested by the defence that Noddy was a 'classic jailhouse snitch' with much to gain and nothing to lose from testifying, the court found his evidence to be coherent and plausible.

The judgment placed weight on the fact that both McCarthy and Steve Collins had testified that Dundon had made a particular gesture to Steve Collins during a previous court case. This involved Dundon pointing to his wristwatch during his trial for threatening to kill Ryan Lee in 2005, which Steve Collins had taken to mean his time had come. On the morning that Roy was murdered, Wayne Dundon had made the same gesture to his brother Dessie in front of his cousin. The court ruled that it was 'not a reasonable possibility' that both Steve Collins and Noddy McCarthy had 'independently fabricated evidence of the gesture'. At the time of Wayne Dundon's 2005 trial, his cousin and four other mob members, including Dessie Dundon, were into the second year of their life sentences for the murder of Kieran Keane in 2003.

Ms Justice O'Malley completed the lengthy ruling with the words that everyone in Limerick had been waiting to hear for a very long time. 'The court therefore finds both of the accused guilty of the offence of murder.' The three judges then imposed the mandatory sentence for murder – life imprisonment. The two dangerous killers showed little emotion as the verdict and sentencing were delivered: they would have a whole lifetime in front of them behind bars to deal with the shock.

And so the final chapter in the horror story that was Murder Incorporated was finally closed. As two more leading members of the most feared gang in Irish criminal history were led away to begin their life sentences for the murder of his son, Steve Collins, the man who had stood alone against their evil, broke down in tears of raw emotion. He had finally got justice for his son and his family. For the first time in almost ten years the Collins family could look forward to tomorrow with optimistic eyes.

Epilogue

Steve Collins struggled through a torrent of tears as he spoke for all the victims of Murder Inc. 'When these Godless creatures killed our son, our hopes and aspirations died with him. We too have been handed a life sentence,' he said, as he read from his Victim Impact Statement following the conviction of his son's murderers.

Only two people in the packed court appeared insouciant as they listened to the heart-wrenching words of the brave father – his son's killers, Wayne Dundon and Nathan Killeen. They watched Steve Collins with cold, dead eyes.

As the Special Criminal Court delivered its monumental judgment in one of the most high-profile gangland cases in recent history, Steve Collins, who'd remained stoic throughout, had finally collapsed in tears in his wife's arms. The court had adjourned for fifteen minutes to allow the family to absorb the fact that they had at long last received justice and to allow Steve to compose himself before he put on record the effect of the outrage on his family's life.

'It has been exactly 1,833 days since these terrorists infected our lives with their hateful poison and destroyed everything that we held dear in life,' Steve continued, his voice faltering with every line. 'Every moment, of every hour, of every day that has passed since that awful day we are numb with grief. Our sense of loss and sadness is so profound that it is impossible to find words to describe it.

'Every day I relive the moment I held him in my arms after he had been shot and, as he gasped for breath, he wanted me to know that he loved me and his mam. The day they murdered my son, they wounded me, and I am slowly bleeding to death. Sometimes I think his loss will kill me. I also have to live with the reality that it was me these savages came for that morning. I would have readily swapped places with my son.'

Steve Collins described in painful detail how the individual lives of his wife and children had been shattered and broken as a result of Murder Inc.'s irrational, blood-curdling hatred. These 'evil men' had ultimately forced his family to leave their relatives and friends behind and enter the witness relocation programme for the rest of their lives. As he read his statement one of the three female judges had tears in her eyes. Even the hardened cops whose tenacity and determination had paid off were misty-eyed. Only Roy's killers were unaffected and unmoved. Dundon began to look bored. Killeen yawned and glanced around as if the proceedings had nothing to do with him.

'All this happened to us because we did the right thing and stood up to terrorists who have ruined the lives of so many others. By standing up I believe that many people were spared the evil wrath of these people. But we have paid the ultimate price for that; one child maimed, another murdered. They burned down our business. They forced us to leave our home, our family, our friends and the country we love – to live in exile in a place where we know no one.'

In that moment of profundity Steve Collins spoke for every man, woman and child in Limerick who had suffered at the hands of Murder Inc. The conviction of the 'Godless creatures' in the dock was a victory for the ordinary decent people who had endured the Dundon/McCarthys' mindless warfare for over a decade. They had left a trail of carnage and human misery on a scale not seen in Ireland since the dark days of the Northern Troubles. Literally hundreds of people bore the physical and psychological scars of an indiscriminate, demented madness that defied any form of logical explanation.

With the convictions of Dundon and Killeen came the last chapter in the story of Murder Inc. – the most violent gang in Irish criminal history. A total of eleven members of the Piranhas are now serving life sentences for murders. Three of the Dundon brothers are among them. No other single gang in Ireland's history ever produced so many killers.

It doesn't mean, however, that the spectre of organized crime will vanish from the streets of Limerick. The remnants of the old entity known as the Dundon/McCarthy gang have since splintered into other mobs. But the city will never see the same level of violence again. The Dundons were the undisputed driving force behind the chaos. Their influence has been emphatically broken. The new drug overlords have learned from the mistakes of the Piranhas.

The story of the rise and fall of this savage mob is a classic one of the battle between good and evil. It was won by the brave men and women of the Garda Síochána in Limerick who were involved in the most intensive and prolonged criminal investigation in the history of the State. Their tenacity finally prised the ancient city from the grip of organized criminal chaos. The peace that now reigns in the city is the fruit of their extraordinary resilience, dedication and diligence. They often went far beyond the call of duty, risking their lives to protect and serve – and deserve to be called patriots.

So, hopefully, this book will go some small way to remember the innocent victims who lost their lives, and to acknowledge Steve Collins and his family and the outstanding work of the Gardaí who ultimately brought down the gang they called Murder Incorporated.

Acknowledgements

This book has been almost fifteen years in the making – ever since the dreaded Dundon family returned to these shores to wreak havoc. As a crime journalist I have covered their blood-soaked story from the beginning right through to the end. Such was their unrivalled reputation for killing innocent people that I first labelled them 'Murder Inc.' in 2008. The name stuck. Never during the past twenty-seven years of covering organized crime and terrorism on this island have I encountered such a group of depraved, remorseless savages. They instilled terror in the people of Limerick the likes of which had not been seen since the darkest days of the Troubles in Northern Ireland. Which is why I want to express my most sincere thanks, gratitude and admiration to the many people, including Gardaí, legal professionals, local politicians, criminals and victims, who shared their first-hand experiences of the sadistic monsters with me through those turbulent war years.

The story of how Murder Incorporated was brought down is a classic tale of a battle between good and evil. Inevitably it created its fair share of real-life, reluctant heroes along the way. People like Michael Murray, the State Solicitor for Limerick, and retired Garda Chief Superintendent Gerry Mahon, whose testimonies in this book are based on previous in-depth interviews. But they are just two of the dozens of truly brave law enforcement officials who took on Murder Inc. and exemplified the best traditions of what it means to be a public servant. I want to sincerely thank all of them for their assistance and trust.

My thanks also to the local Garda force in Limerick City, especially the detective branch, the Regional Support Unit (RSU) and the specialist squad from the Garda National Support Services (NSS) – dubbed the 'Dublin Squad' – who were deployed on the frontline against the mob. In this regard I would like to express my deep gratitude to the former Commissioner Fachtna Murphy, who granted me access to the units when the action on the streets of Limerick was going through its most frenetic – and dangerous – stage.

I also want to use this book as an opportunity to acknowledge the immeasurable suffering and courage of Steve and Carmel Collins and their children, a family who paid the ultimate price after innocently finding themselves in the path of pure evil. I first met this extraordinary man ten years ago, and since then Steve has become a close and cherished friend. As a result I witnessed on a personal basis the appalling suffering and heartbreak inflicted on this family. Steve's capacity for humanity and courage in the face of ferocious adversity has been nothing short of astonishing. Above all else, I hope that this book does some justice in attempting to effectively chronicle the family's experiences.

My thanks also go to my friend and colleague Padraig O'Reilly, who has worked closely with me for almost thirty years. Many of the compelling pictures contained in this book were the result of his courageous work. When it comes to cutting-edge investigative/crime photography, there is no 'snapper' in the business who can hold a candle to O'Reilly.

In particular my thanks, as always, to my extremely talented, and patient, editor, Aoife Barrett of Barrett Editing. I don't know what I would do without Aoife's razor-sharp insights and understanding of the genre. This soft-spoken, intellectual lady from leafy south Dublin regularly shocks her genteel peers with her in-depth knowledge of organized crime.

My thanks also to the MD of Penguin Ireland, Michael McLoughlin, for his faith and unquenchable optimism. Also my gratitude to Penguin Ireland's Editorial Director, Patricia Deevy, Publicity Director, Cliona Lewis, and all the Penguin team in Dublin and London for their outstanding professionalism and support. Thanks also to Charlotte Ridings for her attentive and thorough copy-editing.

And also my thanks to my old friend, libel expert Kieran Kelly – 'the Consiglieri' – of Fanning Kelly and Company, who, like Aoife Barrett, has worked with me on practically all my books.

I want to express my gratitude to Stephen Rae for his friendship and his loyalty through times when it was not fashionable. Such loyalty, which is impossible to repay, speaks volumes about the calibre of a man. In 2013, Stephen, his trusted lieutenant Ian Mallon and I broke the Anglo Tapes story which stunned the nation. On the same day Rae's leadership qualities were acknowledged when he made history by being appointed as Editor-in-Chief of all the titles within Independent News and Media (INM). I also want to thank Stephen and the recently appointed *Irish Independent* editor, Ian Mallon, for their support while I was writing *Murder Inc.*

Finally, as always, my love and gratitude to the people who make life worth living – my wife, Anne, and children, Jake and Irena, for their endless affection, patience and support.